Sena Karasipahi is a Lecturer in the Department of Political Science at Texas A & M University. She received her Ph.D. from the Turkish Studies Department at the University of Leiden.

LIBRARY OF MODERN MIDDLE EAST STUDIES

See www.ibtauris.com/LMMES for a full list of titles

62. *Identity Politics in the Middle East: Liberal Thought and Islamic Challenge in Egypt*
Meir Hatina
978 1 84511 135 9

63. *The New Voices of Islam: Reforming Politics and Modernity – A Reader*
Mehran Kamrava (ed.)
978 1 84511 274 5

64. *The Political Ideology of Hamas: A Grassroots Perspective*
Michael Irving Jensen
978 1 84511 059 8

65. *Reinventing Jerusalem: Israel's Reconstruction of the Jewish Quarter after 1967*
Simone Ricca
978 1 84511 387 2

66. *The State and the Subaltern: Modernization, Society and the State in Turkey and Iran*
Touraj Atabaki (ed.)
978 1 84511 339 1

67. *Sufism and the 'Modern' in Islam*
Martin van Bruinessen and Julia Day Howell (eds)
978 1 85043 854 0

68. *Arab Media and Political Renewal: Community, Legitimacy and Public Life*
Naomi Sakr (ed.)
978 1 84511 433 6

69. *Imagining the Arab Other: How Arabs and Non-Arabs View Each Other*
Tahar Labib
978 1 84511 384 1

70. *Power and Water in the Middle East: The Hidden Politics of the Palestinian–Israeli Water Conflict*
Mark Zeitoun
978 1 84511 464 0

71. *The Zaza Kurds of Turkey: A Middle Eastern Minority in a Globalised Society*
Mehmed S. Kaya
978 1 84511 875 4

72. *Muslims in Modern Turkey: Kemalism, Modernism and the Revolt of the Islamic Intellectuals*
Sena Karasipahi
978 1 84511 783 2

73. *The Arab–Israeli Conflict in the Media: Producing Shared Memory and National Identity in the Global Television Era*
Tamar Ashuri
978 1 84511 814 3

74. *Desert Voices: Bedouin Women's Poetry in Saudi Arabia*
Moneera Al-Ghadeer
978 1 84511 666 8

75. *Britain and Turkey in the Middle East: Politics and Influence in the Early Cold War Era*
Mustafa Bilgin
978 1 84511 350 6

76. *Satellite Realms: Transnational Television, Globalization and the Middle East*
Naomi Sakr
978 1 86064 688 1

77. *Globalization and the Gulf*
John Fox and Nada Mourtada Sabbah (eds)
978 1 84511 144 1

78. *Israeli Cinema: East/West and the Politics of Representation*
Ella Shohat
978 1 84511 312 4

79. *Occidentalism in Turkey: Questions of Modernity and National Identity in Turkish Radio Broadcasting*
Meltem Ahiska
978 1 84511 653 8

80. *Narrating Islam: Interpretations of the Muslim World in European Texts*
Gerdien Jonker and Shiraz Thobani (eds)
978 1 84511 978 2

81. *The Muslim Brotherhood and Egypt's Succession Crisis: The Politics of Liberalisation and Reform in the Middle East*
Mohammed Zahid
978 1 84511 979 9

82. *Palestine in Israeli School Books: Ideology and Propaganda in Education*
Nurit Peled-Elhanan
978 1 84511 813 6

83. *The Emergence of Modern Istanbul: Transformation and Modernisation of a City*
Murat Gül
978 1 84511 935 5

Muslims in Modern Turkey

Kemalism, Modernism and the Revolt of the Islamic Intellectuals

SENA KARASIPAHI

I.B. TAURIS
LONDON · NEW YORK

Dedicated to my parents, Ülkü and Süleyman Karasipahi,
who made me what I am today.

Published in 2009 by I.B.Tauris & Co Ltd
6 Salem Road, London W2 4BU
175 Fifth Avenue, New York NY 10010
www.ibtauris.com

Distributed in the United States and Canada exclusively by Palgrave Macmillan,
175 Fifth Avenue, New York NY 10010

Library of Modern Middle East Studies: 72

ISBN 978 1 84511 783 2

A full CIP record for this book is available from the British Library
A full CIP record is available from the Library of Congress

Library of Congress Catalog card: available

Printed and bound in Great Britain by CPI Antony Rowe, Chippenham, Wiltshire.
Typeset by Oxford Publishing Services, Oxford

Contents

Acknowledgements

The completion of this book would not be possible without the support of number of people. Firstly, I would like to thank my Ph.D. advisor Professor Erik Jan Zurcher for his invaluable support and assistance, whose depth of knowledge and experience illuminated my path extremely. I am greatly indebted to him.

I would also like to thank Professor Michael Meeker and Professor Binnaz Toprak for sharing with me their views and knowledge on the Muslim intellectuals in contemporary Turkey. Additionally, I would like to express my gratitude to Professor Seyyed Hossein Nasr. His precious comments on the subject issue have been very motivating and insightful for me.

In particular, I would like to thank Ali Bulaç, İsmet Özel, Rasim Özdenören, Ersin Nazif Gürdoğan and İlhan Kutluer for accepting benevolently my interview request and answering my questions openly and sincerely. They made important contributions to my understanding of their discourses and their rationale.

Thanks are due as well to Özgür Mutlu Ulus for her important supports, helpful comments and friendship. Special thanks to my sister Özgü Karasipahi Akcakir and my brother Cem Karasipahi for their continuous love and moral support.

Finally, I am deeply grateful to my husband, İbrahim Karaman, for his patience, endless support, kindness and generosity, without which the completion of this book would be impossible.

I would like to dedicate this book to my mother Ülkü Karasipahi and my father Süleyman Karasipahi for their never-ending care and love, their generous efforts, their sacrifices, encouragement and deep trust, which are accountable for my success in every stage of my life.

Introduction

The crisis of the Kemalist modernization process ushered the creation of a new kind of intellectual class in Turkey, who are distinguished by their Islamist stance and rhetorics in contrast to the conventional Kemalist, secular, or leftist intellectual elite. This is the motivation for this present study, which aims to analyse and explain the evolution, thoughts, and beliefs of these Muslim or Islamist intellectuals since the 1980s to the present in contemporary Turkey. During my study, I noticed that this new group of thinkers within the Islamic elite are reclaiming and redefining Islamic values by demonstrating their Muslim identity in a distinctive way unparalleled throughout the Republican history as a reaction to the Kemalist ideology and its project of modernization. That is to say, the inherent peculiarities and paradoxes of Turkish modernity and the subsequent breakdown of its reliability and legitimacy constitute the main grounds for the Muslim intellectuals' critical discourses. I choose six most prominent intellectuals, whom I found the most representative of their groups: Ali Bulaç, Rasim Özdenören, İsmet Özel, İlhan Kutluer, Ersin Nazif Gürdoğan, and Abdurrahman Dilipak. They are all influential and belong to a single, coherent school with their novel understanding of Islam, which sees Islam not as an alternative but the only and single solution. In elaboration, unlike the Islamist thinkers of the nineteenth century and the former conservative Muslim intellectuals of the 1930s–1950s, they try to formulate 'the answer of Islam to the modern world' instead of searching for the reasons for the Muslim world's backwardness as against the West.[1] Furthermore, they are distinguished by their intense and severe criticism and overall negation of Western civilization and by their attempt to deconstruct traditions and conventional interpretations of Islamic discourse.

The struggle for modernization in Turkey dates back to the Tanzimat period of the Ottoman Empire and was continued radically and enthusiastically by Mustafa Kemal Atatürk, the founder of the Republic of Turkey. I contend that the failure of intrinsic contradictions and peculiarities of the Kemalist ideology and its modernization/westernization project together with the domestic and international social, political and economic developments since the 1950s and 1980s laid the ground for the weakening of its ideological legacy and hegemony and enabled the new Muslim intellectuals to re-establish 'authentic' Islamic thought as an alternative to the Kemalist ideology. This is the departing point of my study.

So my prospective study will focus on six of the most leading Muslim intellectuals in Turkey, whom I consider the products of Kemalist modernization in the post-1950 period. More exactly, I am arguing that, in spite of their disapproval of modernity, they benefited from and are affected by the advancements and advantages of the Kemalist modernization project, which I will elaborate on later. I contend that the examination of the Muslim intellectuals in contemporary Turkey is of paramount importance not only due to the transformation they engendered in Turkish intellectual life in general but also in the fundamentalist Islamic discourse. They constitute also a challenge to the Kemalist, secularist worldview. Moreover, they have been playing a significant role in the Islamic revival in contemporary Turkey. It would not be wrong to assert that they will be the role models for young people – specifically 'upwardly mobile' high school and university students both in provincial towns and big cities generally from traditional and conservative circles and middle class origin – in the future.

There is a huge literature and a large number of studies on Islamic revivalism and several general analyses of Islamist intellectuals.[2] However an in-depth and all-inclusive examination, covering all aspects of their ideologies and role in both the reconfiguration Islamic discourse and intellectual life of Turkey, is lacking. Moreover, the cultural aspects of the Islamic resurgence are not researched as much as its political aspects. So this dissertation intends to contribute an elaborate and comparative approach, which will not only concentrate on the problematique of their emergences but also on their particularities and their position in comparison to the most important earlier conservative Muslim revivalists in Turkey and current Muslim intellectuals in other parts of the Islamic world.

Furthermore, this study attempts to answer the following questions: How can we explain the attacks of contemporary Islamist intellectuals against modernity? What is the main content of their discourses? Which factors affect their worldviews? Do they all have the same rhetoric? Are there differences? Do they have similar backgrounds? What is the nature of the present-day Muslim intelligentsia? Are there changes in thinking and in style? Do they repeat themselves? How do they differ from the conventional intellectuals? Where might differences between them and traditional Muslim revivalists lie? Are they radical? Are they traditionalist? Are they involved in politics? Who are their supporters? What are the reasons behind their success in appealing and influencing broad masses?

My study will consist of four chapters. The first chapter is devoted to a critical examination of the shortcomings and contradictions of the Kemalist ideology and its modernization process, in consideration to the social, political, and economic circumstances since 1950s and 1980s that facilitated and enabled the emergence of contemporary Muslim intellectuals.

Since the critique of the official Kemalist ideology and its modernization process constitute an important part of the Muslim intellectuals' discourse, my purpose is also to shed light on their rhetorics and understand the foundations for their attacks. Since the main intention of this dissertation is the examination of the contemporary Muslim intellectuals, the analysis of the Kemalist ideology is given only secondary importance and the treatment of the subject matter is confined to the published views of some of the distinguished scholars, whom I have found the most important, with Mustafa Kemal Atatürk's own statements as illustration.

Certainly I recognize that there exist multiple versions of Kemalisms which have come into being over time, such as rightist/leftist Kemalism, conservative/liberal Kemalism, as well as reactionary Ataturkism and the like during time. However my analysis will concentrate on the Turkish Muslim intellectuals' perception of Kemalism as the official ideology of the single party era, who seems to see Kemalism as a static, unchanging phenomenon and to be out of touch with the debates going on within Kemalism since the 1980s. In other words, their views and critiques of the hard line, state sponsored Kemalist ideology and its monolithic and authoritarian side will be scrutinized.

The emphasis will be placed on the radical transformation of the cultural, social, and political life and the disestablishment of religion from public life by the Kemalist elite for the sake of Westernization, which constitutes the backbone of the Muslim intellectuals' critiques. So, the Turkish version of secularism, which is modeled after French laicism, will be scrutinized in order to give insight into the Muslim intellectuals' ideas on secularism. In fact, they are opposing it on the grounds that it is a construction of Western culture. In elaboration, they also argue that the division between church and state is not experienced in Islam because unlike Christianity, Islam came in the form of a state. Therefore, secularism is irreconcilable with Islam. In fact, they are very sensitive to the elimination of religion from social and individual life.[3]

Furthermore, Michel Foucault's concept of power and Gramsci's theory of subordination and hegemony will be utilized in my research in order to elucidate the authoritarian, forced and top down manner of the Kemalist modernization/westernization project.

At the same time, I intend to make a critical assessment of the Turkish modernization paradigm and reveal its *ipso facto* contradictions and deficiencies together with domestic as well as international social, economic and political developments, which constitute the reasons for the breakdown of the hegemonic character of the Kemalist ideology and its modernization/westernization project for certain sections of society, especially among some parts of the middle class; and the revival of Islam that enabled and facilitated the emergence of Islamist intellectuals in contemporary Turkey after the 1980s.

While I was analysing the origin and nature of Kemalist ideology, I noticed that Kemalist thought has its roots not only in the Enlightenment or positivist trends and ideas of the West but also in the ideology and thinking of former Ottoman intellectuals since the Tanzimat period. This made me go back to that period and analyse the intellectual climate of the prewar period, which affected the thoughts and ideas of Mustafa Kemal and other republican elites. Therefore, I examine the early phase of westernization during the Ottoman Empire and the various views of the 'Young Turks'. Şerif Mardin's study of the modernization of Turkish political ideas has been very informative in this respect.

Moreover, I have benefited from theorems of the modernization process in order to provide theoretical information for a clear understanding of Turkish modernization. In this sense, the Turkish case will be examined as a model for non-Western modernization. It is essential to note that in the current study, the concepts of modernization and Westernization are used interchangeably.

Intellectuals are creators and originators of ideas, who form a 'distinctive grouping of people within a society, set apart from the majority, while at the same time they are a crucial element in society, defining and articulating the communal agreements that provide a sense of legitimacy and basic principles for societal operation and survival'.[4] Consequently, the second chapter deals firstly with the clarification and elaboration of 'intellectual' as a general concept. My intention is to elucidate the specific role, duty, and impact of intellectuals by introducing its various definitions and historical evolution. I will utilize mainly the theories of Weber, Gramsci, and Bourdieu to illuminate the nature and definition of intellectuals and their transformation over time. At this point, the Gramscian distinction between traditional and organic intellectuals has been determinative for evaluating Turkish Muslim intellectuals.

In addition, I contend that it is of paramount importance to give an explanation of the historical evolution of Turkish intellectuals in general. I will trace the development of intellectual currents since the late nineteenth century throughout the Republican period. This historical analysis will be followed by the presentation of biographies of the six important Muslim intellectuals in order to give an objective and elaborate idea about their backgrounds and lives.

The transformation in Turkish intellectual life becomes more remarkable with the increase and overwhelming presence of Muslim intellectuals, particularly after the 1980s, who are differentiated from the conventional Kemalist, secular, nationalist, socialist, and Marxist intellectuals by their stress on morality, ethics, and Islamic values in their intellectual and literary works. In other words, at the heart of their mission lies their aspiration to enhance Islamic consciousness in the society, especially among the young generation, and the realization of an Islamic life as it was lived and practised during the time of the Prophet Mohammad and his Companions. They strongly believe that the current state of stagnation of the Islamic religion is coming to an end and that Islam will be again strong and dominant as it was in its Golden Age. In contrast to conventional convictions, not all of them come from religious and conservative families or circles. On the contrary, some of them have become conscious of the Islamic discourse during their university years. Moreover, although they attack modernity, they owe their intellectual endowment and their ability to diffuse their ideas to a large number of people to modernity.

In addition to these factors, contemporary Muslim intellectuals try to transform and reform society through their intellectual and literary works. They are moderate in their position and are non-revolutionary. Therefore they should not be put in the category of the Islamist radicals, or fundamentalists. Consequently, a critical and general evaluation of Muslim intellectuals is needed to clarify all these aspects. I will describe who they are and what their aims, characteristics, and distinctions are. In addition to these questions, my investigation will also include their methodology, writing style, worldviews, and the reasons behind their popularity.

Contemporary Muslim intellectuals have a distinctive approach towards Western values. Unlike the Islamists intellectuals of the Ottoman Empire during the nineteenth century, who were in favour of the adoption of the material, scientific, and technological achievements of the West without taking its cultural and intellectual accumulations, the present-day Muslim thinkers renounce the West as a whole. In fact, they equate Western civilization with Christianity. Moreover, in their opinion, it is a compact entity, and thus its science and technology can not be considered separate from its culture and religion. So it is a combination of an undividable set of political, economic, moral, philosophical, social, and mental attitudes. Moreover, they argue that profane concepts of the West such as democracy, secularism, and modernism are not compatible with Islam. In fact, their uniqueness among other Islamist intellectuals lies in their rejection of both the 'Islamization of modernity' and the 'modernization of Islam'. Actually, they believe that modernism originated in the West and has a Hebrew–Christian and Greco-Roman foundation, which can not be accommodated within Islam. In other words, modernity is the sum of the Enlightenment's basic conjectures.

Consequently, in order to elaborate these views, the largest and the most significant part of the second chapter is devoted to the descriptive examination of their arguments, thoughts, and beliefs regarding the nature, principal concepts, and ideological products of the Western civilization and its Enlightenment. These concepts consist of democracy, human rights, secularism, modernity, and modern ideologies: Communism, Marxism, socialism, capitalism, and liberalism.

In fact they see the West and modernity as the source of the all evils in society. Related to this argument, Islam is the unique solution for the well-being and salvation of humanity. Furthermore, my intention here will be to provide insight into the Muslim intellectuals' anti-Western discourse and the alternative Islamist paradigm that they offer.

The third chapter continues to elaborate their ideas and thoughts. However the distinctiveness of this chapter comes from the difference in the subjects. In other words, my goal is to convey their thoughts and approaches on issues other than Western civilization and modernity, with which they are highly preoccupied, such as Kemalism as an official ideology of the Republic of Turkey; state and nation; science and technology; religion as a general concept including morality and religious revival, and Islam and history.

During my search through the huge literature on the Islamic discourse of the Muslim revivalists in the Islamic world in general, I noticed that these intellectuals are not ideologues or deep and sophisticated philosophers. In essence, their arguments and thoughts are not original in comparison to those of Islamist intellectuals in other parts of the Islamic world. It is also essential to note here that the contemporary Muslim intellectuals are a part of the Islamic revival process in the Middle East, who are also affected and inspired by earlier Muslim intellectuals and revivalists in the Arab world and in Turkey, such as Hasan al-Banna, Sayyid Qutb, Abul Ala Mawdudi, Ali Shari'ati, Seyyed Hossein Nasr, Bediuzzaman Said Nursi, and Abdolkarim Soroush.

For these reasons, in the fourth chapter I will position current Turkish Muslim intellectuals in a historical and global setting and evaluate their stance, thoughts, and discourses relative to other prominent Muslim intellectuals in the Islamic world (Muhammed Arkoun, Seyyed Hossein Nasr, Nasr Hamid Abu Zaid, and Abdolkarim Soroush) and in Turkey since the 1930s and 1950s (Bediuzzaman Said Nursi, Necip Fazıl Kısakürek, and Sezai Karakoç), who affected and shaped their thoughts predominantly. The main objective is to find out the contemporary Turkish Muslim intellectuals' particularities as well as similarities with these intellectuals and determine their places within the whole Islamist intellectual world. At the same time, social, political, and historical circumstances, which make them unique, will be researched. So both the developments in Turkey and in the Islamic world will be analysed and compared side by side in horizontal (synchronic) and vertical (diachronic) manner.

My research methodology is critical, comparative, post-structural, and phenomenological. I utilize primary and secondary sources. My research is also qualitative and interdisciplinary. I utilize methods drawn from history, sociological and political theory as well as theories of modernization and intellectuals, and the sociology of religion.

Chapter 1

The Emergence of Contemporary Turkish Muslim Intellectuals

Introduction

The project of modernization is undergoing a period of crisis not only in Turkey but also in other parts of the world. Generally speaking, it neither realized even distribution of wealth and prosperity on a global scale nor brought development to underdeveloped parts of the world. On the contrary, those places have suffered and been adversely affected from modernization projects in general. According to one of the leading Islamist intellectuals in Turkey, Ali Bulaç, 'for the first time since the rise of modernity the world has fallen into serious doubt as to the validity and accuracy of the widespread conviction that all problems can be solved within the Western paradigm.'[1] Consequently, this discontent and frustration paved the way for the creation of radical, alternative formations against modernity. This is also true for Turkey, whose struggle for modernization dates back to the Tanzimat period of the Ottoman Empire and was continued radically and enthusiastically by Mustafa Kemal Atatürk and his followers in the Turkish Republic. It is not surprising that the revival of political Islam coincides with the crisis of modernity and the Kemalist ideology. The Islamist intellectuals hold Kemalism and his modernization policies responsible for economic, political and cultural decadence in society and propose a return to the origins of Islam as it was lived and practised in its golden age instead of aping Western civilization.[2]

This chapter aims to analyse the Kemalist modernization and/or Westernization project in Turkey in order to understand the inherent paradoxes and peculiarities embedded in the Turkish modernization paradigm, to which the Muslim intellectuals' critiques and attacks are addressed.

Firstly, the characteristics of the official Kemalist ideology and reforms, which have laid the foundations of Turkish modernity will be studied critically. My objective is not to give an exhaustive and elaborate account of Kemalist ideology but to elucidate it in relation to Turkish modernization. Special emphasis will be given to the Kemalist approach towards the issue of secularism and religion, since an important part of current criticism against Kemalist modernization is concentrated on the repression and neglect of Islam and traditions for the sake of Westernization by the secularist elites. I will then review various modernization theories. My aim is to demonstrate general characteristics of the modernization process, which overlap with the course of Westernization in Turkey.

Kemalist ideology and its modernization project

Kemalism is a 'unique expression of the modern nation-state formation in Turkey'.[3] In other words, it is the attempt by Mustafa Kemal and other modernist elites to establish a secular and progressive nation state after the model of the civilized and modernized West. Furthermore, Kemalist reformers struggled to create a homogeneous society, which provides support and protection for the existing system. To achieve this, they set up a close control mechanism over the society to curb its autonomy. This was authoritarian and paternalistic, which can be explained in Foucauldian terminology by the relationship between the network of 'power' and 'its subjects'. In this context, the state as well as other sources of power tries to ensure a disciplined and docile society, which will maintain this new system. Being the hegemonic power, it aims to legitimize its anti-democratic and authoritarian policies. Similarly, according to Antonio Gramsci's theory 'hegemony'

> was meant to be a strategy of power pursued through a cultural work. It mainly refers to situations of subordination of both individuals and groups. Subordination entails a relation of domination by which the subjects are deprived of their self-reliance as persons as well as citizens. It denotes both a factual condition of powerlessness and a representation of oneself as an impotent hostage in the hands of an ineffable destiny.[4]

The subordination of public sovereignty to that of the Kemalist state by the Turkish modernist elites clashes with the liberal political values of Western Europe. This is one of the contradictions of Kemalist ideology. Indeed, the Kemalist revolution was 'for the people in spite of the people'.[5] In a nutshell, 'like its founding figure', writes Hakan Yavuz, 'Kemalism has been superficially Western in form while remaining rigidly authoritarian and dogmatic in substance. It continues to stress republicanism over democracy, homogeneity over difference, the military over the civilian, and the state over society.'[6]

It is of great importance to examine Atatürk and his policies under the light of the ideological and intellectual setting of the Young Turk era since his world-view is largely affected by those developments. In spite of various important changes, the similarities on the fundamental lines between the Kemalist modernization doctrine and that of the Young Turks demonstrate the existence of the uninterrupted link from the Tanzimat era to the Kemalist ideology.[7] Dumont argues that: 'Mustafa Kemal and his associates rarely borrowed their ideas directly from foreign models. They were guided by convictions that had already inspired several generations of Ottoman Turkish reformers and, duly assimilated, had become part of the national intellectual patrimony.'[8]

As Murat Belge puts it, his feelings are affected by Namık Kemal and his ideas inspired by Ziya Gökalp.[9] Namely, his ideas on nationalism based on 'culture, language, and common ideal' are largely shaped by Ziya Gökalp.[10] Likewise, the Kemalists' quest for oppressing and controlling religion also has its roots in the Ottoman reformers' thinking. The improvement and gradual secularization of the education system together with the establishment of the Military Academy and School of Administration in the Ottoman Empire during the nineteenth century expanded the horizons of the intellectual elite. In other words, not only has the way in which knowledge is acquired changed but their worldview has also become rational, scientific, and positivist since they were exposed to Western positive science and the writings of European ideologues of the Enlightenment era. As Şerif Mardin noted:

> It is possible to observe the firm origins of secularization policies in the journal called *İçtihad* (and previously in the articles published by the journal of *Osmanli*). In general, differently from the Young Turk journals, many themes, which later become the vanguards of Atatürk's reforms, can be witnessed in Ictihad. The importance given to woman's rights, a fundamental reservation towards the sultanate, the belief in the possibility to catch up with the West only by grasping the deep and inner meaning of the Western classics, the necessity of changing ideas and views fundamentally as one of the prerequisites of westernization and to evaluate the universe in a materialistic-biological framework, are the primary factors among these.[11]

In this context, 'the fight for laicization of the Ottoman state', wrote Paul Dumont,

> was spearheaded by Abdullah Cevdet, in his review *İçtihad* (Free Opinion), which sometimes expressed undisguised anticlericalism. We find in this journal, which strongly influenced Mustafa Kemal, a large number of proposed reforms which were later implemented under the Republic: suppression of the *tekkes* and *zaviyes* (convents and monastic cells), closing of the *medreses*, latinization of the alphabet, emancipation of women and prohibition of the *carsaf* (traditional feminine dress), replacement of Islamic headgear by western hats, and the turkification of the Koran and of traditional religious texts.[12]

This transformation in mentality and world-view indicates a break from the tradition of higher religious functionaries, the ulema, which were seen by Kemalists as 'ignorant charlatans rather than as repositories of ancient wisdom', namely because they could not benefit from developments in Western science and technology.[13] So they opposed the dogmatism of religion and consequently came into confrontation with religion, which they regarded as an obstruction to progress.[14] More precisely, as Binnaz Toprak puts it, 'because of the intimate relationship between religious and political authority in traditional societies, religious institutions have stood as symbols of the old regimes in the eyes of revolutionary leaders in France, Russia, Mexico, China, and Turkey.'[15] In fact, the general feeling among the Ottoman reformers was that the Ottoman defeat and backwardness was related to Islam because according to the conditions of that period, religion determined both the ideological, institutional structure and social and political system of the Empire.[16] The Ottomans identified themselves firstly as the 'representative of Islam' and the West as the 'representative of Christianity'. Thus this defeat should be attributed to Islam.[17] So, religion and backward minded religious authorities were held responsible for the decadence since they were seen as the representatives of obscurantism and the existing social order. Therefore, secularism and anticlericalism became the quintessential condition for modernization. In other words, it was used synonymously with westernization. In fact, the Kemalists were largely influenced in their attacks on the clergy by the French philosophers of the seventeenth and eighteenth centuries such as Voltaire, d'Alembert, Holbach, and the right-wing liberals of the French Revolution, who criticized religion 'as a symptom of hysteria, a device of political management, a mark of illiteracy, or a state in historical development'.[18] In other words they claimed that 'the clergy had reduced the level of men's minds and had prevented them from grasping the truths of reason.'[19] Therefore, according to the Kemalists, their autonomy had to be eliminated.

As I stated earlier, Mustafa Kemal Atatürk not only benefited from the positivist and scientific currents in the Ottoman intellectual environment during the late nineteenth century but also went further and radicalized those ideas drastically. 'What distinguished the Kemalist era', writes Paul Dumont, 'was the manner in which reforms were executed; the step-by-step policy of the past gave way to an unconditional radicalism dictated by the new circumstances.'[20] He attempted to eliminate every symbol that had a relationship with the Ottoman–Islamic heritage. In this sense, Kemalism symbolizes a radical break with the Ottoman era. As Hilmi Yavuz noted, conceptually, modernization defined itself as 'a contrario' of the past and therefore renounces it *en masse* without leaving any sign of the past. Therefore, tradition and modernity are considered mutually exclusive, contradictory terms, where the former is sacrificed for the sake of progress and development in Kemalist ideology. More importantly, the Kemalist elite did not only ignore and oppose the Ottoman–Islamic legacy but also the previously traditional parts of the society. This led to dramatic consequences later on, when the gap between the Kemalist reformers and the rest of the society widened due to their anti-traditional, elitist attitude. Namely, Turkish modernist elites disdained the diversity of the traditional culture of its society since they regarded it contradictory to 'Europeanization' or modernization.[21]

To give a sense of Atatürk's thoughts on traditional institutions, let me give the following quotation:

> Could a civilized nation tolerate a mass of people who let themselves be led by the nose by a herd of Sheiks, Dedes, Seids, Tschelebis, Babas, and Emirs, who entrusted their destiny and their lives to chiromancers, magicians, dice-throwers, and amulet sellers? Ought one to conserve in the Turkish State, in the Turkish Republic, elements and institutions such as those which had for centuries given the nation the appearance of being other than it really was? Would one not therewith have committed the greatest, most irreparable error to the cause of progress and reawakening?[22]

In fact, this repudiation of the past has been more radical in societies, which willingly initiated modernization projects such as Turkey, China than colonial societies like India, because in the former case it constituted the basis for their search for a new and modern identity.[23] The abolition of the Caliphate, the Office of Şeyhül-Islam, and the Ministry of Religious Affairs and Pious Foundations (Şeriye ve Evkaf Vekaleti) in 1924, together with the removal of the article that had identified Islam as the state religion in 1928, Mustafa Kemal not only aimed to eliminate the cultural and religious inheritance of the Ottoman empire but also intended to bring religion under the strict control of the Kemalist state.

In correlation to this, as Şerif Mardin pointed out, the terms 'Nation' and 'Western civilization' constituted the backbone of Atatürk's ideology, which explains his thoughts on the role of religion. That is to say, through his efforts to build national 'consciousness' and a 'collective identity' among the Turks in a territory which had not existed previously, he renounced the role of religion.[24] 'It was decided', writes Feroz Ahmad, 'that nationalism would be used as a substitute for religion'.[25] This means that nationalism gradually replaced religion as the quintessential and sole unifying source of Turkish society. However, practically, the Kemalist elites continued to give a role to religion in the form of a 'turkified Islam' originated from the thoughts of Ziya Gökalp, which in their view would facilitate and strengthen national cohesion in modern Turkey.[26] To understand the Kemalist definition of nationalism, let me quote the following statements by Recep Peker:

> We consider as ours all those of our citizens who live among us, who belong politically and socially to the Turkish nation and among whom ideas and feelings such as 'Kurdism', 'Circassianism', and even 'Lazism' and 'Pomakism' have been implanted. We deem it our duty to banish, by sincere efforts, those false conceptions, which are the legacy of an absolutist regime and the product of long-standing historical oppression. The scientific truth of today does not allow an independent existence for a nation of several hundred thousand, or even of a million individuals. ... We want to state just as sincerely our opinion regarding our Jewish or Christian compatriots. Our party considers these compatriots as absolutely Turkish insofar as they belong to our community of language and ideal.[27]

It is essential to distinguish Kemalist nationalism from ethnic nationalism. The former implies a unique version of nationalism, which aspires to establish a homogenous and uniform society devoid of different classes and class conflicts. This is paradoxical because, while the Kemalist reformers were attempting to modernize the country, at the same time they were trying to prevent the differentiation of its society that the modernization would inevitably cause. Namely, diversity is a natural outcome of modernization. However, the Kemalist elites had no tolerance for diversity within the society because they considered it a potential threat to the continuation of the state. Ahmet İnsel names this as 'official' or 'state nationalism', which referred to the combination of required policies for the survival of the Turkish Republic according to the official ideology.[28] Moreover, it is 'secular' and 'cultural' in essence. The striking fact in Kemalist nationalism is the fact that Islam lost its former predominant position and legitimacy as the integrative as well as mobilizing power of the society.

Mustafa Kemal's ideas are guided by his admiration of Western civilization 'as the only civilization to be pursued'. He explained this fact in the following way:

> Our thinking and our mentality will have to become civilized. And we will be proud of this civilization. Take a look at the entire Turkish and Islamic world. Because they failed to adapt to the conditions, they found themselves in such a state of catastrophe and suffering. We cannot afford to hesitate any longer. We have to move forward. … Civilization is such a fire that it burns and destroys those who ignore it.
>
> It is futile to resist the thunderous advance of civilization, for it has no pity on those who are ignorant or rebellious. The sublime force of civilization pierces mountains, crosses the skies, enlightens and explores everything from the smallest particle of dust to stars. … When faced with this, those nations who try to follow the superstitions of the Middle Ages are condemned to be destroyed or at least to become enslaved and debased.[29]

In sum, Western civilization is regarded as 'universal' by Kemalists, who argued that 'there is no second civilization; civilization means European civilization, and it must be imported with all its roses and thorns.'[30] In other words, 'Mustafa Kemal sees the civilization of contemporary Europe', argued Erik-Jan Zurcher,

> not only as the most viable civilization of the time, but as the only civilization: the choice is not between belonging to one civilization or the other, but between being civilized or barbaric. ... He demands a change not only in the realm of civilization, but also in that of culture: where Gökalp wants to turkify private life, Kemal wants to westernize it.[31]

Therefore, according to this idea, the replacement of Islamic culture with the Western civilization was not enough for the Kemalist elite: the transformation of the 'low' or 'popular culture' was also required for modernization.[32]

I believe that Islam is not only a religious faith but also a way of life, which encompasses distinctive cultural, political and social customs, norms, practices, institutions, and regulation systems.[33] 'The emphasis on divine guidance of socio-political institutions', writes Toprak, 'has meant that Islam is not only a belief system in the religious sense but is at the same time a political doctrine which sets the limits of authority and obligation within the Muslim community.'[34] Consequently, this fact makes the secularization issue more problematic, which the same author explains in the following terms:

> Muslim societies have traditionally rested on the premise that there are no distinctions to be made between the secular and the religious. It also points to the difficulty of limiting Islam's influence to a socio-political process through formal secularization. The history of the Ottoman and Republican Turkey is, in a sense, the history of the attempt to cope precisely with this problem of limiting Islam's influence in a predominantly Muslim society where the belief system considers it heretical to separate the religious realm from the secular.

> ... I think that both the political and the organic characteristics of Islam put constraints on the course of modernization that the Ottoman reformers and later, the Kemalist nationalists, followed. Here was a religion which preached a political doctrine. It interpreted the creation of a political community in theological terms. It equated state and society. It considered the distinction between the secular and the religious realms as heresy. It did not allow for the development of an autonomous religious organization. To stay within that Islamic framework and yet change the basic structures of the social and political system was contradictory in terms for it was the religious system itself which had created and given sanction to such structures.
>
> ... The impact of Islam on traditional Ottoman social and political institutions had far-reaching consequences for the developmental process in Turkey during both the last two hundred years of the Empire's existence and the Republican Period. The nature of the religious system set the parameters of what should be reformed and how. It affected the specific manner in which both Ottoman and Turkish reformers responded to problems of modernization, and it put constraints on the process of secularization in general and the separation of religious and political affairs in particular.[35]

Thus, the Kemalist state preferred to implement laicism differently from the Anglo-Saxon version of secularism in the sense that they took a subjective stance by restricting the autonomy and realm of religion radically for the sake of Westernization and progress instead of remaining neutral towards the religious faiths and practices of its citizens.[36] In other words, the Kemalists, with the Jacobin attitude of the French revolutionaries, controlled religion rigorously by excluding it almost totally from public appearance and forced its people to adopt 'state Islam', which is 'privatized' and 'nationalized'.[37] Therefore, I contend that it has a 'militant' and despotic character. As an illustration, the Minister of the Interior Sükrü Kaya argued in the Assembly that 'religions have fulfilled their purpose and their functions are exhausted; they are institutions which can no longer renew their organisms or revitalize themselves.'[38] The recitation of the Arabic *ezan* in the Turkish language, 'turkified Friday sermons' and the establishment of the Directorate of Religious Affairs controlled and dictated by the state are early attempts at the turkification/nationalization of Islam by Kemalist modernizers.[39]

Furthermore, Binnaz Toprak defined the Republic as a 'semi-secular state' and thus argued that 'its brand of secularism is rather unique and should be understood as such'.[40] Namely, a truly secularist state should avoid having any religious function and a 'state religion'.[41] As Paul Dumont also pointed out: 'it is no accident that the Kemalists chose the term *laiklik to* refer to one of the major pillars of their doctrine. Had they so desired, they could have selected a vaguer term; they wanted, however, to stress the principle of separation of religious and lay societies.'[42] However, due to the non-existence of an independent religious entity like the Catholic Church in Turkey, laicism meant more than the disintegration of religion.[43] Actually, some of the Kemalist reformers claimed that the ability to separate religious and earthly affairs is inherent in the Turkish nation, of which the state of the pre-Islamic Turks constitutes a good example.[44] According to them, the preponderance of religion and conservatism was imported from Arabs.[45]

As a result, in order to bring Islam under control by restricting and eliminating its influence in the social, cultural, and political sphere, Mustafa Kemal embarked upon a strenuous social, political, and cultural turkification project by executing the following reforms:

- The abolition of the sultanate in 1922 by a decree of the

Grand National Assembly (prior to the establishment of the Turkish Republic in 1923).

- The abolition in 1924 of the caliphate, which had symbolized the unity of the Muslim ummah. The origins of the caliphate went back to the period after the death of Prophet Muhammed; Ottoman sultans had assumed the title of caliph in the sixteenth century.
- The abolition in 1924 of the office of Seyh'ul-Islam, the highest religious authority in the administration of the Ottoman Empire, one of whose functions had been to oversee the suitability of political decisions to Islamic law.
- The abolition in 1924 of the Ministry of Religious Affairs and Pious Foundations (Seriye ve Evkaf Vekaleti).
- The abolition in 1924 of the Seri'at courts, religious courts based on Muslim law.
- The abolition in 1924 of the medrese, which had been important centres of religious learning in the Ottoman Empire.
- The interdiction of religious brotherhoods (*tarikat*) in 1925, and the ban on all their activities.
- The passage of a law in 1925 outlawing the fez in favour of the western hat; the republican regime also discouraged the veil for women although it did not outlaw it.
- The adoption of the Gregorian calendar in 1925, replacing the lunar Hicri and solar Rumi calendars.
- The adoption of the Swiss Civil Code in 1926, giving equal civil rights to men and women.
- The adoption of European numerals in 1928.
- The change from Arabic to Latin script in 1928.
- The deletion in 1928 of the second article of the 1924 constitution which stated Islam to be the state religion.[46]

Evidently, as I have also mentioned before, these reforms primarily aimed to eradicate all ties with the Ottoman legacy in order to achieve and facilitate the modernization process. The essential thing we have to note here is the top–down character of these reforms. In other words, the modernization process in Turkey did not occur as a result of popular movements. To put it another way, the impetus and demand for change did not come from the people. Rather, it occurred through the Kemalist revolution from above by the intellectual elites. Therefore, it can be called as an elitist movement and 'forced modernization/ Westernization', as Kemal Karpat put it, which created tensions between the masses and the republican elites later on. This fact also contradicts with the populism of Kemalist ideology, in the sense that it renounces the traditional culture of the masses and distances itself against it. As Binnaz Toprak argued:

> In traditional societies where the basis of individual identity is religious, religion may also help bridge the distance between the elites and the masses. Although elite and mass cultures may be different, including differences between the orthodox religion of the elite and the folk religion of the masses, common religious loyalties nevertheless may provide a frame of reference by which the masses relate themselves to the elite culture. On the other hand, in societies undergoing secularization where the process of removing religious influence from political and social relationships has been achieved in elite centres but has failed to penetrate the mass culture, religion may serve as an additional source of divergence between the two cultural systems. In such a setting, it may further widen the elite–mass gap.[47]

This fact is extremely important to our subject because the discontent of the contemporary Islamist intellectuals and the revival of Islam have their roots in this alienation between the ruling elites and the rural people. If we analyse modernization theories, we realize the similarities between them and the Kemalist ideology, although the former emerged later than

Kemalism.[48] In other words, modernist theory is in conformity with the principal tenets of the Kemalist ideology.[49] They both embrace the values of the Enlightenment, positivism, and rationality. According to the Kemalist vocabulary, modernization is equated with 'Westernization', or Europeanization. It is described as the process of trying 'to attain the level of high civilization of the West'. Atatürk clearly underlined this fact in a speech: 'We want to modernize our country. Our aim is to establish a modern, therefore a Western state in Turkey. Is there a nation which has shown willingness to enter civilization but has refrained from turning to the West?'[50] Furthermore, he legitimized his arguments in the following statements:

> We can not easily separate modernity and tradition from some specific tradition and some specific modernity, some version which functions ideologically as a directive. The modern comes to the traditional society as a particular culture with its own traditions. In this respect it has been impossible to divorce modernization from some process of westernization.[51]

In fact, there is a vast literature on theories of modernization. According to Huntington, modernization is defined as 'a multifaceted process involving changes in all areas of human thought and activity'.[52] In addition, Dean Tipps characterizes the modernization process as 'transformational in its impact and progressive in its effects, which not only touches at one time or another virtually every institution of society, but does so in a manner such that transformations of one institutional sphere tend to produce complementary transformations in others'.[53]

Let me review here Huntington's theories of modernization, which generally overlap with the Kemalist modernization project:

- Modernization is a revolutionary process. This follows directly from the contrasts between modern and traditional society. The one differs fundamentally from the other, and the change to tradition to modernity consequently involves a radical and total change in patterns of human life. The shift from tradition to modernity, as Cyril Black says, is comparable to the changes from prehuman to human existence and from primitive to civilized societies. The changes in the eighteenth century, Reinhard Bendix echoes, were 'comparable in magnitude only to the transformation of nomadic peoples into settled agriculturalists some 10,000 years earlier' (Black, *Modernization*, pp. 1–5; Reinhard Bendix, 'Tradition and Modernity Reconsidered', *Comparative Studies in Society and History*, IX (April 1967) 292–3).

- Modernization is a complex process. It cannot be easily reduced to a single factor or to a single dimension. It involves changes in virtually all areas of human thought and behaviour. At a minimum, its components include: industrialization, urbanization, social mobilization, differentiation, secularization, media expansion, increasing literacy and education, expansion of political participation.
- Modernization is a systemic process. Changes in one factor are related to affect changes in the other factors. Modernization, as Daniel Lerner has expressed it in an oft-quoted phrase, is 'a process with so, a distinctive quality of its own, which would explain why modernity is felt as a consistent whole among people who live by its rules.' The various elements of modernization have been highly associated together 'because, in some historic sense, they had to go together' (Daniel Lerner, *The Passing of Traditional Society*, Glence, 1958) p. 438.
- Modernization is a global process. Modernization originated in fifteenth and sixteenth century Europe, but it has now become a worldwide phenomenon. This is brought about primarily through the diffusion of modern ideas and techniques from the European centre, but also in part through the endogenous development of non-Western

societies. In any event, all societies were at one time traditional; all societies are now either modern or in the process of becoming modern.

- Modernization is a lengthy process. The totality of the changes which modernization involves can only be worked out through time. Consequently, while modernization is revolutionary in the extent of the changes it brings about in traditional society, it is evolutionary in the amount of time required to bring about those changes. Western societies required several centuries to modernize. The contemporary modernizing societies will do it in less time. Rates for modernization are, in this sense, accelerating, but the time required to move from tradition to modernity will still be measured in generations.
- Modernization is a phased process. It is possible to distinguish different levels or phases of modernization through which all societies will move. Societies obviously began in the traditional stage and end in the modern stage. The intervening transitional phase, however, can also be broken down into subphases. Societies consequently can be compared and ranked in terms of the extent to which they have moved down the road from tradition to modernity. While the leadership in the process and the more detailed patterns of modernization will differ from one society to another, all societies will move through essentially the same stages.
- Modernization is an irreversible process. While there may be temporary breakdowns and occasional reversals in elements of the modernizing process, modernization as a whole is an essentially secular trend. A society which has reached certain levels of urbanization, literacy, industrialization in one decade will not decline to substantial lower levels in the next decade. The rates of change will vary significantly from one society to another, but the direction of change will not.

- Modernization is a progressive process. The traumas of modernization are many and profound, but in the long run modernization is not only inevitable, it is also desirable. The costs and the pains of the period of transition, particularly its early phases, are great, but the achievement of a modern social, political, and economic order is worth them. Modernization in the long run enhances human well-being, culturally and materially.[54]

Nevertheless, it should be pointed out that every country outside of the West experienced modernization process in a different manner and in its own way. Although we can not deny the pre-eminent influence of Western ideas in Turkish modernization, such as positivism, solidarism, French secularism, rationalism, etc., the immanent social, cultural, and political characteristics of Turkish society have been particularly decisive in the configuration of Turkish modernism.

The modernizing elites in Turkey placed great emphasis on the adoption of the external features of Western societies rather than the institutional and structural dynamics of their systems in the first stage, which consequently resulted in failure and orientation towards the 'fetishism' of Western products and material life.[55] This attitude can be explained by the utilitarian character of the Kemalist westernization process. In fact, this process was initiated with defensive purposes during the Ottoman era in the nineteenth century in order to save the country. Once this mission was completed, the westernization attempts eventually took on a utilitarian and eventually symbolic nature during the Republican era to catch up with the West and develop the country.

To elucidate Mustafa Kemal's emphasis on the change of outward appearance let me give Mustafa Kemal's critics on veil and fez:

> Gentlemen, it was necessary to abolish the fez, which sat on

the heads of our nation as an emblem of ignorance, negligence, fanaticism, and hatred of progress and civilization, to accept in its place the hat, the headgear used by the whole civilized world, and in this way to demonstrate that the Turkish nation, in its mentality as in other respects, in no way diverges from civilized social life.[56]

Gentlemen, the Turkish people who founded the Turkish Republic are civilized; they are civilized in history and in reality. But I tell you as your own brother, as your friend, as your father, that the people of the Turkish Republic, who claim to be civilized, must show and prove that they are civilized, by their ideas and mentality, by their family life and their way of living. In a word, the true civilized people of Turkey ... must prove in fact that they are civilized and advanced persons also in their outward aspect. I must make these last words clear to you, so that the whole country and the world may easily understand what I mean. I shall put my explanations to you in the form of a question.

Is our dress national? [Cries of no!]

Is it civilized and international? [Cries of no, no!]

I agree with you. This grotesque mixture of styles is neither national nor international. ... My friends, there is no need to seek and revive the costume of Turan. A civilized, international dress is worthy and appropriate for our nation, and we will wear it. Boots or shoes on our feet, trousers on our legs, shirt and tie, jacket and waistcoat – and, of course, to complete these, a cover with a brim on our heads. I want to make this clear. This head-covering is called 'hat' (quoted by Bernard Lewis, *Soylev*, ii. 212–13).

In some places I have seen women who put a piece of cloth or a towel or something like it over their heads to hide their faces, and who turn their backs or huddle themselves on the ground when a man passes by. What are the meaning and sense of this behaviour? Gentlemen, can the mothers

> and daughters of a civilized nation adopt this strange manner, this barbarous posture? It is a spectacle that makes the nation an object of ridicule. It must be remedied at once.[57]

Nilüfer Göle defines this type of modernist approach as a general characteristic of all non-Western societies. She propounded that non-Western societies which followed a different path from the West created 'extra-modernity' which is neither the exact replica of the Western modernity nor the opposite.[58] As a result, imported concepts such as 'secularism, nationalism, and equality acquired new and exaggerated meanings' in non-Western societies.[59] This type of 'extra modernity', as I already mentioned, 'takes the form of fetishism eventually'.[60] Consequently, these non-Western nations become more Western than the West itself. This is exactly what we are experiencing in Turkey today. As an illustration, secularism is overemphasized in Turkey to the extent that it took an exceptional meaning as different from French laicism, where it emanated from.[61] Consequently, the existence of 'extra-secularism' precludes the proper functioning of democracy, which constitutes another paradox of the Kemalist ideology.[62] Namely, this contradicts the modernization ideals. In fact, Turkish modernization allows only a 'restricted democratization'.[63]

All in all, the westernization process of Turkish society has not been a change of philosophy but of symbols and images. As I already mentioned, it is proper to stress here its utilitarian and symbolic character. Taha Parla pointed out that the Kemalist reformers preferred to modernize the country by selecting the features of the Western societies which suited and serve their ideology and left the others as they did to the Ottoman heritage.[64] In this sense, the Kemalist ideology is 'pragmatic' and 'flexible' in nature. As Kemal Karpat stated, 'the state policy is distinctly opportunist in its attitude: that is, it is favourable to whatever in Islam is consistent with republican ideals, relentlessly opposed to anything which might endanger Kemalist success, and, for the rest, more or less neutral.'[65] As Şerif Mardin also comments, 'the republic took over educational institutions and cultural practices (museums, painting and sculpture, secularism) from the West without realizing that these were just the tip of an iceberg of meanings, perceptions, and ontological positions.'[66] It did not inherit concepts such as 'human rights, democracy, diversity, civil society'.[67] That is to say, the Republican modernizers adopted the symbols ('such as hat instead of fez, Latin alphabet, Gregorian calendar, European numerals, and metric system') instead of concepts, which left Turkish modernization deprived of a solid base.[68] As a consequence, 'the historical genesis of the state tradition in Turkey determined the choices made by the modernizers in their attempt to delimit the scope of modernity, thus undermining their avowed goal of Westernization.'[69] All these factors prepared the ground for the Muslim intellectuals to criticize and accuse the Kemalist modernization programme of imitating the West.

Breakdown of the Kemalist ideology's hegemony

I am propounding that the failure of the inherent paradoxes of the Kemalist ideology and it westernisation project concomitant with the crisis of modernity and the nation state in addition to the economic, political and social liberalization and developments during the 1980s paved the way for the decline of its ideological attractiveness and hegemonic nature, which instigated political and ideological contestation. This happened on all sides, but one of the most striking results was the emergence of recently urbanized and well educated Muslim intellectuals to reconstruct their identity in opposition to Kemalism.

To elaborate, parallel to the changes in the international arena such as the rise of globalization, development of the international trade and global economy; the collapse of communism and the demise of the Cold War period and the communist threat; political liberalization of Third World countries, the reliability of modernization began to decline. Concomitantly, the Kemalist modernization paradigm also lost its credibility. 'Like all the state-oriented and latently authoritarian concepts of modernization', writes Heinz Kramer: 'Kemalism becomes dysfunctional if the stage of social development has crossed the threshold beyond which the majority of the population is no longer ready to follow but demands to become the master of its own fate. Turkey has reached this point.'[70]

It is hard to argue that the secularist and cultural modernization policies of the Kemalist ideology transformed the countryside as much as it affected the intellectual elites in the large cities and towns, who were already acquainted with Western values.[71] The vast majority of people remained traditional and retained their religious beliefs; therefore, especially after the one-party era, they began to display their discontent towards the oppressive and anti-clerical policies of the Kemalist state against 'folk Islam'.[72]

Moreover, 'the inability of Atatürk's educational reforms to reach the rural masses left a blank in their understanding of social reality, which became critical as social change mobilized large numbers of them.'[73] Similarly, the Kemalists' efforts to reform Islam also failed:

> Because the ground was not ready for it and the inner urge to make such a reform was lacking Reform could have occurred only when modern material and cultural elements were sufficiently entrenched to create a need for spiritual adjustment and to effect that adjustment while preserving their own identity.[74]

In addition, the Kemalist ruling elites' distant and suspicious attitude towards the traditional masses together with their inability to fulfill their promises in terms of social, economic, and political modernization of the countryside reduced the credibility of the Kemalist modernist ideology. That is, the rural people were affected negatively by the growing centralization and influence of the state in most aspects of life. According to the Village Law of 1924, the state imposed various obligations and duties on village people.[75] The establishment of control through the 'central law enforcement as gendarmerie stations through the countryside', the creation of universal military conscription system and regulations on registration and taxation indicate the increasing role and control of the state in society.[76]

It is essential to note that it is impossible to transform the superstructure of a society without changing the infrastructure.[77] The modernist elite of Turkey overlooked this fact. Instead they concentrated their efforts on cultural modernization and disestablishment of Islam.

Evidently, cultural modernization without achieving industrialization created an anomaly, a peculiar kind of quasi-modernity unique to Turkey. The 'forced', selective, and immature westernization project generated 'bourgeoisie modernization', which precluded the formation of a steadfast 'democratic capitalist alternative'.[78]

Besides, fast industrialization with its associated rapid urbanization caused social transformation and differentiation during the late 1960s, which became more dramatic with the crisis of import substituting industrialization (ISI) during the 1970s and rise of globalization. The predominantly rural and traditional profile of the country became urban and industrialized. People realized that the society is not homogenous and classless as the Kemalist ideology asserted.[79] The statist and monopolist strategy of the state prevented the economic development and prosperity of the nation as a whole. As a result there existed uneven social and economic development in favour of the dominantly urban western areas compared to the relatively rural eastern part of Turkey.

Çağlar Keyder explains this fact as follows:

> Regional inequality, with the greater Istanbul area and the

> western provinces in general receiving most of the benefits of economic growth, led to political reaction in smaller Anatolian towns, and fueled ethnic and religious strife. All these conditions were set in an ideological climate where rapid social transformation threatened traditional belief systems and combined them in bizarre forms with a savagely individualistic market ideology and a desperate search for a new source of authority.[80]

As a consequence, all of these factors contributed to the breakdown of the reliability and legitimacy of the Kemalist modernization process. In addition, the vacuum created by its delegitimization was filled with the religious discourse and revival of cultural Islam. Before analysing the reasons for this revival since the 1980s, I should point out that

> value conflicts become most intense in times of substantial socio-political or economic change, the dynamics of which give rise to new systems of thought and value; once the religio-political framework is put to question, there always remain quasi-marginal groups in society whose normative and/or economic interests are threatened by the new kinds of power relationships, economic arrangements, and political activity.[81]

In addition, I contend that the resistance movements against westernization, which are suggesting the return to local traditions and religious values, disprove the widely held belief that diverse cultures and societies are eliminated by the harmonizing effect of modernization. On the contrary, they become much stronger than before as a result of their struggle against modernism. The revival of Islam and the religious rhetorics of Islamist intellectuals confirm this. 'The simpler theories of modernization' as Huntington has suggested,

> implied a zero-sum relation between the two: the rise of modernity in society was accompanied by the fading of tradition. In many ways, however, modernity supplements but does not supplant tradition. Modern practices, beliefs, institutions are simply added to traditional ones. It is false to believe that tradition and modernity 'are mutually exclusive'. Modern society is not simply modern; it is modern and traditional. The attitudes and behaviour patterns may in some cases be fused; in others, they may comfortably coexist, one alongside the other, despite the apparent incongruity of it all. In addition, one can go further and argue not only that coexistence is possible but that modernization itself may strengthen tradition. It may give new life to important elements of the pre-existing culture, such as religion.[82]

So, what were the social, political, and economic reasons behind the increaseing influence of Islamic intellectuals since the 1980s?

The military coup in September 1980 caused a number of political, economic and ideological changes, as a result of which the Islamization of the society and politics accelerated. In order to eliminate the social and political conflict, as well as reunite the society and ensure its solidarity, the military, which has the central and autonomous position in politics of the country as the protector of Kemalist values and secularism, emphasized the role of Islam and supported the 'Turkish–Islamic synthesis'.[83] This ideology was also seen as a panacea for leftist and communist threat. In fact, the 'Turkish–Islamic synthesis', which was formed earlier by the *Aydınlar Ocağı* (Intellectual Hearths) during 1970s, is an amalgamation of 'Turkish nationalism and moderate Islam and its essentials were the family, the mosque, and the military barracks.'[84] So this shift in the state's attitude towards Islam led to the 'Islamization of secularism' and at the same time the 'nationalization of Islam', which accelerated with the prime minister Turgut Özal's liberal approach towards Islam.[85] Initially, religious education became obligatory in public schools by the 1982 constitution.[86] The number of imam-hatip schools[87] rose remarkably 'from 72 in 1970, to 374 in 1980, to 389 in 1992'.[88] At the same time the increasing financial and political power of the Directorate of Religious Affairs, together with the privatization of education, led to the proliferation of religious schools.[89]

Moreover Özal's tolerant and relaxed policies towards Islam also facilitated and increased the activities and public appearances of the Islamic groups. As a result of privatization and deregulation of the mass media, Islamic television channels, newspapers, magazines, publishing houses prospered rapidly.[90] Parallel to these developements, democratization and the liberal environment engendered the creation of a more pluralistic and open society as a result of which the civil society and non-governmental organizations became widespread.[91] A number of socio-cultural Islamic organizations, Sufi orders, Islamic business associations (MÜSIAD), human rights organizations (Mazlum-Der), and trade unions (Hak-İş) prospered during this period. They also became influential and manipulative on the political and economic life of the country.[92] Consequently, through the development of liberal democracy, the Islamic groups were able to carry their messages to the public spaces.[93] In other words, 'the processes of democratization carried political Islamic views and sensitivies from the periphery to the centre of the political forum.'[94] At the same time, a liberal democratic environment strengthened the 'multiethnic' and 'multicultural' society – Islamist and secularist; Turk and Kurd; traditional and modern; rural and urban – which weakened the paradigm of the homogeneous, monolithic and uniform nation state of the Kemalist ideology.[95]

Moreover the liberal economic policies of Turgut Özal, who strongly endorsed an export oriented, free market economy in conformity with the pressures of global capitalism led to impoverishment of the middle and lower classes and exacerbated the income inequality.[96] While only a minority benefited from the economic expansion, the majority was hit by the capitalization of the economy and suffered from high inflation and unemployment rates as well as rising costs of living.[97] Moreover, the incorporation to the global economy and the internationalization of trade and capital and the rise of multinational corporations made the nationalist developmentalism paradigm obsolete.[98] In addition to this, the rapid expansion of the economy during the 1980s also increased social mobility and urbanization, which was accompanied by huge social, cultural change and differentiation. Besides, structural contrasts within the society became sharper.

In fact, as Huntington indicates fast economic growth leads to 'political instability', which can mobilize religious groups:

> Political mobilization, moreover, does not necessarily require the building of factories or even movement to the cities. It may result simply from increases in communications, which can stimulate major increases in aspirations that may be only partially, if at all, satisfied. The result is a 'revolution of rising frustration'.
>
> ... In Turkey, Pakistan, and Burma, the Republican People's Party, Muslim League, and AFPFL deteriorated and military intervention eventually ensued. In party organizations and bureaucracies, marked increases in corruption often accompanied significant declines in the effectiveness of governmental services. Particularistic groups – tribal, ethnic, religious – frequently reasserted themselves and further undermined the authority and coherence of political institutions.[99]

Furthermore, Nilüfer Göle elucidates the resurgence of Islam as a process, which derived from a search for an 'ideal' between itself and modernity by reconstructing the past in today.[100]

So all these developments indicate the collapse of modernity and the hegemonic character of the Kemalist ideology among certain segments of the society. As a result, the Islamist intellectuals become the voice of these marginalized groups, who felt themselves alienated, neglected, and disaffected from the westernization project. As Emile Sahliyeh pointed out, 'religion would presumably restore traditional family values and give its adherents a sense of continuity and direction.'[101] The Islamist theorists' stress on the importance of tradition, religion, and ethical and communitarian values enabled them to gain support from these masses. In other words, these people, who migrate to cities as part of globalization and industrialization, try to overcome the identity crisis and sense of insecurity by resorting to religion and morality. As Binnaz Toprak puts it, 'the Islamic movement not only resolved problems of identity and conservative angst; it became a channel to political power, social status, intellectual prestige, and economic wealth for people who in one way or another had been marginalized by the republican ethos,'[102] Consequently, 'Islam, not as a theological phenomenon but as the ideological expression of a certain contemporary social reality, provided the uniting bond, the common social-moral context, and the common language that enabled the coexistence and cooperation of different groups within the same political organization: urban migrants and rural villagers, Turkish nationalists and traditional Kurds, young educated professionals and small traders and artisans of the central Anatolian townships.'[103]

The striking fact I shall note is that contemporary Islamist intellectuals took advantage of the modernization process by using its tools and instruments, which they criticize. That is, improvements in education, information, and communication systems, mass media, and others, which are the products of modernity, enabled Muslim theorists in contemporary Turkey to spread their ideas more extensively and effectively than before.

As Samuel Huntington suggests:

> Increased communication may thus generate demands for more 'modernity' than can be delivered. It may also stimulate a reaction against modernity and activate tra-

> ditional forces. Since the political arena is normally dominated by the more modern groups, it can bring into the arena new, anti-modern groups and break whatever consensus exists among the leading political participants.[104]

To sum up, in my research I came to the belief that the project of 'Westernization' was carried out superficially in Turkey. It would be unjust to ignore certain achievements of the Kemalist westernization project in modernizing and developing the social, economic, and industrial life of the country such as the education, health and judicial systems, communication, transport, agricultural reform. To give an example, as a result of the establishment of a modern education system, 'the number of schools doubled' from 5602 to 11,040 between 1923 and 1940; the number of teachers increased from 12,458 to 28,298; and the number of students rose from 352,268 to 1,050,159.[105] The foundation of the Village Institutes and People's Houses increased the education level of the people in villages as well as in towns. It is important to note the fact that the Muslim intellectuals themselves are influenced by these achievements of Kemalism. As a result, they were able to equip themselves intellectually with the opportunities of a modern education system and express their ideas freely and broadly. We can state that, as modernity produced rational, positivist, and secular intellectuals, its crisis created the Islamist intellectuals.

However, the accomplishments of Kemalism remained restricted in scale because modernization is equated with westernization and the adoption of West European culture and lifestyles without taking the internal dynamics and characteristics of the Turkish society into consideration. Furthermore, the native traditions and customs are ignored for the attainment of the 'highest level of Western civilization'. In fact, Kemalist reformers followed a 'selective' path in their Westernization project as they have continued to use some of the characteristics of the Ottoman heritage and deliberately ignored the others.[106] As a result of this illusional vision of the West, the modernization process in Turkey could not go further than imitating the material life and the so-called superior culture of the West European countries. These contradictions of the Kemalist ideology and its modernization project constitute today the core of the Muslim intellectuals' discourses.

Chapter 2

Analysis and Explanation of the Contemporary Turkish Muslim Intellectuals and their Discourses

'I have always sensed that the writings of the freedom-loving fighters do not go in vain, mainly because they awaken the sleepy, inflame the senses of the half-hearted, and lay the ground for a mass-oriented trend following a specific goal. ... Something must be happening under the influence of writing.'[1] Intellectuals have been, generally, the pioneers of thought and ideologies, who transform the mental, political, social, cultural, as well as economic lives of their societies by formulating new and original patterns of ideology and ways of thinking. In this sense, their role in history is of paramount importance.

In this and next, I intend to give a broad and inclusive analysis of some of the leading Islamist intellectuals in contemporary Turkey. But before doing this, the concept of 'intellectual' will be examined. Correspondingly, I will ask these questions: who is an intellectual? Should the intellectuals intervene in decision making processes? Is every scholar and educated person intellectual? What kinds of media do the intellectuals use?

Subsequently, I will give an historical account of the Turkish intellectuals' evolution, followed by the presentation of biographies of the leading Muslim intellectuals in contemporary Turkey.

Then, I will investigate the worldviews and arguments of Islamist intellectuals with reference to their understanding and interpretations of both secular and religious issues. Special emphasis will be given to their ideas and critiques on secular values, which are offsprings of modernity, such as democracy, laicism and secularism, human rights, capitalism, Marxism, liberalism, civil societies and technology. However, this does not mean that I will ignore their ideas on religious and theological problems and issues.

Intellectualism as a concept

The use of the term *intellectual* as a name indicating a specific class dates back to the 1860s:

> The term intelligentsia was used in Russia during the 1860s to refer to a self-conscious elite of the well educated, characterized by critical tendencies toward the status quo; the term 'intellectuals' came into vogue through the 'Manifesto of Intellectuals', protesting the French government's persecution of Analysis and Explanation of the Contemporary Turkish Muslim Intellectuals and their Discourses.[2]

Prior to this incident, the term had been used as an adjective meaning 'mental' and 'moral'.[3] In fact, the term 'intellectual' had begun to be used with the emergence of secular intellectuals.[4]

> It is true that in their earlier incarnations as priests, scribes, and soothsayers, intellectuals have laid claim to guide society from the very beginning. But as guardians of hieratic cultures ... their moral and ideological innovations were limited by the canons of external authority and by the inheritance of tradition.[5]

However, as John Esposito points out, 'the development of modern society resulted in a decline in the influence of the older style of intellectuals and the emergence of the secular intellectuals.'

> For the first time in human history, and with growing confidence and audacity, men arose to assert that they could diagnose the ills of society and cure them with their own unaided intellects: more, that they could devise formulae whereby not merely the structure of society but the fundamental habits of human beings could be transformed for the better. Unlike their sacerdotal predecessors, they were not servants and interpreters of the gods but substitutes.[6]

During my search of the literary meaning of the word, I encountered several definitions:

(i) a person, who values or pursues intellectual interests;
(ii) a person professionally engaged in mental labour;[7]
(iii) a person possessing a high level of understanding or intelligence; cultured;
(iv) a person possessing a highly developed intellect.[8]
(v) a person of superior (or supposedly superior) intellect, especially one having an analytic mind; an enlightened person.[9]

In addition to these definitions, Edward Shills described intellectuals as:

> The aggregate of persons in any society who employ in their communication and expression, with relatively higher frequency than most other members of their society, symbols of general scope and abstract reference, concerning man, society, nature, and the cosmos. The high frequency of their use of such symbols may be a function of their own

> subjective propensity or of the obligations of an occupational role.[10]

As stated by Joseph Schumpeter, 'intellectuals are in fact people who wield the power of the spoken and the written word, and one of the touches that distinguish them from other people who do the same is the absence of direct responsibility for practical affairs'.[11] They are not 'a social class in the sense in which peasants or industrial labourers constitute social classes; they hail from all the corners of the social world, and a great part of their activities consists in fighting each other and in forming the spearheads of class interests not their own.'[12]

Furthermore, Edward Said described 'the figure of intellectual as a being set apart, someone able to speak the truth, a … courageous and angry individual for whom no worldly power is too big and imposing to be criticized and pointedly taken to task.'[13]

According to one of the prominent Iranian intellectuals, Abdolkarim Soroush, 'the intellectual is society's critical conscience and the intellectual's main task is to produce ideas.' He identifies their features as: '(1) insight; (2) boldness; (3) theoretical innovation in times of crisis, rupture, and transition; (4) multi-sourcedness' and opposes the idea that 'every educated person is an intellectual' since most of them lack inspiration and the imaginative capacity, which make the intellectuals a distinctive class.[14]

Furthermore, as Timothy Garton Ash explained, the task of intellectual is

> to seek truth and then to present it as fully and as clearly and as interestingly as possible. … He has the role of the thinker or writer who engages in public discussion of issues of public policy, in politics in the broadest sense, while deliberately not engaging in the pursuit of political power.[15]

Soroush puts forward a similar position:

> The task of the intellectual is to fulfill secondary needs, and they are the producers of ideas, art, critiques, and opinions. Their path is thereby separate from – although not necessarily opposed to – that of the state, which must fulfill primary needs. The state uses intellectuals and has to have an intellectual base. But intellectual work, which has no class interest, must not become entangled with the work of the bureaucratic state machinery, which does have a class base. All this calls to mind the famous narrative attributed to the Prophet that says: 'The best rulers are those who serve learned men and the worst learned men are those who serve rulers.' The two must maintain their independence. The state must not wish to see intellectuals as its cronies and servants, for this would only serve to corrupt and distort intellectual work. …
>
> The intellectual must also not make the mistake of thinking that the attainment of power would allow him to exercise a constructive mastery over the country's cultural affairs. … They can be of much greater service to culture and society by staying away from power.[16]

The most prominent factor that characterizes intellectuals is the 'cultural capital' that they own. Weber indicated that 'education is as much capital in the modern economy as are factory buildings or machines.'[17] Likewise, the prominent French sociologist Pierre Bourdieu distinguished four types of capital, which are economic, social, cultural, and symbolic. Accordingly, economic capital refers to money, property and the like, whereas cultural goods, educational achievements and diplomas constitute the means of 'cultural capital'. In other words, it is 'the means of appropriating the mechanisms of the field of cultural production', and its possession provides its owner with 'cultural domination', similar to money as the means of economic capital.[18] In relation to other types of capital, social relations, family or networks of friends designate 'social capital'; and prestige as the source social recognition constitutes 'symbolic capital'.[19] So, all these forms of capital form different sources of 'class power'.[20]

Moreover, Gramsci, who lived between the years that Weber and Bourdieu lived, appropriated for intellectuals an autonomous position and defined their role as the 'formulation of the interests and ideologies of the fundamental social classes'.[21] In fact, he distinguished between two types of intellectuals: 'traditional' and 'organic'. According to Gramsci, 'thinkers, journalists, philosophers, writers, poets constitute traditional intellectuals, who choose intellectual activity as their profession.'[22] They intentionally involve themselves in 'cultural literacy agendas' and educate the masses from above.'[23] Furthermore, the organic intellectuals can come from any occupational group. They can be 'pharmacist, lawyers, teachers, priests, doctors, scientists, researchers, technicians, engineers, military personnel, judges, members of the police', and

> they do not produce knowledge but disseminate information or withhold information in the service of disciplining the body and the mind for the powers that be. These types of intellectual exercise subaltern functions of social hegemony and political government. As agents within cultural and social institutions, they mediate between the interests of power (the owners and controllers of the means of production) and those social groups who serve the interests of the class in power.[24]

He asserts that

> every social group, coming into existence on the original terrain of an essential function in the world of economic production, creates together with itself, organically, one or more strata of intellectuals which give it homogeneity and an awareness of its own function not only in the economic but also in the social and political fields'[25]

Thus Gramsci considers the function of the organic intellectuals more essential.

It is important to point out that with the advent of post-modernist debates, the intelligentsia began to be generally critical, independent, progressive, and questioning the universal project of modernity. 'As historical conditions change', wrote Carl Boggs,

> so too does the role of intellectuals; far from being either fixed or rootless, intellectual groupings are formed and reformed on both the material and cultural terrain.
>
> If modernity expresses certain universal symbols and goals in the form primarily of scientific and technological rationality, its crisis reflects a fundamental challenge to these and other forms of global hegemony against the backdrop of sharpening social contradictions. Whereas modernity entails a revolt against all that is traditional, on the basis of instrumental and secular values, its antithesis (whether called 'postmodernism' or something else) suggests a further revolt yet involving multiple local struggles in a world no longer dominated by all-encompassing belief systems. The assault on modernity thus poses a challenge – or series of challenges – to the ongoing rationalization of all areas of life, leading potentially to an enlarging of the public sphere where critical discourse can be heard and have action consequences.[26]

Alvin Gouldner identified this new type of intellectuals as the 'New Class', which is characterized with its unique 'language behaviour' and 'culture of critical discourse':[27]

> The New Class is a new class: it is neither identical to the old working class nor to the old moneyed class; while sharing elements of both, it also has characteristics possessed by neither. Like the working class, the New Class earns its living through its labour in a wage system; but

> unlike the old working class, it is basically committed to controlling the content of its work and its work environment, rather than surrendering these in favour of getting the best wage bargain it can negotiate. ...
>
> Just as the New Class is not the proletariat of the past, neither is it the old bourgeoisie. It is, rather, a new cultural bourgeoisie whose capital is not its money but its control over valuable cultures.[28]

The evolution of intellectuals in Turkey

The prototype of the modern intellectuals began to appear intensively during the nineteenth century.[29] Before this time, knowledge was monopolized by religious authorities.[30] However, the westernization policies of the Ottoman Empire during the Tanzimat period[31] paved the way to the emergence of the first genre of modern intellectuals. The Ottomans called them as 'münevver', which (an Arabic cognate), signifies 'enlightened' and points at one and the same time to the traditional Islamic concept of divine enlightenment as well as to the humanistic values of the Western enlightenment.[32] The Young Ottomans, 'a group of Turkish intellectuals[33] who attained prominence during the late Tanzimat in the years 1867–78, are considered as the prototype of the modern Turkish intellectuals'.[34] They were 'at one and the same time the first men to make the ideas of the Enlightenment part of the intellectual equipment of the Turkish reading public and the first thinkers to try to work out a synthesis between these ideas and Islam.'[35] That is to say, 'they were the first ideologues of the Ottoman Empire and direct intellectual ancestors of the Turkish Republic.'[36] The Young Ottomans were not against the monarchy; rather they felt the need of reform and modernization in order to save the empire. They did not only introduce the Western political thought into the Ottoman Empire for the first time; they also affected later the ideology of the Republican elites.[37] Şerif Mardin points out that the Young Ottomans established all the necessary intellectual grounds for Turkish modernization 'from simplification of the written language to the idea of fundamental civil liberties'.[38]

As an illustration, Namık Kemal, who introduced for the first time the idea of 'homeland' (*patrie*) in his poems to the Turkish people and popularized the idea of 'liberty', inspired the upcoming generation of Turkish intellectuals.[39] Şinasi, who instigated the thoughts and ideologies of Young Ottomans, published first private Turkish newspaper *Tercüman-i Ahval* (1860) and later *Tasvir-i Efkar* (1860), which disseminated Western ideas and broke the classical rules of Ottoman literature.[40] He is considered as 'the first supporter of Europeanization in the Ottoman Empire and the real founder of the modern Ottoman literature school.'[41]

The 1890s witnessed the generation of the Young Turks[42] (1895–1918), who 'strove for the regeneration of the Ottoman Empire in the late nineteenth and early twentieth centuries'.[43] They struggled for the reopening of the Parliament and re-establishment of the constitutional system, which was abandoned in 1878 by Sultan Abdülhamid II. In fact, what they aimed for was the establishment of a modern bureaucratic system in place of the Abdülhamid's 'neopatrimonial' administration, which is considered as 'a step toward modernization with the mandate of science'.[44] Essentially, the ideology of the Young Turks was 'originally scientific, materialist, social Darwinist, elitist, and vehemently antireligious'.[45] Şerif Mardin defined them as 'raisers of consciousness', who had initiated a search for systematic, internally consistent theory of reform'.[46] Their agenda consisted of 'a strong government, the dominant role played by an intellectual elite, anti-imperialism, a society in which Islam would play no governing role and Turkish nationalism, which became their guiding ideology, especially after 1906.'[47] They were highly influential in the formation of the Turkish Republic's official ideology.[48] As Paul Dumont indicates, Kemalist ideology largely influenced and unbroken originated from the intellectual climate of the second half of the nineteenth century.[49] In other words, 'there is an unbroken continuity in Turkish modernist doctrine from the ideology of Tanzimat to the six Kemalist arrows.'[50] Consequently, 'the anti-clericalism, scientism, biological materialism, authoritarianism, intellectual elitism, distrust of the masses, social Darwinism, and nationalism' of the Kemalist elites have their origins in the thoughts of the Young Turks.[51]

In the Republican era, the intellectuals played a quintessential role in Turkish society, which lacked powerful social groups, in contrast to the West.[52] The intelligentsia continued to have a 'bureaucratic identity' in addition to their intellectual identity.[53] In fact, they had been one of the agents of Turkey's transformation. Furthermore, during the Republican era the term *münevver* is transformed into *aydın*, which designates the Ottoman and Turkish intellectuals' indebtedness to the Enlightenment period of the West.[54]

Generally speaking, the secularization of education (1924), the change from the Arabic to Latin script (1928), the expansion of primary schools to the countryside, and other crucial reforms in education system concomitant with urbanization and capitalist development from the 1950s onwards enabled the creation of a new type of intellectual in Turkey.[55] During the One-Party period, the Turkish intellectuals were dominantly Kemalist and 'elitist' in nature, and strove for the establishment of the Kemalist ideology and the westernisation of the country. As an illustration, people involved in the *Halk Evleri* (People's Homes), followers of Ziya Gökalp, Yakup Kadri Karaosmanoğlu, Falih Rıfkı Atay, Fuat Köprülü, and Yunus Nadi, were the most important among them. In fact, there was intellectual poverty during that time, and these few intellectuals can be considered as organic intellectuals in the Gramscian sense.

Journals were of paramount importance in promoting intellectual activity. During the 1920s, the *Journal of Aydınlık (Enlightenment)* gathered the intellectuals around itself.[56] Şefik Hüsnü Deymer[57] and Hikmet Kıvılcımlı[58] contributed many articles on historical materialism and on the application of

Marxist thought to the conditions of Turkey in the *Journal of Aydınlık* during these years.

Yet, the Marxists were not dominant. The '*Kadro Hareketi*' (Movement of Cadre) around the journal *Kadro*, published by Yakup Kadri Karaosmanoğlu and Şevket Süreyya, was essential in the intellectual life of the 1930s. It not only attempted to solidify the Kemalist regime and its ideology but also the idea of 'nationalism'.[59] It aimed to establish the idea of 'nationalism' in place of 'class concept'.[60]

In addition, there were also ultranationalist intellectuals. Among them, Nihal Atsız, a significant Pan-Turkist thinker, historian and literary figure, was the most remarkable. He committed his life to represent and spread the Turanist ideology through his pan-Turkist journal *Orhun* and his articles, novels, poems, and books. His aspiration was to unite the entire Turkish nation including those are living in irredenta.

After the Second World War, we witness a completely different environment. The famous poet and Muslim thinker Necip Fazıl Kısakürek, who actively opposed the Kemalist regime since the 1930s, and his pro-Islamist intellectual and literary magazine *Büyük Doğu* (The Great East), which was suspended several times by the government, was very influential in the formation and diffusion of the Islamist worldview.[61] In this journal and in his other writings, Necip Fazıl Kısakürek opposed the Jacobin secularism of the Kemalist state.[62] In fact he resisted the secularist and authoritarian policies of the Republican People's Party's (RPP).

Later during the 1970s, Necip Fazıl Kısakürek's role was taken by Sezai Karakoç, who was also one of the most prominent conservative Islamist intellectuals and poets – with a very strong Islamic agenda. His pro-Islamist intellectual and literary magazine *Diriliş* (Revival), which was published during the years 1974–78, aimed to increase the Islamic consciousness of the public and particularly the young generation. In fact, the current Muslim thinkers were nurtured and influenced by this journal and its thoughts.

In addition, the journal, *Markopaşa* was published by Sabahattin Ali and Aziz Nesin during 1946–48. It was a comic paper with a socialist outlook, which preponderantly criticized the existing political and social system.[63] Moreover, there were other journals, such as *Yeni Adam* (New Man) and *Yurt ve Dünya* (Nation and the World); but *Markopaşa* was the most influential and successful journal of its time.[64]

The 1950s were marked by the journal *Forum* (Forum) which put great emphasis on 'scientific thought' and had an 'anti-communist' character.[65] Later during the 1960s, the journal Yön (*Direction*) replaced *Forum*. This journal had a neo-Kemalist position, which saw Kemalism as the panacea for all political and economic problems.[66]

In fact, the Ottoman and Turkish intellectuals between 1860–1960 are state-oriented and bureaucratic in nature that sets them apart from the West. However from mid-1960s onwards real leftist and Marxist intellectuals emerged, who contested Kemalist ideology. Nevertheless they spoke a different language and hence it was a debate within the elite. So there was not large public support.

Capitalist development, industrialization, urbanization, and the demise of the one-party era after 1950 and the relatively relaxed and tolerant attitude of the state towards religion with the beginning of the multi-party period allow the emergence of culturally conservative, but economically and politically liberal intellectuals in contrast to the conventional, secular, Kemalist elites or socialist intellectuals.[67] They supported capitalist growth and had more organic relations with the rest of society compared with other intellectuals.[68] Their practical influence was greater than their intellectual capability.[69] Moreover, we can observe the occurrence of a 'technological intelligentsia'[70] as a result of the advance of capitalism during the 1960s and thereafter. Nilüfer Göle, described them as 'engineers, who represent the technical elite and have been agents of social and economic development and who have taken an active part in political movements, supporting some of the dominant ideological trends of the times.'[71]

Finally, it can be stated that the bureaucracy played a significant role in the formation, and functioning of intellectuals in Turkey, as a result of which the independence and creativity of the intellectuals remained restricted.[72]

Muslim intellectuals in contemporary Turkey

In the light of these factors, the concept of 'intellectual', which has always been conceived in connotation with the humanist, secular, positivist, socialist or Marxist, or nationalist type of intelligentsia in the modern Turkish Republic, has changed with the emergence of the Islamist[73] thinkers, who are writing in a journalistic, intellectual, or scholarly vein from an Islamist point of view with a Muslim identity. They are considered as public intellectuals. The Muslim intellectuals are newspaper columnists, authors, government officials, or academicians, and mostly they are doing all of these professions at the same time, so most of them are supported by a government salary and consequently are not thoroughly independent intellectuals.

Other than this, they know each other and they collaborate. That is to say, they are not entirely independent in this sense.

Moreover, literature and poetry constructed the aesthetic ground for some of the Islamist intellectuals' thoughts and shaped their ideas.[74] That is to say, they use literature and poetry and their artistic creativity as a means to convey their beliefs in their search for truth. Particularly, two of the leading intellectuals, İsmet Özel, (who began his intellectual life as a poet) and Rasim Özdenören (as a novelist), are significant for their work and contributions to literature and poetry.

The Muslim intellectuals became more and more influential and publicly visible in the late 1970s and especially since the beginning of the 1980s. They critically and thoughtfully investtigate the contemporary problems of the world system in general and that of Turkey and Islam in particular in their columns in newspapers and journals, in television and radio programmes, panels, conferences, or in their books. Due to the spread of the mass media, the proliferation and privatization of television channels, and the political liberalization and democratization under the former Prime Minister Turgut Özal, their appeal to wide masses is facilitated. So they took advantage of the elimination of the state monopoly. Consequently, in contrast to earlier intellectuals, they are able to appear more frequently in media and thus have a larger public. That is to say, if there were only the state's official broadcasting channel (TRT), these Muslim intellectuals would not be able to reach this vast public.

Before embarking upon an in-depth analysis, let me briefly give the biographies of Ali Bulaç, İsmet Özel, Rasim Özdenoren, İlhan Kutluer, Ersin Nazif Gürdoğan, and Abdurrahman Dilipak, who I have chosen as the most prominent representatives of Muslim intellectuals on the basis of their popularity as well as intensity and prominence of their intellectual work.

Biography of the Muslim intellectuals

Ali Bulaç (journalist and author): he was born in the southeastern city of Mardin in 1951, where he completed his elementary and high school education. He became acquainted with religious knowledge and the Arabic language during his seven years of study in a medrese in Mardin. He then immigrated to Istanbul to study at the Istanbul Higher Islamic Institute in 1975. Later, he also studied sociology at Istanbul University. He founded the journal *Düşünce* (Thought) in 1976 and established the İnsan publishing house (1984) and the journal *Zaman* (Times) (1987). His articles have been published in magazines such as *Düşünce* (Thought), *İlim ve Sanat* (Science and Art), and *Hareket,* (Movement). Furthermore, he has been a columnist in various pro-Islamic magazines and newspapers such as *Zaman*, *Milli Gazete*, *Yeni Devir*, and *Yeni Şafak* and he is currently writing in *Zaman*.

İsmet Özel (poet, author, journalist): he was born in the central Anatolian city of Kayseri in 1944. He completed his pre-college education in Kastamonu, Çankırı, and Ankara. For a while, he attended the Faculty of Political Science of Ankara University. He then completed his university education in French Language and Literature at Hacettepe University in 1977. Together with Ataol Behramoğlu, İsmet Özel published a socialist journal called as *Halkın Dostları* (Friends of the People) in 1970. In the following years, his worldview changed dramatically and he began to write from an Islamic point of view as a true believer. *Geceleyin bir Koşu* (A Run in the Night) (1966), *İsyan* (Rebellion) (1969), *Cinayetler Kitabı* (Book of Crimes) (1975), *Celladıma Gülümserken* (While Smiling to my Executioner) (1984), *Erbain* (Midwinter) (1987), and *Bir Yusuf Masalı* (A Tale of Yusuf) (1999) are some of his books of poetry. He wrote in the newspapers *Yeni Devir* (New Age) (1977–1979, 1981–1982) and *Milli Gazete* (National Newspaper), which has an Islamic stance and flavour. He is currently writing in the journal *Gerçek Hayat* (The Real Life) and speaks both French and English. More importantly, he is a prominent poet in Turkey and gives lectures on poetry at Bilgi University. As Michael Meeker pointed out, he had been an inspiration for other Islamist intellectuals such as Ali Bulaç and Rasim Özdenören.[75] To put it specifically, in his first book *Three Problems: Technique, Civilization, Alienation* (1978), he refused to accommodate Western science and technology with Islamic beliefs and life.[76] This is one of their significant particularities that place the contemporary Muslim intellectuals in a unique and different position in comparison to nineteenth and early twentieth century Islamist elite.

Rasim Özdenören (journalist, author): He was born in the south-eastern city of Maraş in 1940. He attended primary and high school in Maraş, Malatya, and Tunceli, and then completed his studies at both the Law Faculty and the Institute of Journalism at Istanbul University. Afterwards, he worked in the State Planning Organization as an expert. After completing his Master's Degree in Development Economics (1970–71) in the United States, he became consultant and inspector in the Ministry of Culture (1975). He has written columns in the newspaper *Yeni Devir* (New Age). He is specifically interested in literature and philosophy. He has published various novels and five volume-length stories such as *Hastalar ve Işıklar* (Patients and Lights), *Çözülme* (Dissolution), *Çok Sesli Bir Ölüm* (A Very Loud Death), *Çarpılmışlar* (Touched by the Spirit), and *Denize Açılan Kapı* (A Door Opening to the Sea). He is presently columnist in the pro-Islamic newspaper *Yeni Şafak* (New Dawn).

İlhan Kutluer (academician, author): he was born in Biga in 1957. After completing primary and high school education in Biga, he studied philosophy at Istanbul University, where he also pursued his graduate degree on the programme of 'History of Turkish–Islamic Thought'. He finished his Ph.D. thesis in the Faculty of Religion of Marmara University, where he worked as research assistant. His Ph.D. thesis was entitled as 'The Emergence of Morality in the History of Philosophy of Islam'. He is currently associate professor in the Faculty of Religion at Marmara University. *Modern Bilimin Arka Planı* (The Unseen Agenda of Modern Science), *Erdemli Toplum ve Düşmanları* (The Virtuous Society and its Enemies), *Akıl ve İtikad* (Reason and Faith), and *Modern Bilimin Arka Planı* (The Background of Modern Science) are among his important books.

Ersin Nazif Gürdoğan (academician, author): he was born in Eskişehir in 1945. He received his bachelor degree in Mechanical Engineering at Istanbul Technical University. Later, he did his MA in Business and Administrative Sciences at Istanbul University in 1968. He worked as an expert on project evaluation in the State Planning Organization. He did research for one year in England. Gürdoğan got his Ph.D. degree on production methods at Ankara University (1975). He became professor in 1994. He is a columnist in the newspaper *Yeni Şafak* (New Dawn) and appears in TV programmes on religious channels. *Kirlenmenin Boyutları* (The Dimensions of Pollution), *Görünmeyen Üniversite* (The

Invisible University), *Kültür ve Sanayileşme* (Culture and Industrialization), *Teknolojinin Ötesi* (Beyond Technology), and *Yeni Roma* (New Rome) are some of his most popular books.

Abdurrahman Dilipak (author, journalist): he was born in Haruniye, Adana in 1949. He completed Religious High School in Konya (1969). He then studied Arabic and Persian Language at Istanbul University for a while. Afterwards, he studied at the Institute of Journalism and Public Relations of İstanbul Ticari İlimler Akademisi (Istanbul Academy of Commercial Sciences). He was one of the founders of the pro-Islamic newspaper *Yeni Devir* (New Age). He has written in various newspapers and journals such as *Cum'a* (Friday), *Milli Gazete* (National Newspaper), *Akit* (Contract), *Yeni Şafak* (New Dawn), *Aylık Görüş* (Monthly View), and *Gazete Gazetesi* (Newspaper of Newspaper), and taken part in many television programmes. He is currently writing in the Islamist newspaper *Vakit* (Time).

Definition and analysis of the Muslim intellectuals

The contemporary Muslim intelligentsia in Turkey can be characterized as intellectuals, or thinkers, who analyse and approach the issues from an Islamic standpoint with a Muslim identity. More elaborately, Michael Meeker defined the Muslim intellectual as:

> a new kind of believer who arises in response to the special challenges of contemporary life. His task is not to rework Islam so that it takes the form of yet one more modernist construction, but to show how its beliefs and practices remain a sufficient foundation for community in contemporary life.[77]

Although we identify them as 'Islamist Intellectuals' due to their Islamic stance and rhetorics, they favour being named 'Muslim Intellectuals' since they 'write as true believers'.[78] As Nilüfer Göle has stated, the term 'Muslim' denotes a 'religious identity' whereas 'Islamist' refers to a 'political consciousness and social action'.[79]

In general, the Muslim intellectuals write in an ironic, comparative, eloquent, and critical style. They combine investigative and analytical thinking methods with a considerable amount of sarcasm and cynicism. Generally speaking, they have an articulate, smooth, and fluent writing style. Among the Muslim intellectuals, İsmet Özel's style in particular appears derisive and aggressive. In contrast, Abdurrahman Dilipak is distinguished by his satiric, witty, and ironic outlook. They all use polemical language.

They constantly talk about morality and ethical issues, and take Islam as their reference point in all issues. That is to say, Islam and the principles of Sharia based on the Koran, Sunnah, and Hadith[80] are the measurement for the value and validity of everything. They often give citations from the Qur'an and use Islamic concepts.

It should be also stated here that in terms of their strong emphasis on the purity of the faith and adherence to the original sources of Islam, they belong to the group of puritanical Muslim revivalists.

Moreover, if we analyse their evolution from the 1980s through the 1990s, we do not see any remarkable change in their thinking. In other words, we observe that they repeat the same arguments, criticisms, and proposals. As İsmet Özel points out, their ideas throughout time did not alter; rather they have become more consolidated. So their worldviews and beliefs remain the same. Recently, İsmet Özel decided to discontinue his writings in the Islamic newspaper *Milli Gazete* (National Newspaper). He stated that he will devote himself only to poetry from this time onwards. The reason for this is not a change of his Islamist stance or views, as many people assume, but the demise of his belief in the sincerity and spirit of the commitment of some of the Muslim people, who are supposedly struggling for an Islamic way of life. In other words, he no longer believes that they will take action in order to realize an Islamic way of life.

Although the Islamist intellectuals often propose the replacement of the modern world order with an Islamic way of life, they do not mention clearly how this process will be realized. Binnaz Toprak also makes this point. She states that 'there is talk of a political struggle, but exactly how this struggle will be carried out remains unclear; there is to be a transformation in the course of which modern technology and industry will be destroyed, but what precisely is to replace them is unclear; a reduction of the intricate social, political, and economic relationships or a relatively complex society to their simpler forms is advocated, but no nuts and bolts discussion of the process is undertaken. At this point the new Islamist ideology seems to be geared toward raising religious consciousness alone.'[81] It seems to me that their objective is not to establish an ideology. In fact, the Muslim intellectuals state their aims as expressing and elucidating the truth and increasing the knowledge and awareness of the people. Ali Bulaç explains the objective of his writings as follows:

> the book is written for the young generations who feel the need to understand the cultural and social environment in which they live, especially for those students who are in the course of their lycee and higher studies, and for researching and investigating intellectuals. Its aim is to provide them with true, realistic, and healthy information regarding the socio-economic orders that makes up the modern world, and in doing so to offer criticism and open up alternative avenues of research.[82]

So they try to be functional. İsmet Özel points out that his aim in writing in the mass media is not to draw attention but to concentrate people's thoughts on the Qur'an.[83] In other words, they do not propound any kind of armed struggle or revolution for the transformation of the existing system. Therefore, it would be incorrect to define them as radicals. Essentially, they believe that this transformation can only be initiated through the inner development of the individuals through obeying the rules and principles of Islam.[84] In other words, the creation of an Islamic life is only possible if each and every individual in a society becomes a 'true Muslim'. So as they suggest, the revolution should occur within the self of the human being. Ersin Gürdoğan underlines that people who transform their inner world can change the outer world easily.[85] Furthermore, the new world order will be created through these people, who have matured within the culture of Islamic mysticism.

In fact Sufism (*tasawwuf*)[86] has an important place in Turkish Muslim intellectuals' thoughts and writings. In their view, *tasawwuf* is 'all the efforts, struggles, and actions of the people to understand the essence of the orders of Shar'ia and thus it is the continuation of the Sunnah.'[87] They often refer to the teachings of *tasawwuf*. Accordingly, this world is deficient but it is neither autonomous nor insignificant; rather, it has an esoteric meaning, which can only be grasped thorough the Heart instead of Reason because the projection of the Intellect is found in the Heart.[88] Consequently 'Heart is the centre of all humanly activities.'[89] They believe that the performances and teachings of *tasawwuf* enable the transformation of man's inner world, which liberates him from the chains of Ego and the material world and takes him to the Ultimate Reality.[90] Consequently, the new world order can be created with the culture of *tasawwuf*.[91]

In addition, Islamic intellectuals often resort to comparisons between West European culture and Christianity on the one hand and Islam and the Islamic way of life on the other. Generally speaking, they equate the West with modernity and consider it as evil and miserable factors which they assume are the source of each and every problem in the contemporary world. In other words, the denunciation of Western society as well as its culture and exaltation of the original form of Islam is the common language of the Islamist intellectuals. Consequently, they belong to the group of apologist Muslim intellectuals, because of their attack on modernity and the West, their defence of Islamic principles, and their reclamation of a glorified Islamic past.

In correlation to this, they constantly attack the Kemalist ideology and Republican policies, which, in their views, desacralized Turkish society. Moreover they envisage the rebirth of an Islamic community that will be based solely on the Koran and Sunnah, the original sources of Islam. In this way, the Islamic faith will be purified of all the derivative and alien elements brought by history and tradition. Paradoxically enough, although their Islamist discourses are against modernity and Kemalism, we should note that they have been educated in the secular institutions of this regime under the predominance of modern values and methodology. After completing high school (lycee) in their hometown in southern or Central Anatolia, they moved to large cities for their university education and eventually settled there, and broke the urban monopoly on intellectual debate. They are the products of the opening up of the provincial towns, migration, and social mobility as well as the spread of education. That is to say, the diffusion of education facilities and the expansion of printing presses facilitated the intellectual awakening of Muslim intellectuals.

In addition, they belong to approximately the same generation. That is to say, they completed their university education roughly in the mid-1960–1970s. So it would not be incorrect to assert that contemporary Muslim intellectuals are the products of the Kemalist Republic and the political liberalization of the multiparty era in Turkey. Actually, they are highly impacted by political events and upheavals in Turkey. In other words, it would be wrong to evaluate them independently of Turkish political, cultural, and social life and dynamics. Thus we can argue that they are molded within the framework of these specific conditions. Another remarkable point is the fact that they all have studied and specialized in social and administrative science and the humanities instead of engineering or the natural sciences.[92] Moreover, they learned at least one foreign language:

English, French, or Arabic. İsmet Özel is bilingual; Rasim Özdenören, Ersin Gürdoğan, and İlhan Kutluer have graduate degrees. Some of them have spent some time in Western countries. Ersin Gürdoğan lived one year in England, and Rasim Özdenören did his Masters in the United States. Therefore, we should state that their criticism is not a radical Islamist's repudiation of the West, who despises the West blindly. Rather, they are criticizing it from the point of view of an intellectual with a western education.

As a result, they are all impacted by and acquainted with the Western ideology and life style. Their dress and appearance are like those of the Westernists rather than Islamists, and they also use modern-day Turkish in their writings and speech, unlike the earlier Islamist intellectuals.[93] Since they have been educated through the secular institutions with modernist methods and values, they frequently use the tools and terms of modernity. They benefit from analytical thinking and refer often to historical analysis, statistical methods, and data. Moreover, their ability to read and write a foreign language gives them the opportunity to make constant reference to Western thinkers – especially the Western philosophers of the Enlightenment period – in their books and articles. In fact, most of them have a twofold education: Islamic and secular. Therefore, they have deep knowledge both of Islam and modern ideologies. Consequently, they are familiar not only with Muslim philosophers and intellectuals such as Ibn Sina, Farabi, Ibn Fadlan, Bediüzzaman Said Nursi, Necip Fazıl Kısakürek, Sezai Karakoç, Seyyid Hüssein Nasr, Seyyid Qutb, Abdulkarim Soroush, and Ali Shariati but also Western thinkers and writers such as Sartre, Camus, Kafka, Spinoza, Hume, Popper, Heidegger, René Guenon, Dostoyevsky, Tolstoy, Hemingway, Steinbeck, James Joyce, and Virginia Woolf, have been influential in the formation of their thinking.[94] Likewise İlhan Kutluer states during my interview:

> While reading the project of *Virtuous Society* of Farabi, I do

> not overlook Karl Popper's *Open Society and its Enemies*. While reading the ontology of Ibn Sina or Ibn Arabi, I do not neglect the ontology of Heidegger. The classical thought tradition of epistemology takes me to the books of Carnap, Ayer, Popper, Kuhn, and Feyerabend, who are prominent in the modern philosophy of science.[95]

They discuss not only religious, moral, and philosophical issues but also national and international politics, economics, science, history, culture, art, and so forth. It may seem contradictory, but they criticize almost the same things about the problems of the contemporary world order as their opponent, namely the secular intellectuals. So 'the new Muslim intellectual'

> is very much the product of the post-1950 secular Turkish Republic. This background differentiates him from earlier Islamist thinkers in Turkey. While he is more or less indebted to a century of Islamist criticism of Westernization, the new Muslim intellectual is very much the product of the post-1950 secular Turkish Republic. The kind of language he uses, the literary works he cites or analyses, the stance he takes toward Westernism and secularism, together with less tangible features of his discourse, are unprecedented, even though much of his thinking falls more or less squarely within what might be called a tradition of Islamist resistance and opposition.
>
> ... In effect, the Muslim intellectual as a believer who is now, perhaps more than ever before in the history of the Republic, responding to the same problems and experiences as the secular intellectual.[96]

However, the solutions they offer to social and political problems are different from the solutions of the secular intelligentsia. As Ersin Gürdoğan stated in our conversation,[97] they were a different 'generation of 1968', who did not see the remedy in the West but in the genuine sources of indigenous culture and history.[98] This fact constitutes the backbone of Muslim intellectual's ideology. That is to say, their proposals for the problems of the modern world are different than the secular intellectuals in terms of their strict adherence to Islamic doctrine and parameters. Furthermore, according to my findings, their close and intimate attitude towards the public is another factor that differentiates them from conventional intellectuals. To put it differently, they are not appealing to society from top down by remaining distant and reserved to the public. On the contrary, they are within the society, and they use informal language. In this respect, they can be called public intellectuals. They always identify with those people, who are alienated and negatively affected by social change. So, urbanization and upward social mobility concomitant with globalization engendered the dissolution of the traditional society. This process is described as the transition from the *Gemeinschaft* to *Gesellschaft* by sociologists.[99] In other words, there emerged an identity crisis, as the people moved to big cities, and found themselves in this 'artificial' and 'constructed social environment'.[100]

> In contrast to their experience of a given personal identity in a moral community, they were faced with choosing who to be, with whom to associate, what to think, even with choosing how to dress, what to eat, where to go, and what to see, all matters that were more or less socially given in Anatolian villages and towns. Consequently, these young people were pressured to work out for themselves a new form of identity, one that required the ideologization of experience. As they left behind their provincial identity, which was not chosen but determined as a fait accompli, mental maps of social reality became all the more important to them. And because they were moving from a given to a constructed social environment, these mental maps tended

> to take the form of ideologies, often tenuously related to social realities past and present.[101]

In sum, they have been successful in appealing to and share their sufferings with a wide mass of people who have similar backgrounds and who experience same feelings of alienation and disillusionment. As Gramsci indicated with regard to the ideas of Marx and Lukacs, 'every social class needs its own intelligentsia to shape its ideology, and intellectuals must choose which social class they are going to become an organic part of.'[102] The Muslim intellectuals have been the ideologues of the Islamists, who belong to the class of uprooted, migrated urbanized people. Consequently, we can argue that the contemporary Turkish Muslim intellectuals are organic intellectuals in the Gramscian sense.

On the same token, Edward Said argued that the 'true' intellectual places himself on the 'side of the dispossessed, the unrepresented, and the forgotten'.[103] So, 'the Muslim intellectuals have managed to give a voice to these young people and,'

> in doing so, to make them aware of themselves as a distinct group among Turkish believers. Across the range of traditional, neo-conservative, radical, and extremist opinion, it is the Muslim intellectuals who have argued the need to think through the consequence of a European existence, that is, an existence touched by politically competing cultural identities which separate Muslim from non-Muslims. The audience of the Muslim intellectuals, which did not exist in any appreciable numbers only a few decades ago, is itself a product of the Westernizing policies in Turkey. Like the Muslim intellectual himself, his reader is a believer who is likely to have had a secular education, may hold a higher degree, may know something of a European language, may have visited Western Europe, has read bits and pieces of Westernist literature, philosophy, and social history, and is familiar with progressivist and modernist ideologies. In

> effect, both writer and reader are 'Republican Muslims', believers whose outlook has been decisively shaped by the secularist institutions of the Republic and the Westernizing of Turkish society.[104]

Consequently, not only religious people but also people who do not actively practice religion read their books and writings, attend their conferences, and follow their ideas.

Indeed, current Muslim intellectuals in Turkey are not leading philosophers, ideologues, or original, profound thinkers. Rather, they are impresssive and popular public intellectuals. They are remarkably influential and popular especially among high school and university students, who are coming from similar backgrounds. In fact, they are conscious and aware of their public role and impact within Turkish society. During my research, I noticed that clear, open, and plain presentation of the ideas in their books, writings, and speeches enables these young readers to increase their knowledge and awareness not only on the Islamic philosophy and thinking but also of the Western ideologies and concepts.

Apart from these factors, we should also point out the Islamist intellectuals' distinctiveness as compared to other conventional, Muslim writers and thinkers in their approach to Islam and modernity. Unlike them, the Islamist intellectuals consider Islam not only as a faith or as one of the elements of Turkish national identity but also as a *sine qua non* worldview and way of life by itself. Furthermore, in addition to their criticisms to the anti-religious policies of state, they also denounce modernity as a system, in which these procedures are entrenched. However, other Islamist groups try to conciliate with modernity in this or that way. In short, contemporary Muslim intellectuals neither accept the modernization of Islam nor the Islamization of modernity.

Furthermore, the Islamist thinkers underline and support strongly the significance of diversity in society. According to them, the Truth is single, but it expresses itself in multifarious ways. Hence life is also pluralist. Thus, they argue that the people should not be condemned to a single, particular paradigm. So Muslim intellectuals believe that diversity is not a source of conflict or differentiation, but an appropriate and fruitful base for cooperation.

The fact that modernity facilitated and increased the expansion of critical intellectual work explains the Muslim intellectuals' ability to reach large number of people and places. In other words, we are living in a technological era and in an information society, in which this new genre of intellectuals can present and express their opinions in numerous alternative ways. Consequently, the force of intellectuals in this post-Fordist era surpassed their occupational roles and made them more influential in social and cultural life, unlike the traditional intellectuals.[105] As Carl Boggs put it, 'the high-tech revolution has deepened the trend toward more dispersed locales of learning, cultural life, and opinion making associated with computer networking, cable TV, self-publishing, mini-magazines, electronic books, and similar forms, where technological innovation converges with intellectual work.'[106] The Muslim intellectuals in modern Turkey have been benefiting from the possibilities of modernity and technology, which they denounce. They have their own publishing houses, newspapers, journals, book stores, and television channels. As a result, they are able to disseminate their views and ideas more efficiently and broadly.

Moreover, their books have a steady and good selling rate by Turkish standards. The publication of their books reaches roughly five to ten per person, and sells between 2000 and 15,000 copies.

As a final statement, it should be noted that just as the Turkish intellectuals of the nineteenth century introduced the thoughts of the Western philosophers and determined the contours of Turkish intellectual and ideological life in the twentieth century; contemporary Turkish Muslim intellectuals present the ideas and views of prominent non-Turkish Muslim intellectuals such as Seyyid Hussein Nasr, Seyyid Qutb, Abdulkarim Soroush, Ali Shariati, Adul Ala Mawdudi, Hasan Hanefi, and Mohammed Hamidullah. It seems to me that this will have an impact on the intellectual climate of the future.

Now let me scrutinize their ideas about West European civilization and its fundamental ideologies, which constitute the main agenda of the Muslim intellectuals.

West European civilization

According to the Islamic intellectuals, Western or European civilization is identified with Christianity, capitalism, the free market economy, and democracy.[107] In addition to this, they conceive Europe as a cultural and religious entity. They emphasize its Christian nature and its incompatibility with the Turco–Muslim culture and heritage. To elaborate this let me cite Ersin Gürdoğan's definition of Europe:

> what comes to our mind if we mention Europe is not a continent. Europe is a symbol of a culture. If there are attempts to keep Christianity and Judaism alive, and the names of Caesar, Aristotle, and Socrates are respected, there we can speak of Europe. Because, as Paul Valery pointed out, 'each race and nation, which becomes successively Roman and Christian and adopts the thought system of ancient Greece, is purely European.'[108]

Likewise, Rasim Özdenören contends that according to a Muslim, the West is a matter of mentality rather than a geographical location.[109] Ali Bulaç considers it in its totality as a whole set of political, economic, moral, philosophical, social, and mental attitudes.[110] Similarly, İsmet Özel defines the Western civilization as a set of mentalities and moral values, which emerged as a result of humanity's redefinition of its existence in this world as opposed to conventional religious belief.[111] Since every concept is shaped by its own culture, Western concepts, in their views, do not have a place in Islam.[112] Likewise, according to İsmet Özel, it is imperative to know the intellectual and cultural environment before adopting modern concepts.[113]

Moreover, Muslim thinkers reject being identified as 'European' because

> the origins of our culture and European culture are completely different. Our history is the history of a 1500-year long conflict between European and Islamic culture.
>
> ... We are not Westerners. We are not European either in spite of our long existence on European soil. Therefore, we have to concentrate our efforts on this distinction.
>
> ... We will be given the role of being Europe's enemy as America is given the mission of being Russia's enemy for a long time. This is not a simple hostility as in its literal meaning. That is only one dimension. The real confrontation will be in culture, art, literature, social structure, and economy.[114]

There is a general tendency among the Islamist intellectuals to consider Western civilization as the source and reason of all the ills and problems of the contemporary world.[115] Allegedly, it symbolizes chaos and contradictions. The West, claims Bulaç, 'is for us the destruction of our culture, denial of our personality and identity, the continuation of political society, recession of civil demands, and annihilation of fundamental rights and liberties. ... It is not just "humanism"; at the same time, it is crime, robbery, exploitation, filth, and destruction.'[116]

One of the most criticized aspects of Western civilization is its colonialism and materialist culture. In his book 'Contemporary Concepts and Orders', Ali Bulaç says:

> It should not be forgotten that our age is a materialistic age. The beliefs and ethics of the bourgeoisie class are solely

> capital. Capital is the God of Western people. We can not solely connect the colonial movements, two world wars, and current rebellions to the Christian conservatism and religious expansionist policies of the crusaders. The whole issue is the superpowers' desire to share the world. Today only imperialist aspirations constitute the foreign policies of the highly developed capitalist countries, as is the case in Western Europe and the US.[117]

He regards the West as the 'biggest thief', which considers theft as freedom.[118] Likewise, Abdurrahman Dilipak defines the Western people as 'despicable colonialists, plunderers, torturers, and terrorists, who have destroyed the dignity of humanity.'[119] Furthermore, the West, Dilipak argues:

> founded its entire civilizations on the grounds of the usurped rights, blood, and tears of other people. The basis of Western civilization is colonialism. It is the character of the West. The democracy of ancient Greek can not be considered as a unique Western culture. An order constructed on the grounds of the usurped rights of others that culminated in failure and dissatisfaction can not be presented as a model for the rest of the world.[120]

Supposedly, the origins of materialism in Europe can be found in the paganism of ancient Greece and the Roman Empire, which were influenced and shaped by Judaism to a great extent.[121]

According to their argument, all of the philosophers of the Enlightenment period were impacted by the thinking of the ancient Greeks. According to Ali Bulaç, every belief and social system that stems from paganism is 'sophistry' because it is deprived of divine wisdom.[122] Moreover, they are condemning Europeans for secularizing philosophy in the Age of Reason, where humanism replaced the divine order.[123]

> As Europe renounced wisdom after the Renaissance, philosophy became secular and the divine order was replaced by a humanist one. Furthermore, in the eighteenth and nineteenth centuries, all metaphysical and divine things were removed from philosophy, and consequently philosophy was split from science. However, only thinking systems based on wisdom could reveal the ways to freedom. Humanism together with social and positive sciences put humankind in the prison of this world. As the human being cut his ties with metaphysics, he became solely interested in this world, which is material and limited.[124]

More elaborately, the humanistic philosophy placed the human being at the centre of life by detaching him from the divinity and the principle of God's unity and consequently destroyed *vis-à-vis* 'high culture'.[125] In other words, humanism designates the effort to find a scientific basis to the claim that everything begins and ends with the human being.[126] Not only humanism but also other philosophical movements like rationalism, positivism, and idealism attempt to assign the human being an equal status *vis-à-vis* God, which emerged as a reaction against religion in the West.[127] To put it differently, people began to worship themselves, and refused the unity and the omnipotence of God.[128] Finally, humanism together with positivism incarcerated human beings in the prison of this world, as a result of which they lost their vision and freedom.[129]

In addition, the brutality and destructiveness of the European people, who regard themselves as the 'lords of the universe' are harshly criticized. With its technological and economic superiority, the West devastates the historical, cultural, as well as traditional values of the countries which it penetrates and replaces them with its own values based on the historical accumulations and social structure of European civilization. Moreover, in comparison to Westerners, the Eastern people, propounds İsmet Özel, live in harmony and peace with their environment.[130] In

Islamist intellectuals' opinion, the Muslims owe the 'superiority of their behaviour and morality to Islam'.[131] In this sense, it is said that 'Western people are in total stupidity'.[132] As we see, there is general tendency among the Islamist intellectuals to assess the Europeans according to Islamic criteria. Allegedly, for Europeans, life is meaningless.[133] That is to say, they lack any goal in life to fight for.

Moreover, both Ali Bulaç and Rasim Özdenören also call our attention to the cultural aspect of Western imperialism, which deliberately attempts to make their way of living and culture universal and dominant by imposing it on the rest of the world at the expense of diversity.[134] This, argues Bulaç, is another characteristic of the progressive and egocentric Western culture. These homogenizing efforts never existed in Islam, which tolerates and supports cultural, ethnic, traditional, religious, and regional plurality.[135] Correspondingly, Rasim Özdenören asserted that what is going on in the universe is Europe's attempt to create a uniform and 'global culture'.[136]

However, İlhan Kutluer indicates the impossibility of this project: 'what we have is not a universal Western civilization but a way of life, which dominated every civilizations other than itself on a global scale. Even the issue whether the modern West is truly civilized or not in comparison to Muslim civilizations throughout history is controversial.'[137]

Rasim Özdenören argues that ethnic and racial discrimination constitutes another negative attribute of the European civilization, on which Western imperialism depends.[138] To be more specific, allegedly, the European imperialists considered the non-Western world as uncivilized and inferior. 'The West', states Ali Bulac,

> puts all cultures other than itself out of the world's cultural heritage. At the same time, it takes some elements of all other cultures through translation, anthropology, orientalism, and the like, while imposing the idea that the other cultures have to follow the West in order to be civilized

> since the ability to create thought, art, science, and culture only belongs to the West. From this perspective, the Western civilization is culturally racist and paranoid.[139]

This attitude continues even today in many parts of the world.[140] Ersin Gürdoğan shares the same concerns with other secular and European scholars about the future of Europe.[141] In his book *Culture and Industrialization*, which is a compilation of his previous articles, Gürdoğan argues that Europe exhausted the resources of Asia and Africa as a result of its incessant exploitations. However it has had reached its limits and consequently at the present time, we observe degradation in European civilization.[142] In order to support his argument, he gives the names of several Western secular intellectuals (Oswald Spengler, Albert Camus, André Malraux, Arnold Toynbee,William Faulkner), who are also pessimistic about the imminent future of Europe.

It would be appropriate to designate here a conventional belief of the Islamist thinkers. According to them, since Europe lost its former power and influence, now its time is up. In other words, Europe has completed its historical mission and is far from offering hope even for the European people.[143] 'The era in which the West had the leading role came to an end. Its role as the pioneer of the world is terminated. Nevertheless, at the moment, only very few people can realize this.'[144]

Thus, assert the Islamist elite, it is Islam that will bring salvation. As a result, they envisage that dominance will pass to Muslims.[145] Moreover, they warn the Muslims to avoid from appearing the same as the Europeans in every aspect of life from dress style to consumption patterns, ways of greeting.[146] Finally, they believe that what the Muslims have to do is to discuss every paradigm of the West.[147]

Democracy

In general, the Islamist intellectuals define democracy not only as a system of government but also more importantly, as a 'thinking style' and mentality.[148] It reflects the social, economic and cultural accumulations of Western culture.[149] The fact that the source of sovereignty of the European democracy arises not from God (Allah) but from the nation makes the subject more dubious and controversial for the Islamist intellectuals. The striking point is its secular and profane character. They argue that from this perspective, Islam is not democratic. The Muslim intellectuals indicate that in Islam, sovereignty and final judgement belong only to God. In other words, Allah is the only legislator. They do not question whether there exists democracy in Islam or not. Rather they investigate the place of democracy from the perspective of Islam.[150] In other words, according to Rasim Özdenören, we should ask where democracy is in accordance with Islam rather where Islam is in accordance with democracy.[151] They argue that in Islam, the rights that are determined by democracy come from revelation and divine sources, and the ruling elite do not have the right to manipulate the rules and rights determined by Sharia.[152] So Rasim Özdenören claims that 'Islam and democracy are as different as bird and cat.'[153] In the same way, Ali Bulaç states the impossibility of a comparison between Islam and democracy.[154] In other words, Islam should be compared with something similar that belongs to the same category such as Christianity, Buddhism, Judaism, because Islam is a 'religion' while democracy is a 'ruling method'.[155] Ali Bulaç proposes that:

> If it were possible to speak of 'Islamic democracy', then this would not be an absurd process, in which Islam reassesses and even revises itself according to democracy; but on the contrary, it will be realized by offering a new approach and the new fundamentals of a distinctive political theory to the Western democracies.[156]

Moreover, they imply that it would be hard to reach democracy in a non-Western country that is not familiar with the

European mentality. Because 'like the other political institutions in Turkey', states Özdenören: 'democracy is also imported from the West. Democracy did not originate from Turkey's own cultural sources and historical conditions. Therefore, it can operate only under the guidance and manipulations of the West.'[157] Likewise, Bulaç clarifies this point:

> It is possible to say that democracy is specific to the Western traditions and political culture in terms of its existing political values and mechanisms. From this perspective, we should not forget to consider democracy with its historical class struggle and differences among religious sect together with the organic alliance of the aristocracy with the clergy in absolutist monarchies. We can not regard the West independently from its unique historical, social, religious, political, and economic conditions and we can not pose the question why democracy did not develop anywhere else by overlooking this reality.[158] … the late occurrence of democracy and the multiparty system in our country is not accidental; on the contrary, this is related to our social structure, which is organized on the basis of religion and law, or socio-cultural structure instead of a socio-economic one.[159]

Turkish democracy is therefore restricted and deficient. Furthermore, Ali Bulaç draws our attention to the fact that democracy is a system of majority instead of plurality in its Western form: 'In its existing form, pluralism is the most distant thing to the socio-cultural and political model of the West. This model is based in theory on the majority principle. Western democracies, which choose representation, Machiavellism, and majority rule as a valid method, are in a serious crisis today.'[160]

So, Bulaç does not consider the principle of political majority sufficient. For him, if social and cultural plurality is not present in the public and civil life, then there occurs a 'monolithic and totalitarian' system and this is the quintessential weakness of modern democracies.[161] Hence we can hardly speak of the occurrence of 'public will' in such a system. Ali Bulaç calls this system as 'despotism of the intellectuals', in which the Jacobin elite established despotic regimes by acquiring their legitimacy from positivism and rationalism.[162]

Nonetheless, Bulaç admits that 'democracy is the most 'advanced' ruling system compared to its opponents such as oligarchy, monarchy, and aristocracy.[163] But still, it is incomplete. According to him, it would be erroneous to consider Western democracies as the ultimate phase and paradigm for the rest of the world.[164] Moreover, he also condemns the Western democracies for applying double standards and not acting in accordance with the ideals and rules of democracy.[165]

Similarly, İlhan Kutluer analyses democracy through the lenses of the prominent medieval Islamic philosopher Farabi:

> In fact, democracy as a regime of 'cahiliye'[166] is open to all forms of Hedonism; it prepares appropriate grounds for the satisfaction of all kinds of lust and greed and does not allow the rule of virtuous people. Nevertheless, democracy is the most suitable regime among other 'cahiliye' regimes that can be transformed into a virtuous rule.
>
> ... Freedom is the excuse and guarantee of immorality. Freedom is developed at the expense of morality. The fulfillment of essential needs, satisfaction of banal desires – current Materialism, Hedonism, and Machiavellism – nourish indecent behaviours. In such an environment of freedom, the preferences of the majority are determined by their libidinal energy and drive of domination; or these preferences can be manipulated easily within this framework.[167]

Furthermore, Bulaç quotes from Max Weber that the functioning of the politics through a party system implies ruling with the interest groups.[168] Thus, he contends that only the wealthy and powerful people can benefit from democracy. He refers to Laslie Lipson's argument that decisions are not taken according to the needs and aspirations of the masses; this is 'deception'.[169] There are other realities behind it. More precisely, he contends that people's desires and thoughts are manipulated by the powerful groups organized within the state and that the constitution is prepared by these people instead of representatives of the public.[170] In this respect, their views are reminiscent of Gramsci and Foucault. With an apologetic attitude, he refers here again to Islam to show it as a model for true democracy, which prefers ethnic, cultural, and religious pluralism. He claims that this system guarantees to protect the rights of even the smallest minority groups:[171]

> In the Islamic Plurality Model, which constitutes the basis of the Medina Contract, all the problems related to democracy are solved. The basic framework is based on the acceptance of the idea that each social group lives together according to the legal principles which are chosen by their free will during the contract. Priority is given to the fact that the social groups – instead of a single nation – within the political structure identify themselves and create a valid legal system. This is required to secure religious freedom and free choice. Consequently, uncertainties will be eliminated and standards for each social group will be determined. This model rejects the superiority of 51 to 49, but it claims to protect all fundamental rights of 1 even against 99.[172]

So Muslims can redefine and develop the concept of democracy.[173] Therefore, the idea that democracy is identified with Westernization is renounced by the Islamist intellectuals. Allegedly, the public will can also be realized without Westernization.[174]

Human Rights

As a secular and modern concept that originated in Western Europe, the human rights issue is not embraced by the Muslim intellectuals. To elaborate, the common attitude of the Muslim intellectuals is their ironic attack against this concept as being the product of Western civilization and 'human effort'. In other words it is created within a specific cultural environment. Thus İsmet Özel regards the issue in this context as 'human rights imperialism.' So, since it does not originate from God's will, it is secular and profane and therefore not acceptable. In his book 'The Misery of the New World Order', Rasim Özdenören stated that:

> All the rights collected under the name of human rights, finally, originated from the need to provide free thinking against the church and create laws to protect themselves against the church. The subject is both secular and profane due to its content. Despite of this fact, it is conceived as sacred and taboo in its secular and profane structure since it is a product of human effort.[175]

Consequently it is conceived in Western Europe by the people themselves against the omnipotence of the church. It did not get its legitimacy from divine sources but from the revolt of human beings. Özdenören argues that as a result of this, people can idolize themselves, since they asserted their law making capacity against the church.[176] Özdenören regards the human rights issue as insecure and fake. The reasons for this, he explains,

> is the eurocentric definition of the human being, which is the product of the imperialist Western culture. According to this definition, a human being is someone who comes from the Arian race and belongs to the Greco–Roman culture and Christian religion. Therefore, whether the other people who do not meet this criterion are human beings or not is doubted. Even if they are considered so, ultimately they are

> savage and barbaric. Hence they need to be civilized by the West European people. Only they (and naturally the American, White, Anglo–Saxon, and Protestant people 'WASP') are subjected to human rights. Others deserve only to be exploited and need to be ruled.[177]

He attempts to deal with the issue not only in political and judicial terms but also as a 'social phenomenon' in order to perceive its precariousness and incompatibility to our culture.[178] To put it another way, according to the same author, the concept of 'human rights' implies a distinct meaning in our culture from the other modern values such as democracy, secularism and liberalism.[179] It is adopted from outside and in a top–down manner. For this reason, there is a striking discrepancy between the evaluations of the subject matter made from the point of view of our culture and theirs. Not surprisingly, his reference for culture is Islam. He brings the discourse to the superiority of Islam, in which these rights already exist.

Correspondingly, Ali Bulaç mentions five fundamental human rights, which are guaranteed by Islam as the 'protection of religion, life, property, reason, and generation.'[180] According to Ghazali, says Ali Bulaç, these rights are 'the fundamentals of all judicial systems and the remaining rules and laws are only derivatives of them.'[181] Furthermore, he claims that both the Magna Carta (1215) and the United Nations International Declaration of Human Rights (1945) lack two of the fundamental rights stated above: the protection of reason and of generation. He concludes that this fact proves the supremacy of Islamic fundamentals in comparison to Western human rights made by human beings according to the needs and features of the European people.[182]

Furthermore, İsmet Özel regards the human rights issue in its current version as a means of subjugating and controlling the people by exploiting their weaknesses.[183] Thus it implies for him human rights imperialism.[184]

Both Bulaç and Özdenören criticize the hypocritical nature of the subject under question. As an illustration, Ali Bulaç points out the inequality of income distribution on a global scale, as a result of which a large majority of the world population is driven into poverty and a life of low quality whereas only a small minority is living in affluence.[185] He gives statistical evidence. For example, 80 per cent of the world's resources are consumed by only 17 per cent of the world's population. Likewise, 54 per cent of the total national income in the US is consumed by just 1 per cent of its population.[186] He claims that this contradicts the ideals of International Declaration of Human Rights.

At the same time, Özdenören accuses the West of applying double standards by remaining indifferent in the headscarf (or *türban*) issue in Turkey. In other words, they are blocking one of the human rights. Along the same lines, he considers the 'directive and manipulating secularizing policies' in Turkey imposed on the Muslim majority as contradictory to human rights.[187] In other words, the Kemalist state prohibited the religious freedom of its Muslim population by secularizing all aspects of the social life.

In a nutshell, according to present Muslim thinkers in Turkey, the human rights issue is insincere, distrustful, and forged in its eurocentric version. And therefore, in their views, we have to refer to the authentic Islamic jurisprudence, which offers genuine fundamentals for the area under discussion.

Secularism and laicism

Islamist intellectuals point out that laicism, like other concepts of modernity, is initiated outside of their country and culture. Their arguments are centred on the fact that Islam, in contrast to Christianity, occurred initially in the form of a state; so religion and state were not separate things.[188] In other words, Özdenören states that the division between mosque and state never existed in Islam as happened in Christianity between church and the state.[189] Consequently, the Muslim intellectuals concur on the impracticality of laicism from the perspective of Islam.

Rasim Özdenören defines laicism technically as 'separation of the state's authority from the authority of the church'.[190] In addition, the same author describes secularism as 'the acceptance of the human's will instead of divine judgement as the reference point in every aspect of life including legislation.'[191] Moreover, he contends that laicism and democracy are different concepts and thus they do not require each other necessarily.[192] Likewise, Abdurrahman Dilipak points out that laicism is not a prerequisite for democracy, human rights, or modernization as is supposed.[193] To prove his argument, he proposes that laicism does not exist in England, which is a democratic and modern country.[194]

To elucidate Ali Bulaç's ideas on laicism and secularism let me give the following statements:

> Laicism is defined in the Arabic language as '*ilmaniyye*'. That is to say, it means to be scientific, and proposes to establish society on the basis of scientific principles and data. The concept of laicism in Arabic language involves non-religiosity in administration; positivism, and positivist philosophy in thought. The third concept next to positivism and positivist thought is secularism. Namely, it means to make religious things worldly and to destroy religious belief. This concept originates especially from the Latin language. ... Although it encompasses the meaning of laicism, secularism designates being contemporary.
>
> ... In its philosophical root there is a description of an unspiritual life, which is not sacred. In other words, the universe is entirely profane. Everything begins in this world, and terminates in this world too. In fact, what aimed with secularism is modernization. And modernization is synonymous with westernization. ... We can claim that secularism intends to eradicate every positive aspects of religion from the society and replace it with Western values.[195]

So, as stated by to Ali Bulaç, secular culture is 'kufur',[196] which occupies all of human consciousness and impels people ultimately to atheism, in which there is no place for religion and God.[197] In a nutshell, in Bulaç's words 'laicism is potential agnosticism' and even atheism.[198] That is to say, it rejects everthing that exists outside of this material world.[199] On the contrary, according to Ali Bulaç, Islam invites man to contemplate and be conscious about the esoteric meaning of the things and the metaphysical world, which exists beyond the limits of the material world.[200] In his view, this does not necessitate a detachment from this world.

Laicism as an imported concept for Turkey is scrutinized elaborately by Abdurrahman Dilipak in his book entitled 'Laicism'. Laicism is more a 'philosophical concept and legal term than a political technique.'[201] First and the foremost, he points out is that Turkey never experienced laicism in reality.[202] Allegedly, in fact, Turkey applied 'Kemalist theocracy' as laicism.[203] More exactly, Dilipak is of the opinion that in practice laicism in Turkey constitutes a challenge for the Republic, democracy, and human rights instead of securing them. In his words, 'laicism is used as an instrument of oppression against the Muslims in order to protect the regime.'[204] To put it differently, he describes the impact of secularist policies as a total regeneration and transformation of the country in every sphere of life.[205] The object of the Kemalist laicism project is investigated:

> A non-sacred society is aimed for by the Kemalist reformers. You realize how ignorant and distant the so-called intellectuals are to their own society's fundamental values, beliefs, history, and culture... An illiterate, poor, and immoral community is aimed for. Headscarf is guilt, but the income of the brothel is considered as sacred. Religion is 'irtica',[206] but anti religiousness is regarded as a precondition for becoming an intellectual. Religion and pious people are held to be dangerous and attempts are made to seclude them from the rest of the society. Why? ... This is an antidemocratic and dictatorial attitude.[207]

Although laicism is imported from Western Europe by the state elites,[208] its application is different from the Western pattern. Ali Bulaç argues that the state in Turkey did not give autonomy to religion. On the contrary, the Byzantian–Ottoman model was adopted, which gave the state the possibility to intervene and manipulate religion as an independent power.[209] As a result, religion was dissolved and absorbed by the state. Thus, according to Dilipak, in the Turkish case, with the advent of laicism 'national sovereignty' supplanted 'divine sovereignty'.[210] He denounces the state's intervention in the religious belief and practices of people, which is not found in the West. He claims that in the West, only the legal system is secular, not the people but.[211] That is to say, the society can practice its religious faith freely. In this sense, he rejects the idea that human beings can be secular.

Moreover, Dilipak elucidated the impossibility of laicism in Turkey due to the non-existence of the clergy in Islam[212] because laicism was initiated in the West in order to eliminate the omnipotence of the church and the clergy. As argued by Dilipak, the state in Turkey thus attempted to organize the clergy without success. He mentions the opening of the religious middle schools (Imam-Hatip) in 1951 as an indication of this fact. Dilipak condemns the state for being disrespectful and hostile to religion. He describes this attitude of the Turkish state as 'Byzantinism', which tried to manipulate religion according to the needs of the governments by eliminating its autonomy as a civil institution. In addition to this, he indicates the flexible use of the concept during the Republican period. To put it in other words, laicism took diverse meanings and forms in different situations in Turkey.[213] So there is not a uniform and consistent interpretation of laicism. As an illustration, the leftists were opposed to religious education whereas right wing forces made it obligatory in order to assure that Islam would not constitute a barrier for Westernization.[214] He contends that the right wing took a milder stance and used religion for its own ends. On the other hand, he emphasizes the 'top down' nature of Kemalist laicism.[215] More precisely, it is proposed that Kemalist laicism denotes the repudiation of religion, history, and society's own culture.[216] Allegedly, it is 'extremely conservative and dogmatic.'[217]

Abdurrahman Dilipak also specified the difference between the Ottoman and Kemalist laicism processes. According to him, laicism during the Ottoman period was more liberal than laicism in the Republican era. Moreover, he uses a dialectical method. He explains both the Islamic and western patterns and shows the Islamic paradigm as the ideal one:

> If we consider secularism as modernization, we can offer humanity a modern world in the name of Islam. All dynamics to make such a future possible are existent in the essence and doctrine of Islam. If laicism denotes saving the civil people from the monopoly of the clergy, than Islam already renounces the priesthood. If interreligious peace is meant with laicism, than Islam already stipulates this. If laicism is a means of freedom and peace, Islam already makes arrangements to provide this.[218]

Finally, it is asserted that the Kemalist type of laicism has no chance to survive: 'Kemalist laicism has no future. Laicism, which is the guardian of liberalism that defines tolerance among different religious sects in the West, is transformed into coercion against religion; and antidemocratic, militarist, Jacobin conspiracy in our country.'[219]

To put it briefly, both laicism and secularism are rejected and despised by the Islamist intellectuals in their present form in Turkey.

Modernity

According to the Muslim intellectuals, modernism was initiated as a reaction to tradition in the West. Accordingly, İsmet Özel calls it as 'a product of Western culture' supported from both Hebrew,

Christian, and Greco-Roman backgrounds.[220] He believes that Europe exported it to the rest of the world in order to assure its survival and continuity.[221] He points out that the crystallized version of modernity is 'Americanisation'.[222]

Likewise Ersin Gürdoğan describes the concept of modernity as a European project that aspires to establish Western values, ideas, and life systems in the Muslim world.[223]

Ali Bulaç defines *modernity* as the 'aggregation of the Enlightenment's fundamental philosophical premises'.[224] According to this idea, Western civilization projects a new universe, which is based on individualism, secularism, and nation state.[225] This model is introduced to the globe through modernization politics, which are, according to Ali Bulaç

> coercive policies, which are based on colonialist, assimilative fundamentals supported by a so-called philosophy of history and anthropological and sociological data.[226]
>
> ... In every historical era, modern times are regarded only as a period of 'bid'at' (*innovation*). More importantly, in spite of its splendor, the modern world is not 'new' or entirely 'unique'. Modernism is imitation. It is a humane and fake imitation of the divine one. We can claim that the pioneer of the modern world is Satan. Because according to an ancient dictum, 'Satan always imitates God.' Modernism too is the repetition of the divine being with all essential philosophical hypotheses, promises, and reasons.[227]

According to İlhan Kutluer, modernity, as a concept of mentality, designates the 'blessing of the present and the new'.[228] Moreover, contemporaenity means to live with the needs and requirements of the current age.[229] He is convinced that contemporaneity does not have to comply with modernity.[230] To put it differently, the fact that we are living in the same period, where modernity is the dominant system, does not necessitate becoming modern.[231] Contemporaenity signifies both being 'beyond history and within history.'[232] Supposedly, Muslims do not surrender themselves to modernity; rather they struggle to 'leave a mark' on their age under the light of 'rationality and reality' identified by Islam.[233]

Ali Bulaç dates back the history of modernity to the eighteenth century. However, he argues that its transformation to modernism, which encompasses social, cultural, and economic developments, occurred after the Second World War.[234] Bulaç indicates that the modernist ideology, which originated from the idea of westernization, is transformed into a modernization paradigm from that time onwards.[235] In fact, according to modernization theory, developed in the post-Second World War period during the 1960s when the decolonization process in Asia and Africa began, the newly emerging nation states and underdeveloped countries should modernize according to the Western model in order to progress. From this time onwards, the term 'modernization' began to be used in place of 'Europeanization' and Westernization.[236] So it does not have a long history. According to modernization theory, the Third World countries will pass ultimately from the traditional and primitive stage to modern, capital intensive, industrialized, and technological stage.

Ali Bulaç finds the Turkish modernization problematic and monolithic due to following reasons: (i) it is determined by the state; (ii) it means Westernization, Europeanization, and even to become French; (iii) it excludes religion.[237] So, Bulaç suggests that the state should leave the decision on the modernization issue to society and the individual. He draws our attention to non-Western modernizations such as India, Japan, etc. Essentially we should state here that he does not propose to cut ties with the West completely. In his view, the West is a great experience for us, and we should benefit from this experience as much as we can. However, as Bulaç notes, this does not require us to imitate the Western civilization and to follow its path.

Furthermore Bulaç also analyses modernity from the perspective of Islamic philosophy. He focuses on its relation with divine truth and evaluates it according to this criterion. In fact, such a tendency is very common among the Islamist intellectuals.

> Since the modern human being and 'advanced society' cut its relations with the source of life, it is spiritless, unexcited, and meaningless. Although the human mind is focused solely on material activities, still he does not possess a genuine idea about the objects, each of which represents a distinct symbol and meaningful code. If we detach the World of Existence from its own source of life then there will be left numerous objects to be worshipped. Each of these objects becomes a God. So modern philosophical thinking degraded the material world, which it considers as the single truth, to a state of old fetish with a primitive mentality. Consequently fetishism is reborn. And even in the name of science, rationality, progress, civilization, development, and humanism.[238]

This point is also elucidated by İsmet Özel. He considers modernism as the new form of 'atheism', in which we worship the market, machines, money, theories, organizations.[239] So in this period, which Özel calls 'Middle Age', all these objects are mystified and even deified. In other words, money and profit become the measurement of everything.

Furthermore, modernity detached the people from their roots and identity and compels them to pin their hopes on a fictitious future.[240] Bulaç asserts that this fact prevents modern man from enjoying the happiness of the present moment in which he lives.[241] In other words, he has lost both his past and his future. As a result of this, his life has become futile, absurd, and meaningless. Ali Bulaç names this as a deviation of modern man from knowledge of divine truth.[242] According to the same author, the modern human being is restless as well as prejudiced and thus he needs to discover the ways to Divine Wisdom and faith.[243]

We should question why we have to modernize instead of how we can modernize. Ali Bulaç analyses the problematic with an

Islamic interpretation. In his views, we are all missing our actual homeland, which we lost temporarily, and thus we are struggling to regain it.[244] He hardly believes that modernism can bring us back to paradise from where we were driven out. In fact, Muslim intellectuals believe that the modernity project is a manifestation of humankind's unconscious desire to recapture that past, but that is an illusion.

> Modernism, which is a natural expression of progress, promises us a perfect and infinite life in the future. In this time span of evolution, happiness and satisfaction will be realized. In fact, there is an overlap between the promise of an everlasting life and the Paradise informed by religions as a reality. What does not overlap is the impossibility of modernism's desire to carry that paradise to this world.[245]

The argument that modernity is the ultimate stage in the history of mankind that can be reached in terms of wealth and development is unequivocally denied by the Muslim intellectuals. Ali Bulaç pointed out that this perception leads to 'spiritual and mental deviation', which makes the West and western products enormously attractive.[246] Moreover, the aim of modernism is not to offer happiness but to make people more and more dependent the West, and in this respect it is both an ideological and political term.

Another objective of modernity is to create a 'monolithic and single' world and thus it destroys customs and traditions all over the world. In relation to this argument, Ali Bulaç points out that 'Modernity, which intends to transform the world into a small village, attempts to eradicate the cultural identity as well as independence of every nation and people with its worldwide organizational capability.'[247] Nevertheless the Islamist intellectuals strongly assert that this eurocentric plan, designed in accordance with the interests and benefits the Western people, can not be a model for the entire world.[248]

In addition, the destructive effects of industrialization and consumption patterns connoted with modernity are condemned:

> Modernization is an incessant process. It entails continuous change and renewal. Modernism is built up on this destructive logic. The modern system offers us new requirements everyday and wants us to meet them in all possible ways. In fact, from the advent of humanity, the needs are same. So what has changed is not their essence but their redefinition, and marketing methods. ... And this process is called modernism.[249]

Ali Bulaç also examines the effects of modernization on cities. It is argued that engineers, who are deprived of wisdom and divine truth like modern positivist social scientists, built inhumane and mechanical cities in place of the organic ones.[250] In other words, these cities are designed statistically as places, in which the masses can be manipulated and controlled.[251] The aesthetic and spiritual components are neglected. Evidently, modern society is transformed into a 'complex, disintegrated, but controlling and oppressing machine.'[252] Consequently, in these modern cities, human beings are driven into a sense of powerlessness and loneliness. Hence, the concept of private life increases in importance as the single place where the disgraced human being can take refuge.[253] So Ali Bulaç points out that modern man gets lost in abundance and disengages itself from the Divine Being, which ultimately leads to his death.[254]

This alienation, solitude and, unhappiness of modern people lead to the emergence of marginal groups and facts such as heavy metal music, feminists, and hippies. That is to say, these groups and people try to express their discontent with their action and rhetoric.[255] He proposes that 'modernism suppressed the unrest and marginalized it; so the marginalization of opposition is the myth of contemporary individualization.'[256] Allegedly, aggressiveness, drugs and alcohol addiction, and high rates of suicide are connected with the displeasure and frustration of modern individuals. İsmet Özel indicates that this 'disappointment and suffocation of the human soul' is the essential characteristic of the modern age.[257] Ali Bulaç insists on the idea that even atheists do not renounce the existence of God in reality; rather they are rebelling to the secular and immoral design of modern life, in which is there is no place for God.[258]

As a conclusion, Ali Bulaç argues that the replacement of unity (Vahdet) with affluence (Kesret) led to chaos, and that what is occurring in the modern world currently is this state of chaos.[259] His suggestion is to replace the 'world view of modernity' with the Islamic idea of Universe (Alem).[260]

Modern ideologies: communism, Marxism, socialism, capitalism, liberalism

The Islamist intellectuals approach contemporary order not as a social, economic, or political system but as a way of thinking and living. In their opinion, these systems are the offspring of Western cultural values, and hence they represent the secular and profane mentality and lifestyle of the West and have a meaning only for those cultures. For this reason, from an Islamic point of view, they are inefficient and unacceptable. Let me now introduce their opinions about modern ideologies and the reasons for their incompatibility with Islam.

According to the Muslim intellectuals, capitalism, which symbolizes economically wealth and power, is the source of all devastations on the globe.[261] In effect, in Bulaç's opinion, it is capitalism that impoverished many countries and hindered their development.[262] Moreover, it is the origin of all of the colonialist movements, which have acquired a new and modern outlook. Indeed, Ali Bulaç identifes it as the 'universal name of modernism.'[263] He indicates the non-humanistic nature of capitalism. Accordingly,

> Although its philosophical basis is humanism – the glorification of the human being – the system exhausted the

> human and transformed it into an ordinary component of a huge mechanism, which is based on profit, production, and market. Due to its intrinsic individualistic culture, it makes its preference in favour of the individual, when a capitalist conflict arises that causes the defeat of society by the individual. Besides, the madness of consumption constitutes another weakness of this system. Production, which is realized through the utilization of thousands of people, finds markets by instigating the desires and ambitions of millions of individuals. This fanatical consumption passion exhausts rapidly all known natural resources and the world is approaching an ecological calamity.[264]

Hence the Muslim intellectuals concur on the idea that it must be overthrown. So, they propound the total elimination of the current system rather than correcting the deficiencies of capitalism.

Like capitalism, communism is also an offspring of western thought. Therefore, Ali Bulaç claims that the social climate, which prepared the ground for capitalism, also laid the foundations for the emergence of communist societies.[265] That is to say, he indicates that both capitalism and communism are products of ancient Greek and Roman philosophy.[266] So they are both profane. Yet, they are hostile to each other as a result of the manifestation of God's Will, who let the oppressors struggle with each other.[267]

In fact, communism is characterized as a system of 'oppression and exploitation' that clashes with the essence of human beings, its honor, and its dignity.[268] Allegedly, in contrast to its promise, communism legalizes social inequality through the force of the state.[269] Bulaç points out that the reason for communism's inability to eliminate class distinctions, imperialism, and oppression, has its roots in Westernist culture and thought.[270] By the same token, Rasim Özdenören argues that Christianity's diversion from its truth by the West is the cause for all of depression and disorder in humanity, as a result of which the individual came into conflict with its values.[271] Özdenören explains the emergence of capitalism and communism with this deviation:

> The expulsion of Christianity from the realm of the individual's daily life brought the Western people undesired lifestyles. All the love and clemency suggested by Christianity could not be reflected in the gloomy souls of the Western people. For this reason, they tried to develop a non-Christian way of life, which is oriented to goods and commodities. Inevitably the Western individual took refuge in them, as they were left as the single alternative. This provided him with two cruel lifestyles, which are based fundamentally on profit making. Currently, these two oppressive systems are competing. Although both of them consider each other as tyrannical, yet they concur on the subjugation of the human through domination of goods and commodities.[272]

İsmet Özel defines socialism as the byproduct of modernization, which questions the global income distribution.[273] In Özel's words, socialism is an improved version of capitalism, deficiencies of which are eliminated. However since socialism too, is based on rationality as other systems are, it can not go further than being a different phase, or form, of the system.[274] Likewise, Ali Bulaç contends that in spite of their opposition to capitalism, socialism and Marxism have a common basis with capitalism in terms of worldview, essential philosophical propositions, and ultimate objectives.[275] So socialism and Marxism principles are nothing more than the consumption and production of commodities, which are provided by capitalism.[276] Moreover İsmet Özel points out the impracticality of socialism for Turkey:

> We will observe with a realistic attitude that Turkey, which is trying to continue its existence as a country during the

> globalization process, can benefit neither from socialism nor from a nationalist approach. The socialist view will counteract globalization only with a global response. As Karl Marx and Friedrich Engels acknowledged the bourgeoisie as the most revolutionary social class ever seen, and as Vladimir Ulyanov [Lenin] played a role in making people consider state capitalism as socialism by depicting imperialism as the ultimate stage of capitalism, current socialists too can be the last link in the chain of deception by claiming that the sanctity of globalization comes from its ability to make the conflict between labor and capital more visible.[277]

Therefore, he proposes that socialism can not be an alternative to capitalism. In effect, the cause of the problem is directly the system of the West itself, in which socialism and Marxism are also located.[278]

Liberalism is considered by the Muslim intellectuals as a mindset and way of living as democracy. It instigated the emergence of philosophical systems such as positivism, rationalism, and Enlightenment ideas.[279] According to Rasim Ozdenören, its determinative components are 'rationalism, individualism, humanism, cosmopolitanism, democracy, and nationalism', which are completely secular and profane.[280] In effect, he argues that the environment of freedom and liberal thinking paved the way for the development of these principles. The same author elucidates rationalism as materialism, individualism as a kind of egoism, humanism as a compilation of the cultural values of the West, cosmopolitanism as something contrary to the Islamic concept of ummah, democracy as the human's declaration of its sovereignty as against of God as the source of ultimate power, and nationalism as a system in which the nation state in contrast to the ummah ideal are constructed in order to escape the Church's authority.[281] Thus, all of these principles are intolerable according to Islam.

Ali Bulaç analyses the implications of liberalism for the free market economy:

> The democratic mechanism, which is tightly attached to Western values, imposes the free market economy as the primary condition. And through this way, the countries in which democracy and the free market economy is applied opened their economic, natural, and human resources to the exploitation of the industrialized countries. It is conventional to allocate some share to the native collaborators. This leads to deterioration of the national income rapidly and increases poverty. So, as scarcity, famine, unemployment, inflation, pervasive prostitution, increasing criminality, social unrest, and the like augments and opposition to the existing system intensifies, the status of the people who defend the status quo is secured with human rights. The oppression and criminal policies of the party in power are supported and even the military coup d'état are regarded as legitimate so that the 'democracy of the future' will not be threatened.
>
> This fact displays clearly that a complete and continuous democracy in poor countries, which are opened to the free market economy, is not possible. That is to say, the free market leads to political and social instability due to its character that enhances poverty and income inequality, and in these countries the unsteadiness is suppressed by military interventions and dictatorial regimes. This phenomenon will continue as long as the Western countries equate 'free market' with liberalism and exploitation and consequently they will be responsible for anti-democratic regimes and violation of the law.[282]

In a sense, the free market economy is considered as uneven competition. The industrialized countries of the West are in an advantageous position *vis-à-vis* less developed countries, which are forced to accept liberal economy.[283]

It is believed by the Muslim intellectuals that both communism and fascism came into being as a remedy to the problems created by capitalism.[284] Their failure to cure the illnesses of capitalism tells us how epidemic and deadly the plague of capitalism and liberalism is.[285] In fact, as described by Ersin Gürdoğan, neither liberalism nor central planning is the effective source of production. What is more important is the believing human being, firmly attached to moral values.[286] That is to say, it is the human's action that constitutes the essence of the social structure, and his actions are determined by religion.[287] And Gürdoğan proposes that the legitimacy of all of the modern economic and social systems are destined to vanish in the face of the truths of religion.[288]

In sum, according to contemporary Muslim thinkers in Turkey, all modern orders are created by the West and thus they represent secularism and profanity. In other words, these ideologies represent different fractions of modernism. They are all oriented to the satisfaction of human desires, and based on the human's dominance and control over nature, independent from God.[289] Injustice, oppression, exploitation, and alienation are the common characteristics of all these systems.[290] Although they promise heaven on earth, none of them has been able to bring peace, equality, and happiness to mankind. In effect, the Muslim intellectuals believe that humanly doctrines, which are the products of a certain culture, society, and history can not bring order contentment and peace.[291] To conclude, let me give a typical Muslim intellectual's statements:

> We are not idealist or materialist. More elaborately, all humanly doctrines are deceiving and create unhappiness. Therefore idealism and materialism as a thought; capitalism, socialism and Marxism as an action; and the system obscure the consciousness of the human being and prevent him from grasping the existence of God and makes him unhappy.
>
> So in sum, neither does materialism, which is the theoretical fundamental of Marxism, nor idealism, as the philosophical basis of capitalism, comply with Islamic thought. Since the attitudes of both systems towards

religion are the product of Western ideas, in the materialist explanation, religion is approached with hostility.

... Capitalism, communism and fascism no longer offer any benefit for humanity. As long as these doctrines shape social systems, upheavals, turmoil, and depressions will continue. We are living in an impure world and indecent life. We believe that humanity needs new thought, a fresh world view, a distinctive morality, and a novel way of living. Such a system will not have a humanistic nature; rather it will be a way of living based on the belief in God's unity outlined by divine revelation, which takes human beings and society into consideration in all their dimensions; which carries an authentic message from the world of reality or the other world; and which invites us to benefaction, maturity, and peace with people, nature, and ourselves: our essence.[292]

Chapter 3

Examination of the Muslim Intellectuals' Thoughts on Concepts other than West and Modernity

Introduction

In this chapter, I will examine the Muslim intellectuals' views on different issues which are not directly related to Western civilization or modernity. In particular, my analysis will concentrate on their views about (1) Kemalism as an official ideology of the Republic of Turkey; (2) state and nation; (3) science and technology; (4) *religion* as a general concept including morality and religious revival; (5) Islam; (6) history.

Kemalism

The denunciation of the Kemalist ideology[1] and its policies implemented by the Kemalist bureaucrats constitute the backbone of the Muslim intellectuals' discourses. Their criticisms are centred mainly the on the negation and elimination of the cultural and religious values of the Turkish society by Mustafa Kemal and its followers for the sake of Westernization. They emphasize its fundamentalist character in transforming the country in accordance to the Western pattern. It is argued by Rasim Özdenören that from this perspective, Kemalism, which does not consider Westernization as the amalgamation of the indigenous culture with the Western culture, is unrivalled among other pro-Western currents.[2] So it envisions an encompassing transformation of society through Western values and lifestyles. They believe that Westernization attempts were not only aimed at modernizing the country but that it tried to make Turkey a part of Europe.[3] Özdenören elucidates the Westernization model of Kemalism in comparison to similar efforts in other countries:

> As Kemalism 'officially' attempted to put Western civilization in its totality in place of our indigenous culture without taking the alleged distinctions into consideration, then people began to reflect on Westernization. Indeed, Kemalism resembled neither the Japanese nor the Russian model of Westernization. It was a unique type of Westernization. At the same time it can be claimed that the Kemalist paradigm was superior. That is to say, it would not confine itself merely to the adoption of Western technology as Japan did. In addition, it did not attempt to take only one among dozens of ideas as a guide and follow that path, as Russia did. Kemalism envisaged straightly that we should become a Western country by denying our civilization and incorporating Western civilization as a whole.[4]

Moreover he emphasizes the conservative character of Kemalism and notes that it has completed its mission during the 1920s and 1930s. In addition, forced modernization policies are identified as despotism by the Muslim intellectuals.[5] 'Turkey's experience during the One-Party era', says Ali Bulaç,

> is very close to totalitarianism. The use of national unity and solidarity for purposes of glorification of the state; the

> dependence of the regime on the Kemalist reforms and principles; the removal of religious and traditional institutions with radical and authoritarian methods; and the expansion of this restructuring process to the extend of transforming religious life, theology, and praying forms designates the close relationship of the new Republic's regime with totalitarianism. … In Turkey, Islam is designed in accordance to the national character of the Turkish people, and correspondingly Ezan is converted from Arabic to Turkish.[6]

In addition, these radical westernization policies of the Kemalist cadres at the expense of native culture and religion engendered cultural and political pollution. Ersin Gürdoğan says:

> The value conflict, which intensified during the Republican period, increased the gap between the army and bureaucratic administration on the one hand and the public on the other to a great extent. As the conflict between the values of the Anatolian people and that of the state gains momentum, political and cultural pollution deepens. That is to say, there is a correlation between the value clash and political as well as cultural corruption. As this friction intensifies, the political and cultural decay augments.[7]

The Muslim intellectuals believe that this corruption can be prevented by returning to the essence of the native culture and values. Moreover, Abdurrahman Dilipak believes that there is a Kemalist theocracy in Turkey. To put it differently, he evaluates Kemalism as a 'religion of civilization'.[8] In addition, he criticizes Mustafa Kemal for modernizing the country with oriental methods, as a result of which there occurred an identity crisis that still continues today.[9] He contends that the country neither became western nor remained eastern but is stuck in between. And this situation is aggravated by the practices of the subsequent Kemalist elites. Ersin Gürdoğan contends that we have been witnessing a 'cultural purification' process in the last thirty years in Turkey to regain an authentic identity.[10]

In fact, Samuel Huntington indicates that modernization is a long and painful process and thus the transitional period in traditional societies is full of crisis and troubles.

On the other hand, İsmet Özel denotes that Kemalist ideology entails some elements of bolshevism, fascism, and National Socialism.[11] Hence he argues that both leftist and rightist political formations are in fact different 'versions' of Kemalism.[12]

As a final point, according to Ali Bulaç a purely secular plan never exists in the universe; and even modernity is an 'inverted religion', which situates itself with reference to religion.[13] Thus, argues Ali Bulaç,

> it is more clearly understood that a modernization paradigm in spite of religion is not possible. Consequently, the seventy years long experience shows us that the Kemalist modernization project has resulted in total fiasco in comparison to the models of Japan, South Korea, Singapore, and even Latin America, Mexico, and Argentina. Currently, we are living in a period in which the secular modernization paradigm that has been proved to be ineffective and wrong will be replaced with a new one.[14]

In my view, this new project will be based on Islamic norms and principles.

State and nation

The concept of political state has an Islamic connotation in Islamic intellectuals' thoughts. We witness again the condemnation of the modern nation state, which emerged as a product of the mentality change in Europe as a result of the Enlightenment process and the French Revolution following the Renaissance and Reformation. İsmet Özel analyses the evolution of the current form of the state as follows:

> Today the instances which are presented us as the history of modern state are in fact the history of new and different state undertakings. The world system has reached its current form by eliminating novel and divergent types of state enterprises, which it has considered as rivals. The conflict between the secular rule and the Church after the collapse of the Roman Empire; consolidation of the concept of state-religion by the subsequent Protestant movement, and eventually the success and dominance of the state, which had reached its complete form with the independence of the United States, is offered as a prototype valid for all other countries and rights. Nevertheless, this is just 'one' type of state. In terms of value system, it is far from Islamic mentality, in terms of morality it is unrelated with Islam, and from the perspective of worldviews, it is based on the eradication of the Islamic way of life.[15]

Before analysing the critiques by the Muslim intellectuals of the nation state let me give Ali Bulaç's definition of the state:

> We consider the state only as an organizational model, and therefore we think that it had to be evaluated in a separate platform independent from all kinds of sacred, philosophical, and ontological foundations. The state is neither the manifestation of Divine Will, nor the privilege of the elite families; nor collective intellect, or the tool of a mission that modernizes social life. A state is the political organization of the people, who have to live together. In order to live collectively, organization is imperative; consequently a state is not a way of life that is uniform and homogenous, but in contrast, it is the legal base of the multifarious modes of lives based on different religions, beliefs, and philosophical views.[16]

So the Muslim thinkers agree that the state exists in order to ensure the people's rights and freedom and that it is not monolithic but embraces diversity within the society.[17] However, the nation state put an end to this heterogeneity by creating artificial homogenous communities. In other words it tries to create a single type of nation and Turkey is a good example for this kind of state, which attempts to modernize everybody by any means. Bulaç indicates that 'modernism is uniformity in which all the multiplicity, divergences, and autonomous units are dissolved:'

> The modern despotic state achieves this with the concept of 'mass society'. This is a huge melting pot, in which the personal, unique, and all the divergent identities are melted. This melting process is given fictitious names such as dynamism, movement, development, homogenous, universal state, progress, and the like. In fact, what is happening is the existence of a widespread and penetrating totalitarianism.
>
> ... As the individuals, societies, and regional autonomous groups are reidentified and put into the pot of 'nation', the state makes the decision instead of the people. The nation is the projection of a worldly ideology, which violates the sanctity of religion. So, as Gellner said by departing from Durkheim's religious analysis, nationalism means the self-worship of a society, which is classified as a nation. If nationalism is the self-worship of the people, then in its roots lies the secularization of religious matters, which has the sense of worship in its core. The Christian community of the Catholic Church has split apart because of nationalism but the sacredness of the Christian universal community is transferred into the parts, in which the nations are divided. Subsequent to this, the liberation that is believed to be acquired by being devoted to Jesus is degraded to modernity, which is supposed to be achieved by the modern national state. Here, Satan imitated God.[18]

These ideas sound very similar to Benedict Anderson's and Eric Hobsbawm's views on nations and nationalism. On the other hand, Rasim Özdenören also indicates that this model of state is deprived of all kinds of sanctities, which superimposed the rule of humans by renouncing the authority of the Divine Being.[19] This designates the replacement of Islamic law by the profane jurisdiction of the modern authoritarian state.[20] And what seems paradoxical for Özdenören is the adoption of this system by Turkey and other Islamic countries, which did not experience similar historical events in their past.[21] Moreover, in Muslim scholars' opinion, the nationalist disposition of the modern state engendered division, discrimination, and conflict among societies.[22] The First and Second World wars and current massacres and ethnic cleansing in different parts of the world prove this. Let me elucidate at this point their thoughts on nationalism.

Ali Bulaç calls it 'materialism' because he contends that the ontological constituents of the nation – race, ethnicity, colour, language, land – are related to the 'material and historical' characteristics of a nation.[23] In addition, it aims to modernize non-Western societies with the aid of nation states. Thus nationalism is a product and agency of modernism. Moreover the 'otherization' of different groups depending on these factors destroys the belief in 'Tevhid',[24] which aims to gather mankind on the basis of the concept of 'Unity of Truth'.[25] For that reason, nationalism is considered as 'schismatic', 'dangerous' and 'disintegrative' and a potential motive for polarization as well as conflict.[26] At the same time it is a means of domination and tyranny.[27]

In addition, İsmet Özel believes in the inseparability of the idea of 'religion' and 'nation'.[28] In other words, according to this idea, 'people who belong to the same religion should not form two different nations, just as people who become a nation should not belong to different religions.'[29] That is to say, the fundamentals that determine the nationality of a community shape and constitute at the same time the essence of the religion of those people.[30]

On the other hand, he also points out that nationalism in Turkey has a different meaning in comparison to other nationalisms in diverse parts of the world.[31] According to Özel, nationalism occurred as an element of European culture parallel to the development of capitalism in the world.[32] So, allegedly, nationalism is seen as a byproduct of capitalism. Actually, this is the thesis of Ernest Gellner (a prominent social anthropologist and theorist of modernity) who sees nationalism as a by-product of industrialization and economic progress. In other words, Gellner argues that 'nationalism was the only possible outcome when industrialism burst into an ethnically differentiated world.'[33] In his book *Nations and Nationalism*, Gellner states that 'if an industrial society is established in a culturally heterogeneous society, then tensions result, which will engender nationalism.'[34] He argues that 'while other forms of society are either indifferent to common culture or even hostile to it, industrial society requires shared systems of communication, establishes them by means of formal education, and thus promotes the formation of nation.'[35]

Likewise, in İsmet Özel's opinion, since Turkey neither experienced feudalism nor capitalist development, nationalism has a distinctive foundation. In other words, Özel says that nationalism gained a meaning only as a result of world system's integration into Turkey.[36] So nationalism in Turkey is different than the development of nationalism in Europe. In fact, he points out that Turkey is the only country that has been able to form a national entity in spite of its unfamiliarity with capitalist development. Thus he contends that Turkey can lead the beginning of a new kind of nationalism.[37] However, these views of İsmet Özel should not make us believe that he defends nationalism.

On the other hand Rasim Özdenören considers nationalism as one of the requirements of Kemalism and argues that it constitutes a great obstacle for the development of Turkey.[38] Likewise Ali Bulaç believes that nationalism is a means of oppression and regards it as very dangerous. He notes that it appeals to the human ego and necessitates the domination of the strong side over the weaker one. Furthermore he stresses that nationalism attempts to dissolve different groups of people in its own identity, which eliminates plurality.

Moreover, the Muslim intellectuals contend that the problems of humanity are universal and global; hence it is impossible to solve them with national agendas. As a result, they anticipate that just like other secular and modern ideologies, nationalism too, will fade away soon.[39]

Now let me turn back to the issue of state and look at the views of İsmet Özel on the subject. He agrees with the Spanish philosopher Ortega Gasset's contention that 'the state is a plan of activity and programme of labour division.'[40] Accordingly, the state emerges when divergent and separate groups of people have to build a common life. In other words, for the formation of state, the common ideal is essential. İsmet Özel indicates that this objective generates the state.[41] He has reservations about giving a name to the community over whom the state exerts its authority. He states that they can be called nation, ummah,[42] society, or public. However this is not the crucial factor that we have to deal with because each of these forms constitutes a different type of manifestations of the state's power.[43] He emphasizes that the important thing is whether the form of the state complies with the character of the community or not.[44] What he tries to say is that the state and the nation (or whatever it can be called) has to come from the same essence.[45] Otherwise the state will become distant to its community. And this is exactly what has happened in Turkey between the state and the nation. Abdurrahman Dilipak also stresses this point and suggests that the state in Turkey can only preserve its unity and reach success by empathizing with the beliefs and worldviews of its people.[46] This point is affirmed by Ali Bulaç. 'Since the state', claims Bulaç,

> does not cease to consider itself separate and distinctive from the public, it always stands insecure when facing civil

> society and its developments. Since the state in Turkey is constructed from the top down, it never remains satisfied without molding the people according to the determined pattern. Thus the state tries to eliminate its distrust by reinforcing the bureaucracy; in a sense it struggles to ensure its safety.[47]

Another feature of the state according to İsmet Özel is its materialistic character after the rise of capitalism. He proposes that the generative element of the modern state is the drive for profit:

> It would not be a fantasy to claim that in spite of the existence of different flags, national frontiers, various languages, and several administrative units on earth, there is only one state and this is the capitalist state, which has its leaders in the metropolis.
>
> Today the alleged world system should be considered as the last form of the state of our age. Everything from the sport contests to economic success should be regarded as an effort to acquire a niche in the system. Firstly you are adopting the value system, moral principles, and the interpretation of life, and consequently you try to prove how successful you are on these judgements, principles, and interpretation. In a nutshell, you are expected to join the 'state' when they call you to realize that objective.[48]

Moreover, the Muslim intellectuals draw our attention to the authoritarian power of the modern state. Bulaç asserts that the modern state is the most despotic and autocratic state humanity has ever seen.[49] Accordingly, the state dominates and penetrates in every sphere of the individual's and society's life with the aid of modern science and technology.[50] Here Bulaç often resorts to the ideas of two prominent postmodernist philosophers, Michel Foucault and Gilles Deleuze. In relation to their ideology on power politics, 'the state is a giant war machine', and to remain outside of its control, which is consolidated by the capitalist system, would mean the acceptance of being labeled as schizophrenic because according to the modernist ideology, schizophrenic people are those who refuse to surrender to the system.[51] So, as Bulaç states, the freedom of individuals is curbed by the modern state significantly, in a manner unparalleled throughout history:

> The modern state is transformed into a huge and sophisticated octopus, which operates not only within assigned limits but also in all aspects of social life; which controls strictly the individual's life and which makes decisions for the people on its own. So, we are confronted with a political society that decides for us in every matter from health to communication; from child education to family planning; from entertainment to worship; from culture to extra-curricular activities; from commerce to defense and from economy to law, in short from what we have to do, to how we have to live.[52]

In addition, the Muslim intellectuals denounce the current corruption in the political sphere in Turkey. They elucidate this issue with the power of the political authorities, who misuse the social and economic prerogatives that the ruling post has offered them. That is to say, the state is the biggest shareholder in the economy.[53] Ali Bulaç elucidates this point by saying that:

> In countries such as Turkey and the like, saving the state is equated with capturing it, and this has always been a very profitable task. That is to say, since the state has to create its own affluent and intellectual class, it is at the same time a means of wealth and social status. The individuals who are backed by the state become wealthy; acquire high status in the society, and if employed in the bureaucracy, they can control the public.[54]

Thus, Abdurrahman Dilipak urges us to discard the strong state and strong parties, which have huge economic powers.[55] Ersin Gürdoğan argues that the political parties avoid putting human beings at the core of economic, social, and cultural life.[56] He criticizes political parties for behaving amorally and considering every means justifiable to achieve political power.[57]

The Muslim intellectuals point out the transformation of the modern state into a gigantic firm thanks to globalization. What they try to indicate is the increasing responsibility of the state in struggling with the multinational and transnational corporations and to resist successfully relentless international competition.[58] As the globalization process advances, the legitimacy of the nation state begins to fade. To put it another way, henceforth the states will be long lasting as long as they adapt to global transformations.[59] Otherwise, they will be driven out of the global system. So the Muslim intellectuals criticize the modern state for pretending to be national but eliminating and restraining simultaneously the cultural and traditional elements unique to that nation for the sake of globalization.[60] However Bulaç strongly emphasizes that the declining legality of the nation state does not imply the weakening of the modern state; on the contrary, it indicates the consolidation and expansion of its totalitarianism as well as despotism.[61] Furthermore, he predicts that the decadence of the nation state will facilitate the strengthening of the ummah spirit, which envisions a social project that exceeds the purely political model of the modern state.

Let me now analyse this project by referring to the Muslim intellectuals' explanations of the Islamic state. They define this as the 'self organization of the ummah within a political framework', in which the people are protected with greater rights and in which the individual become stronger *vis-à-vis* the state.[62] More elaborately, the Muslim scholars underline three essential characteristics of an ideal state:

1. Politics should not be detached from religion and morality.

But this should not be confused with the 'religious state' or theocracy. The state should have an 'official ideology of religion;' however, it should also have ethical aims and ideals, and these can be nourished by religion as well.
2. The presence of a capable subject, who is responsible for his own life and actions; and politics, should take him into account.
3. The existence of broad civil spaces, where the individual is protected.[63]

The contemporary Islamist thinkers propose that God's Will is manifested in ummah instead of the state or in political leaders.[64] They underline the impossibility of theocracy in Islam since the administrators are elected people, who are authorized by the public.[65] The decisions are taken by ummah, the public, who are accountable for the results of their decisions.[66] The Islamist intellectuals stress the temporality of the government and state and the permanence of ummah. Thus ummah is considered more essential than the state, which is dependent on divine law (Shari'a).

Ali Bulaç states that the *raison d'être* of the state is to facilitate the advance of ummah and eliminate the existing obstructions. In addition, he portrays the classical functions of the state as 'the provision of internal security; legislation, the collection and spending of taxes for collective and indivisible services; general fiscal and monetary policies; foreign policy and defense'.[67] Moreover, according to Bulaç, other issues like economy, education, health, commerce, art, culture, communication, and sports should be left to civil society.[68] So contrary to the modern nation state, in this system the state does not decide on and intervene in everything, but gives the people great autonomy. Moreover, according to this model, the quintessential responsibility of the state is to govern with justice and ensure the security, freedom, and essential rights of its people, who belong to different religions, beliefs, or ethnicities.[69] The same author clarifies this point as follows:

> Since not every religion, belief, or ethnicity has the chance to become an independent nation, there is no solution to make various identities live together with realistic plurality and organize the public sphere according to this pluralism. One of the duties of the state is to prevent the hegemonic dominance of any identity, community, or social group over the others.[70]

In order to realize this, Ali Bulaç offers the Medina Charter[71] as the single pattern that is 'the legal document of a political union' signed by the Prophet Mohammad with the non believing Arabs and Jews of their free will on the basis of reciprocal conciliation to organize mutual relations.[72] It has aimed to enable different communities to live together in peace and harmony and been seen 'as the prototype of an Islamic constitution'.[73] In this respect, the Medina Act was 'pluralist and participatory', where Muslims, Jews and non believing Arabs were considered as an ummah.[74] Technically, this concept of ummah indicates their existence as a political union.[75] Each community in this political unification had religious and judicial autonomy.[76] So the Shari'a was applied solely to the Muslims. For other people, who had to live with the Muslims, there had been no enforcement of living according to the rules of Islam. In other words, they were free to organize their lives in conformity with their own religion, beliefs, and laws. Thus they were independent within the realm of their autonomy. Furthermore, the shared and indivisible tasks such as internal security, tax collection, and defense were carried out by the elected parliaments, whereas legislation, education, trade, economy, science and the like were left to civil society.[77] All in all, the Muslim intellectuals contend that this pattern is the most effective and ideal form of the state, in which the dominance or supremacy of any group was precluded and the maximum contentment of every person was provided.

Finally, the pace of globalization diminished the role and legitimacy of the nation state. Yet this did not weaken the subjugating power of the modern state. Therefore, the Muslim intellectuals propose the Islamic model as the single alternative, which will offer the necessary solution to the increasing problems of humanity.

To give a better idea, let me conclude this section with Bulaç's statements below:

> In relation to globalization, the problems of humanity are constantly increasing. Nevertheless, the existing paradigm and its product of the modernity project are far from offering any solutions to these problems.
>
> The anti-dictatorial pluralist project of Islam, which is far from theocracy, is a choice on its own. In this age, in which the humanity and our planet are approaching total demise, for people who are preoccupied with Islam and the problems of the world, it is their first and foremost responsibility to move towards the universal ummah project. Otherwise, Muslims too will not be able to resist this global process and escape from being integrated into the world system.
>
> ... If so, today is a new day, and let us start this new day with a new beginning and let us 'construct a new Medina', as the Prophet Mohammad had constructed Medina with the Medina Act.[78]

Science and technology

At the heart of the Islamist intellectuals' arguments lies the repudiation of all the elements that exclude the Divine Being. Hence they concur on the idea that a concept of science that excludes spirituality is erroneous and deficient. In other words, the essence of the subject lies on the duality between God's *revelation* (Vahiy) and *reason*; or the purely *divine* and *humane,* which prevailed throughout history.[79] Consequently, the source and objective of knowledge are of paramount importance for the subject under consideration. From an Islamic perspective, reason is not the source but a 'significant instrument for collecting, developing, classifying, and interpreting scientific knowledge.'[80] Moreover, according to Rasim Özdenören there is not a single path of reason, as rationalism suggests.

In contrast to revelation, argues Ersin Gürdoğan, reason utilizes solely the data that is perceived by our five senses.[81] It is unable to explain the metaphysical world and thus its power to reach the Truth is limited. Consequently, information from divine revelation is imperative in order to understand human beings, nature, and the cosmos.[82] It is not 'irrational;' on the contrary, it is 'beyond and further' than reason.[83] Parallel to this, Bulaç also argues that knowledge originates only from revelation and divine wisdom. In other words, God's revelation is the sole source that differentiates truth from falsehood.[84] He clarifies this point by claiming that:

> The most trustable way to resist Satan passes through *Knowledge and Wisdom*. If God's revelation (Vahiy) is not the source of knowledge, it is still possible to obtain information about the Universe, human beings, and history, but this is only a kind of knowledge that had existed during the time of pre-Islamic Arabian paganism and the age of ignorance (al-*jahiliyyah*). The philosophy, worldview, and institutions that depend on this sort of knowledge keeps the material and cultural structure of infidelity (Küfür) effective. 'Küfür' is a dark cover that disguises and obscures reality. Unless the knowledge that comes from God removes this cover, humans can neither perceive the essence and purity of reality nor acquire Wisdom.[85]

In short, this kind of knowledge does not only give us information about the cosmos, life, and human beings but also equips us with the knowledge of God, the Angels, the Afterlife (*Ahiret*), and Eternity (*Dar'ül Beka*).[86]

The detachment of science from divine sources with the

Enlightenment in the West created the belief that science is unquestionable and perfect. Ali Bulaç defines this separation as an epistemological break, in which the essence is transformed and reduced to a mathematical and physical reality.[87] The same author proposes that:

> In the past, the sciences were the legal instrument and powers that display the methods of the Truth. However, current science caused the people to live in profound unrest. Pythagoras began to call the wise people philosophers (not the people of wisdom but the people, who love wisdom) as he realized for the first time that human beings has lost Divine Wisdom. As he was using sciences such as Mathematics, Geometry, Astronomy and Music as techniques to reach from plurality to the Unity in the Universe of Existence, today the same sciences are transformed into a method, which provides the expansion of the sphere of quantitative, objective, and material growth. In Pythagoras and other Chinese, Indian, Persian, Babylonian, Egyptian, and Islamic cultures, mathematics is a sacred way to know God, which is the unique principle and the source of the Universe of Existence. Geometry searches the movements of the planets and stars within the space and their own orbits, which are a kind of praying and dance. So the music of their divine voices is determined and this cosmic and universal reality was meant to be discovered by these four sciences. After Descartes Mathematics and Geometry were distorted from their conventional objective and transformed into a simple instrument used in the counting of the quantitative world. Modern astronomy is being used presently for the capture of space by the hunters of nature, who have completed the conquest of the world. It would be futile to mention Music. Now, it is not a science; rather it is a noise, in which electronic, sexual, and acrobatic madness go hand in hand.[88]

Similarly, İlhan Kutluer defines the replacement of the God-centred view of the cosmos with the human-centred, humanist viewpoint after the Renaissance as a deviation in human history, which was a consequence of the human mind's revolt against the Divine Being.[89] Bulaç describes this secularization of knowledge as the challenge of modern man to the sacred objective and meaning of life and even to its own existence.[90]

According to the Muslim scholars, the aim of science is firstly to 'help and guide humans to know Allah (God), and then to make their lives more efficient, productive, and easy'.[91] In this sense, the attempt of science is to enable people to perceive the essence of Existence and to reach from the particles to the Whole and vice versa.[92] According to Ali Bulaç, knowledge does not provide any benefit if it is devoid of faith in God.[93]

However, Westerners utilize science and technology in order to dominate mankind and produce mass weapons for the continuation of their exploitations.[94] According to modern ideology, Westerners consider the world a place for exploitation and thus waste natural resources for technological ends.[95] In other words, Ersin Gürdoğan argues that present scientific studies are carried out in order to increase the amount of production and stimulating material consumption instead of exploring the essence of the substance and the meaning of life.[96] Moreover, human beings are the measure of everything and thus everything is designed accordingly.[97] Consequently, modern science offers indisputable universal realities that appeal to all of mankind.[98] Nevertheless, Bulaç propounds that not all knowledge is universal and absolute as they are different expressions of the unique Truth.[99] In relation to this, Kutluer argues that modern science is 'immoral and value free':

> The transformation of modern science systems into a moral activity is not possible because, with its inherent epistemological values, modern science offers us an indirect worldview; indeed it proposes us an angle. It commands us

to look from this angle and within its confines. Modern science produces knowledge that is oriented not directly to action but to technological application. If it is possible to create an Islamic science model, then the major problem of this project would be centred on the question of how to ensure the relation between knowledge and action, because theoretical models are not sufficient. It should be put forward what the practical responses to these models could be. However, before engaging in such a project, it is necessary to understand the concept of 'science' according to Qur'an in the Qur'anic manner.[100]

In contrast to Islam, which regards science as a 'path and method' that leads people towards God, the West considers science itself as a 'God' or 'idol'.[101] Therefore with the Enlightenment period, science replaced religion and positivism became the new faith of the West.[102]

Rasim Özdenören points out that science has become the new taboo of humanity:

> The scientists eradicated the dogmatism of the previous ages; however, the cost of these old dogmas has been the emergence of new dogmas. For the time being, science is the new taboo of humanity. Science exists as an impediment to the free thinking of mankind. People are obliged to think as science commands. In reality, human beings, who battled against dogmas, reached a new kind of dogma.[103]

Abdurrahman Dilipak proposes that science is not capable of explaining everything because, he explains,

> according to modern science neither Satan nor Jinn nor the Archangel Gabriel exist. Consequently, there is no prophet, Heaven, or Hell. The important thing for a believer is not to what extent religion conforms to this ideology of science,

> but the degree to which science complies with religion. ... Religion is a transformed version of an eternal and all-encompassing divine project into a belief system.[104]

The idea of progress, which is one of the pillars of modern science, is criticized by the Islamist intellectuals. According to that idea, science and technology are continuously developing on a linear basis. Moreover it is also claimed that science and technology are 'abstract processes', produced by two interconnected phenomena. To elaborate, contemporary modern man regards the notion of progress both as an 'idea' and 'contract'.[105] Consequently, belief in progress has acclaimed the superiority of reason and is transformed eventually into a profane 'ideal of the humanity'.[106]

What the Muslim intellectuals do not agree with is the imposition of this process on human beings, who are considered by the West as 'the subjects of a universal destiny'.[107]

Ali Bulaç claims that scientific knowledge is created and employed as a means of power by the West:

> After Descartes, the Europeans embraced a new worldview under the light of Cartesian philosophy. And as they decided to embark upon colonialism; they found the theory of Aristotle highly useful, which suggests that 'knowledge is power, and whoever seizes this power rules over the issue of knowledge.' The Europeans put this theory at the centre of all their operations.[108]

Bulaç argues that this power is 'expansionist' and 'totalitarian' in its essence.[109] In relation to this, current improvements in computer technology and electronics enhanced the dominating and absolute power of science together with its effects on social, economic, and political transformations on a worldwide scale.[110]

Thus from this point of view, science is considered by Bulaç as a 'means of oppression'.[111]

> As Muslims, who are dependent on revelation, we are against the contemporary idea of science. In fact, this is not science; rather it is a means of oppression. This science, which produces nuclear weapons, bacteria bombs, toxic gases, and puts them in the hands of the hegemonic powers, causes the total destruction of humanity and threatens the future of our planet. We can not approve of this outrageous age and its perception of science. We can not approve of this science, which spends billions of dollars for rearmament and puts the people of underdeveloped countries more and more on the margins of poverty and misery instead of investing in the improvements of their economic, medical, and social conditions, and which annihilates them when they rebel.[112]

Similarly, İsmet Özel points out that this oppressive character emanates from the contemporary Western idea that recognizes the omnipotence of science as the single and absolute way to reach the truth. In addition to this, its effort to interfere in every respects of human's life beyond the limits of its own duties gives science the right to oppress people.[113] Allegedly, the results gained through the distortion of science with the claim of its absolutism in the West are replicated in Turkey, which has led to the creation of 'science despotism' without any benefit for society.[114]

Ali Bulaç relates the emergence of the social sciences to the birth of modern nations.[115] In accordance to this argument, psychology was initiated in order to assign human beings the status of 'individual'.[116] Likewise the science of sociology attempted to imprison people into a uniform social pattern.[117] He elaborates:

> In sum, the social sciences, which are claimed to be independent from any value, are not so due to their existence as a technique and method. The most resorted method of the sciences according to their subjects is to

> divide the world of the materials and objects into the parts and categorize them according to certain measures and subsequently to ensure the control and determination of this manipulated world by the central authority.[118]

The pointless friction between science and religion, which is engendered by the adoption of a distorted version of science particularly in underdeveloped countries, is also another significant point that the Islamist intellectuals indicate. İsmet Özel denounces the fact that in societies including Turkey, which are reluctant to question the fundamentals of science, religion and science are regarded as opponents.

Now let me concentrate also on the Islamist intellectuals' opinions about technology. Ali Bulaç defines technology as the 'practical application of science', which consolidates the certainty and absoluteness of science.[119] Ersin Gürdoğan delineates it as the collection, categorization, interpretation, and application of the knowledge accumulated throughout history. The core issue is not the effectiveness or usefulness of technology but our ability to control and rule it.[120] In other words, the Islamist intellectuals are not against technology; but they have a critical attitude towards it. They argue that it should be put under human control.[121] According to the Muslim intellectuals, technology is a product of humanity and is identified as the expressions of infinite human desires.[122] Thus, unless the people's desires are restrained, it is hard to dominate technology. However, they also believe that humanity lost its determining and guiding influence on science and technology with modernity. In other words, technology took control over the economy and the economy began to rule society. In a nutshell, modern man has become the prisoner of this 'iron cage' [technological civilization], which is created by himself.[123] According to Ali Bulaç:

> Technology is a grand and concrete evidence of the collective masochisms of the individuals, who create the

> fiction of the modern society in an organized and coordinated manner. Once the collective masochism is transferred as technology, it consumes the individual; controls society with its autonomous and objective institutions, and grows more and more every day as a destructive power on nature and the ecosystem.[124]

Nevertheless, Ersin Gürdoğan contends that the Muslims have the crucial values and beliefs to overcome the tyranny of technology.[125] In accordance to this conviction, technology is not the quintessential element but only a tool in Muslims lives.[126] To put it another way, society should not be oriented according to the needs of technology. Bulaç states that technology is not absolute, and opposes the idea that everything which is obtained from technology is good and useful.[127] Since the most essential endeavour of the believers of Islam is to attain the target determined by the Islamic religion, technology does not keep them spellbound.[128] The Islamist scholars consider this fact as the significant advantage for Muslims compared to Westerners.[129]

Moreover both Ali Bulaç and Ersin Gürdoğan argue that technology is not neutral. That is to say, it is not independent from the value system in which it has originated.[130] In accordance to their argument, a system that disregards divine sources cannot understand the individual and the true meaning of life and hence could not produce technology that is efficient and useful for humanity. Ersin Gürdoğan illustrates this point in the following way:

> The Egyptians acquired great affluence as they utilized the water of the Nile river for irrigation. However, they consumed this wealth not for the enrichment of the human soul but for the construction of the giant pyramids for their self satisfaction, which did not provide any benefit for the society. On the other hand, the Muslims used the wealth that they had obtained as they came to Asia Minor not for

> the fulfillment of their own desires but for the exaltation of the name of the God (Allah) and had generated magnificent creations. They have built Blue Mosque and Süleymaniye. So this is the difference between two kinds of cultures; culture that is nourished by divine sources on the one hand, and culture that is disconnected from it on the other. For this reason the essential factor in the production of technology is the human being's relation with God.
>
> ... We can compare those mosques with pyramids. The pyramids, which were constructed at the expense of many lives, represent ineffectiveness; however the Süleymaniye mosque symbolizes that the principal function of the human being is to comply with the divine revelation by emphasizing the impermanence of worldly prosperity and power.[131]

Let me also give the similar statements of Rasim Özdenören about this point:

> Technology is not evil on its own. This evil arises from its programming. In other words, the determining force is human intention in approaching technology. One can obtain benefits from technology according to its target. Without human intervention, technology does not provide any gain on its own. To put it differently, the technology of the Muslims will be different than the technology of the non-Muslims. Or the same quality product that is obtained from the same technology may be used with different purposes.[132]

In relation to these arguments, according to İsmet Ozel, technology has imposed its own morality. 'Technique' he proposes,

> is constituted not only of a machine and its rules of functioning. You are confronted with a technique, which is created by several conditions of a certain civilization and reached to the dimensions unique to that culture. This

> technology, which has grown and developed in the Western civilization, undertook a specific mission for them: to break off the relations between reason and existence. Approaching technology without understanding its purpose would mean to fall into its trap. That is to say, technology is not innocent as it is assumed. Apart from serving the Islamic society with its present features, it is also far from bringing peace and tranquility to the society of disbelievers. ...
>
> In order to identify the identity of the Western technology, we have to know firstly that technical development is not spontaneous. It is an extension of a certain social organization and a means of the interests of a specific social group, which emerged in a particular time span. Technique is a power that is generated in conformity with the ideals of Western civilization in order to serve the bourgeoisie. This power has a specific intention and meaning. Occasionally it operates in accordance to its purpose and mission independent of humans.[133]

So technology is a culture that removes divergences between various systems. Therefore the Muslim intellectuals are cautious about the export of every kind of technology. Here the quintessential thing is to export technology with a particular mentality rather than with the expectation that it will bring a certain outlook.[134] Indeed, Western technology will bring its culture with it. As indicated by the Islamist scholars what we have to do is not to adapt to this new culture but to remodel it according to our own culture.[135]

Another view of the Muslim intellectuals on the subject is related to the inefficiency and destructiveness of high technology. They are of the opinion that modern technology makes life even more unpleasant and complex.[136]

> Although the people are reluctant to accept it, the main problems of the world arise from high technology rather

> than 'underdevelopment' as in the cases of nuclear station accidents. The scientific and technological dimension of the West, which is considered as its strongest aspect, constitutes at the same time its weakest and most vulnerable side.[137]

Ali Bulaç also accuses high technology of harming the ecosystem and nature. He explains this point as follows:

> The Chernobil accident in Russia demonstrated clearly how a huge nuclear station in an advanced industrialized country can cause a horrible disaster. Apart from Russia, a part of Eastern Europe and Northern Turkey was affected by this calamity in a few days. The Western media took again the backward and cumbersome industry of Russia instead of technology itself accountable for this accident.
>
> ... For the sake of comfort and prosperity, the ecosystem and nature are impelled to pay heavy costs. The price of all these costs are; some doubtful benefits, namely 'welfare and civilization', which are promised by technology. There are simple indications of the fake happiness that is supposed to be provided by welfare and development: more televisions, more air conditioners, and more deodorants and similar things.[138]

Simultaneously, the Muslim intellectuals believe that with the improvement of science and technology the humanity lost its dignity and superiority when the people began to believe in machines instead of God. Consequently, modern society, which is organized according to the provisions of technology, created 'dehumanization'.[139] This point is described by Ersin Gürdoğan as the detachment of the individual from earth by being enchanted by the comfort and contentment that technology offers. As a result, people begin to loose the essence of their existence and humanly values.[140] So, in Rasim Özdenören's words, human beings turn out to be the servants of technology, which they have created.[141]

Finally, although science and technology transformed material and social life, they were not able to explain how we need to live.[142] Let me conclude this section with İlhan Kutluer's statements on the issue of what science and technology ideally should be:

> In the modern age, an Islamic paradigm should be established, which would be able to determine beforehand our observations and experiments; the questions that we will pose, and the answers that we will find to these questions. However, the creation of such a paradigm is closely related to the establishment of an Islamic socio-cultural environment. Such a paradigm will designate our way of thinking.[143]

Religion

Religion is defined by Abdurrahman Dilipak as 'the aggregation of belief and rules that are accepted as the source of truth and its reality.'[144] In elaboration, he categorized three meanings of religion:

1. Its meaning as provider of order within the society.
2. Its psycho-social meaning that is preoccupied with good and evil inside the people and is engaged with their praying as well as morality. In this sense, it presumes that the people act properly, justly and righteously.
3. Its meaning as a social institution that ensures the religious freedom of the people.[145]

So in a sense it regulates the economic, social, cultural, and political activities of a society by organizing the acts and thoughts of the individuals.[146]

In addition to this explanation, İsmet Özel clarifies the term 'religion' in its Arabic context. Accordingly, religion means:

1. Primacy, preeminence, being superior.
2. To be in service of an authority.

3. Customs, rules, laws, and conducting oneself in conformity with laws.
4. Judgement.[147]

Simultaneously, Özel contends that religion is a way of life that involves every issue related to humans and their relations with other creatures.[148]

On the other hand, Ali Bulaç accepts the Qur'anic definition of religion as 'the path that humans follow in this world and a belief and way of life'.[149] According to this definition, Marxism, atheism, liberalism, socialism, and the like are also a religion.[150] In addition to this description, he identifies religion as 'honesty'. In elaboration, religion means 'being fair and just towards Allah, nature, creatures, other human beings, and to oneself.'[151] Essentially, religion, which is based on divine sources and revelation, also regulates principles of faith.[152]

The Muslim intellectuals of Turkey assert that religion encompasses everything and consequently nothing can exist outside of religion.[153] Insisting on non-religiosity is an illusion or fantasy on which the modern world is constructed.[154] According to this idea, non-religious people can exist within the society; yet the continuation of the community is provided by believers.[155] In relation to this, Ali Bulaç points out that:

> Religion is the first and foremost source of knowledge. This source guides, shapes, and creates the essence of wisdom and culture. An entirely non-religious culture existed neither in our age, nor throughout the history of humanity. That is to say, whether human beings believe in God or not, ultimately he is equipped with certain thought and beliefs about the universe, life, society, and mankind. So, all these facts are characteristically religious and belong to religion. Thus, the wisdom and culture of human beings are reproduced on the basis of knowledge, beliefs, and perceptions that are existent within religion.[156]

In addition, religion is not a 'mystical' phenomenon outside of the boundaries of life that provides spiritual gratifications. On the contrary, it is a living set of orders and prohibitions according to which we have to arrange our actions.[157] Rasim Özdenören puts forward the thesis that science, ethics, jurisprudence, and everything else acquire their meaning with reference to religion.[158] That is to say, 'religion is faith, knowledge, action, honesty, advice, and in short, life.'[159] Therefore Bulaç also emphasizes that religion is a living thing; otherwise, it would be just a 'claim or a fancy ideology, or a hypocritical philosophy'.[160] As argued by Dilipak, the main task of religion is to complete good moral qualities because virtue is the first and foremost factor for the success of the system.[161] To achieve this, religion enhances the perception and spiritual richness of the individual by inspiring metaphysical thought.[162] It makes human beings pray and praise God and shows the means of ascension to the status of God's servant.[163] Consequently, people begin to search for the reality of life, which makes their lives more meaningful.

İsmet Özel holds the West accountable for the mystification and segregation of religion. 'Before capitalism, in Asia, Europe, and other parts of the world' says Özel:

> the concept of 'religion' in its present context and meaning did not exist. People did not separate their religions from other personal characteristics. ... In short, religion was not an issue of conscience that people were carrying individually. The detachment and emancipation of religion from working life, state administration, education, and entertainment is a consequence of capitalist civilization.
>
> ... Religion in the lands of Western civilization has been from the beginning in connotation with prohibition, subjugation, and suppression. From these facts we understand not only that the idea of religion designates the clerical authorities, which states prohibitions but also that the partition of life in religious and non-religious forms that

> constitutes the basis of the Western ideology. Consequently, we can realize that in our age, in which the Western lifestyle pervades everywhere, religion designates a kind of private psychological situation. For a modern individual, religion is important as emotionality, which has completed its course. According to him, religious life is a system of morality, where the guarantor is the modern individual.[164]

Now let me mention the Muslim intellectuals' comparison of religion with ideology and philosophy.

Ideology is a product of the human mind, so it is entirely humane and worldly.[165] On the other hand, religion originates from divine knowledge. That is to say it is 'a conception of the universe, which also includes and surpasses this world'.[166] So it is equipped with knowledge of the known and unknown and the seen and unseen, whereas ideology is only capable of revealing the truths of the concrete and visible world.[167] Moreover, religion, and Islam in particular, is seen as more realistic than all modern ideas and philosophies.[168] Bulaç argues that:

> Idea and its systematic knowledge, that is to say ideology, can not lead us to Divine Truth and genuine happiness. In effect, idea is the product of a perception that is gained through this Level of Existence. The Truth and its principles are intrinsic to revelation, which is with and beyond this Level of Existence. Therefore pure idea is a futile effort and should be exceeded.[169]

In addition, Bulaç warns us against reducing religion to pure ideology because this will mean the politicization of religion by segregating it from its spiritual, cosmic, and intellectual dimensions.[170] So the Muslim intellectuals reject both the involvement of religion with politics and politics with religion, which will lead to Cartesian dualism.[171]

On the other hand, unlike philosophy, religion has unique

methods and rules of thinking. In philosophy, the acceptance of an idea is arbitrary and not obligatory.[172] However, according to religion, the state of believing is not left to the decision of the individual.[173] To put it differently, since revelation appeals to the whole of mankind, every person is subjected to it and thus responsible.[174] Moreover, religion does not attempt to prove its statements.[175] In other words, it is not an issue of religion. But from the perspective of philosophy, proof is the most essential thing.[176] That is to say, according to Rasim Özdenören, philosophy cannot function without verifying the accuracy of its ideas.[177] Finally, deed and action are the crucial responsibilities of believers of religion, which does not exist in philosophy.[178]

Moreover, religion is considered by the Islamist writers as the 'sole source' of morality. In fact, religion and morality are not separate or disconnected things. 'Morality is the expression of a universal attitude, which is intrinsic to religion.'[179] In relation to this, the morality of an individual requires him to behave in accordance with divine order and stance.[180]

Moreover according to Rasim Özdenören, morality is 'the reflection of culture in the form of human behaviour'.[181] So, it designates the norms and rules of conduct of a certain culture and therefore changes according to the different value systems of distinctive societies.[182] Hence, according to Rasim Özdenören, it would not be wrong to derive the conclusion from this fact that the denial of Western morality would mean the negation of its culture and its products in entirety.[183] So, the concept of morality is not independent from the value and belief system of a certain civilization.

In addition, since morality is based on religion, which is the fundamental source of everything, modern distinctions such as 'science ethics', 'religious ethics', or 'secular ethics', can not exist.[184] In a nutshell, ethic and morality can not exist autonomously or independently as different phenomena.

Moreover the Islamist intellectuals proclaim the revival of religion after an interregnum period.[185] They observe that with the crisis of modernity, people began to realize the importance of religion as they lost their confidence in modern rhetorics.[186] In fact, it is essential to note here that religion is considered as the 'alternative paradigm' of modernism.

Consequently, in contrast to the general belief, more and more people from diverse backgrounds and sections of society become interested in religion.[187] Bulaç explains this revival as follows:

> The return to religion in our age is human beings' return to God, as they realized that all of his (man's) efforts had resulted in tragedy after having a profane and secular life for a long period of time. As history reveals too, atheism and nihilism are marginal belief systems, and only religious beliefs and sacred traditions have been significant throughout history.
>
> The revival of religion as an effective phenomenon both in the East and West and its existence behind the social and political movements all over the world is the indication of the beginning of a deep transformation in the perception, consciousness, and thought of the human race.[188]

Thus, in the Muslim intellectuals' view, the future will be determined by religion and modern ideologies; also, doctrines will cease to be effective and the future will be illuminated with the 'light of Islam'.[189] In fact, from the Islamist intellectuals' point of view, 'since the holy sources of Islam are not distorted and since it did not surrender to modernity and is still resisting to it', Islam is considered as the 'single alternative' among other religions.

Likewise, Ernest Gellner contends that it would be erroneous to say that 'secularization prevails in Islam. Islam is as strong now as it was a century ago. In some ways, it is probably much stronger.'[190] He answers Islam's resistance to secularization unlike other religion and belief systems in the following way:

> Why should one particular religion be so markedly secular-

> ization-resistant? This is an important question. ... The central doctrines of Islam contain an emphatic and severe monotheism, the view that the Message received by the Prophet is so to speak terminal, and that it contains both faith and morals – in other words, it is both doctrine and law, and that no genuine further augmentation is to be countenanced. The points of doctrine and points of law are not separated, and Muslim learned scholars are best described as theologians/jurists. There is no canon law, but simply divine law, as such, applicable to the community of believers, rather than to the organization and members of some specialized agency.
>
> ... The fact that, in this way, legislation is pre-empted by the deity has profound implications for Muslim life. It does not merely mean that a fundamentalist may have difficulties in accepting modern law and legislative practices; it also means that a certain kind of separation of powers was built into Muslim society from the very start, or very nearly from the start.
>
> ... Another striking and important feature of Islam is the theoretical absence of clergy. No distinct sacramental status separates the preacher or the leader of the ritual from the laity. Such a person is naturally expected to be more competent, above all in learning, but he is not a different kind of social being. Formally, there is no clerical organization. Muslim theology is in this sense egalitarian. Believers are equidistant from God.
>
> ... Islam knew rapid and early political success, which is perhaps one of the reasons why a church/state dualism never emerged in it: the original charismatic community had no need to define itself as against a state that still remained alien. It was the state from the very start.[191]

In conclusion, according to Islamist writers, 'the modern era taught us that human beings can not plan a real world without the existence of religion.'[192] In other words, man can not live in spite of God.[193] Once life is detached from the sacred and divine sources, people become the servants of ideologies, which are the products of narrow-minded systems.[194]

Islam

The Muslim intellectuals in contemporary Turkey note that Islam is first and foremost a religion, which can not be compared to any doctrine, philosophical dogma, or worldview.[195] Ersin Gürdoğan defines it as the 'last version of the Divine Truth', which uniquely preserves its 'authentic value', unlike other distorted religions.[196] In a similar way, Ali Bulaç points out that Islam is not an ordinary religion 'the religion', which has distinctive features.[197] He exemplifies this distinction by presenting Islam as the religion, which 'continues and represents the divine religions', sacred doctrines, wisdom, and knowledge heritages'.[198] Moreover, according to Ersin Gürdoğan, it is 'the only religion, which stipulates with its universal message respect and love for the single God and numerous prophets'.[199]

Moreover Ali Bulaç describes Islam as the 'project of a pluralist society and collective living, which is based on religious and judicial autonomy and the assurance of human beings' fundamental rights and liberties'.[200]

According to İlhan Kutluer, Islâm is the religion of 'salvation and freedom', which is obtained thorough surrender in God.[201] Concomitantly, the Muslim intellectuals argue that man is living in an 'iron cage inside of the cave of the modern world and has lost Divine Wisdom'.[202] Thus, according to Ali Bulaç, 'the task of Islam as a tenet based on revelation is to liberate this human being from the closed system of modernity and then to teach the meaning and reason of the World of Existence'.[203] That is to say, as Bulaç proposes, the Islamic doctrine represents the ultimate and definite reality, and its objective is to take the individual to this reality, which is the 'gist and purpose' of Creation and Existence.[204]

Similarly, in the analysis of Rasim Özdenören, Islam provides mankind with the ability to grasp the universe and its existence in its totality with all its details without feeling the need for evidence or the intervention of Reason.[205] So, by the same token, Islam enlarges the perception and vision of man.[206]

The Islamist intellectuals renounce the alien and derivative elements that are carried into the Islamic belief throughout history with culture and traditions. They contend that these non-Islamic and even modern influences spoil the purity of Islam. Therefore these elements should be purged from Islam:

> We can offer a cure for the sick hearts of people with neither traditionalism and conservatism spoiled with superstitious beliefs; nor with rationalism and modernism that try to interpret Qur'an with absolutist reason and positivistic facts. More importantly, it is completely erroneous to present Islam as it is constituted of a purely ideological and political struggle and to transform it into a functional instrument for the worldly and material pleasures of human beings. Islam is a religion which guides toward the true faith and happiness. This religion requires fundamental changes in the material and spiritual, cosmic and moral, economic and political realms of people and society. The transformation is only possible with realization of the Qur'an under the guidance of the Prophet.[207]

Accordingly the essential requirement is to live and understand Islam in its genuine form.

Aside from this, Ali Bulaç differentiates the Islamic movements throughout history in the forms of 'official' and 'civil' Islam.[208] Accordingly, official Islam is a top down and totalitarian Islamization movement, in which the power of the state is employed to create an Islamic society according to an official ideology.[209] To illustrate this, various Islamist movements and groups – ranging from extremist and revolutionary to democratic and conciliatory – in Iran, Pakistan, Algeria, Egypt, Jordan, and Turkey (Welfare Party) are belonging to this category.[210]

We should state here that the Islamist intellectuals disapprove of politicization of Islam because this will lead to determination of Islam by the principles and needs of state and politics.[211] That is to say, the disengagement of Islam from two genuine sources (Qur'an and Sunnah) and its confinement within a closed political and humane circle will lead to the creation of a 'totalitarian Islam'.[212] Therefore political Islam is regarded as 'a bad copy of the modern world' and should be avoided.[213]

On the other hand, civil Islam is based on a social project and therefore addresses society and the individual.[214] In other words, it aims to seize the society instead of the state and thus ummah is more important than the state.[215] Ali Bulaç evaluates Bediüzzaman Said Nursi and his followers as being within this group.[216] In my view, Bulaç and other Muslim intellectuals belong to this latter category. Their goal is to transform the society in accordance to 'authentic Islam' from below.

Another important fact we have to clarify is their thoughts on the revival of religion in Turkey. As mentioned earlier, they argue that the state in Turkey reduced the autonomy and freedom of society and religion. As a result, the state manipulated religion. However, from the Muslim scholars' point of view, the social transformation that intensified after constant migrations from the countryside to large cities made these policies of the centralized state ineffective and obsolete.[217] So according to Ali Bulaç, the revival of Islam should not be considered as 'fundamentalism' or a 'reactionary movement'.[218] Rather Islam 'came to the agenda in contemporary Turkey as a social consensus and an international ideology of an economic and political order'.[219] Moreover, they strongly emphasize that Islam constitutes the building bloc and 'cultural texture' of Turkish society.[220] Bulaç proposes that Islam in our culture is as essential and vital as iron is to concrete.[221]

Besides they emphasize the non-theocratic nature of Islam. To elaborate this point, Bulaç asserts that in theocratic societies, the clerical class is the ultimate power. In addition, although religion dominates everything, its relations with the state on the one hand and social and economic life on the other are separated.[222] Contrary to these facts, in Islam, the sovereignty of the clergy does not exist. In other words, society is governed by civil people in accordance to the principles of Islam. Furthermore, Bulaç notes that Islam is a 'total religion, which considers life as a whole'.[223] Hence it involves itself not only in religious or spiritual matters but in all aspects of life, for example, social, political, and economic affairs. So it encompasses life in its entirety. As a consequence, Islam is not a theocratic religion.

Another point that the Islamist intellectuals make is the discouraging situation of contemporary Muslim societies. They accuse current Muslims of living in conformity with non-Islamic systems.[224] In other words, these Muslims are evaluating Islam with the concepts and mentality of the current modern system, which is secular and profane. Hence, the Islamist scholars renounce their life style, which is not relevant to the reality of Islam.[225] To put it differently, contemporary Muslims are blamed by the Islamist intellectuals for being integrated into the capitalist order. In their view, a Muslim should reject to be 'an element of his age' by having a mentality different than the thought system of his era.[226] In effect, in the intellectuals' view, incorporation into a certain system leads to the adoption of that system's morality as well.[227] So, the fundamental problem is the need to overcome the 'modern world'.[228] Therefore the Islamist intellectuals suggest that contemporary Muslims purify their minds from the filth of the profane modern order with the tenets of pure Islam as it was practised in its golden age, which is called as the 'Age of Happiness' (*Asr-ı Saadet*). Indeed, the Muslim intellectuals try to demonstrate that the interruption of the Islamic way of life since a few centuries ago created a 'cultural gap' between the perfect Muslims of Asr-ı Saadet and the present Muslims. Hence it is stated by Bulaç that this model of 'Asr-ı Saadet' is the sacred objective that motivates contemporary Muslims to the 'best and ideal' one.[229]

It is noteworthy to mention here that according to the contemporary Muslim intellectuals, this 'golden age' or 'Age of Happiness' does not correspond to a historical, symbolic or nostalgic view of the past. More than that, it represents a 'dynamic process' and a 'life style' that encompasses past and the future.[230] In a nutshell, authentic Islam with its universal messages for the problems of the modern era is seen as the single solution not only for the non-Muslim world but for contemporary Muslims as well:

> Islam is a religion that does not have to relive its own history. That is to say, it possesses authentic sources (Qur'an, Hadith and Sunnah), with which it can criticize its situation in history as well as at the present time. Islam is able to reproduce itself all the time, question history, and assign itself a genuine position that grasps the realities of its age. At the same time, the current message of Islam offers solutions not only to the problems of the Islamic world but also of industrialized Western societies. Western individuals, who are alienated and driven into despair and hopelessness by the political elites and atomized by giant institutions, has nothing to do except to give consideration to Islam as the last message of God. Islam, both in the East and West, is the hope of salvation for suffering people, who are weakened by a small number of secret or open oligarchic powers in the material, economic, political, emotional, and mental sense.[231]

As a final remark, they note that after a long period of interregnum, Islam is reviving. They conclude that the dawn of Islam is imminent and the earth will be brightened with the holy light of Islam.[232]

> The Islamic world has lived an 'interregnum period' since the beginning of the twentieth century. However, we are

> observing today that this era is culminating. We experienced great sufferings, wars, oppression, and torture. Nonetheless, we did not lose our hope and endurance. The 'days of God', in which we will live again independently and honorably, are approaching.
>
> ... Yes, Muslims have always believed in their permanence in history. The same conviction, spirit, and hope are today also fresh, and it heralds the completion of the interregnum period.[233]

History

The Muslim intellectuals have a distinctive explanation for history, completely different than its modern definition, which is very similar to the medieval view of history. They recognize history not as a section of social science as a 'knowledge of wisdom', which helps us to grasp the journey of mankind from the inception of the universe to its demise from a different point of view.[234]

Let me elucidate their understanding of the subject in detail. The Islamist scholars identify history not as a series of single, independent events. On the contrary, they approach it with a holistic attitude. In this regard, they argue that there is a divine rationale and wisdom behind all events in history. This wisdom is constituted of 'the conflict of justice and oppression'.[235]

In fact, Marxism and even positivism have a similar approach towards history, although in a secular manner. According to the Marxist theory of history, people do not make their history independently. In other words, 'history itself has no independent standing or substance, nor has it any aim, purpose, or direction of its own.'[236] So, the historical change has a general trajectory, which is explained by 'evolutionary and teleological reasoning'.[237]

According to Özdenören, the believers of Islam, who accepted the unity of God, represent 'justice', whereas the non-believers symbolize 'oppression'.[238] Similarly, Bulaç also contends that human beings are composed of two groups; that of the believers on the one hand and the infidels on the other. Consequently, this clash between justice and oppression constructs the substance of history,[239] and human beings are the natural components of this unremitting chain conflict.[240] In addition, according to the Muslim intelligentsia, the divine will is the determining factor in history. In this sense, Muslim intellectuals reject the role of coincidence. Let me quote the following arguments of Ali Bulaç about his understanding of history:

> The nature and the general world of existence are under the influence of God's power, and open to His intervention all the time. There is no doubt that human beings invite the intervention of God, though in any case the single power that is only able to interfere is God. He interposes history. From this perspective, by arguing that the divine will plays a formative role, we want to say on the one hand that history does not occur as a result of random accidents and on the other hand that we reduce the powers, whose numbers can be multiplied till infinity, to the One. There are not two wills in the course of history, as there are not two spaces in Existence. Undoubtedly, peripheral factors always play influential roles, and it is necessary to know the function and significance of these effects in order to understand the patterns of change in history.[241]

In the Muslim intellectual's views, the crucial things in history are identified as 'change and maturity' instead of 'evolution and progress'.[242] Indeed, what is changing is not the essence of man but only the 'forms and shapes'.[243] Thus the 'progressivist' idea of history, which considers advancement as absolute and certain, is rejected. As alleged by Islamist intellectuals, incessant movement, which makes change possible is vertical.[244] That is to say, with reference to Qur'an, the direction of historical change is from bottom to top or vice versa rather than from backward to forward.[245] The movement from bottom to top is called by the

Islamist intellectuals 'maturity or perfection' and its contrary 'deterioration'.[246] So according to the Muslim intellectuals there exists only 'exaltation' or 'deterioration' in history instead of 'progress' and 'regression'.[247] Essentially, in Bulaç's opinion, 'the eventual objective of human's history and the Existence is to construct the future from bottom to top.'[248]

Furthermore, history is also regarded as the 'human's walk towards God'.[249] In this regard, human beings, who are the subjects of history, are defined as 'passengers' on this journey. Thus, divine will and objectives in this expedition that lead humans to God is seen as quintessential. According to the Muslim intellectuals, our situation on such a journey, if it disregards the will of God, will resemble the situation of an individual on a train, who can only walk between the compartments and still regards himself as capable of influencing the direction of the train.[250]

Conclusion

In sum, the Muslim intellectuals believe that the westernization process carried out by Mustafa Kemal with Jacobin policies resulted in failure.[251] In other words, they argue that the authoritarian and directive modernization policies caused social upheavals, conflicts, and identity crisis not only in Turkey but everywhere.[252] Moreover they strongly emphasize that the Kemalist elite made a mistake by excluding religion in their modernization project. This is the crucial point of their criticisms.

In relation to their views on state, the Islamist intellectuals concur that the modern state is profane, despotic, and egocentric. They argue that although it glorifies and propagates the human rights, democracy, and similar values, it operates not for the public but in spite of the public. Moreover, the public should be more powerful than the state. However, the modern state has curbed the autonomy of the individual and generated a rigid control mechanism over the society. Consequently, they believe that the ideal state is based on the Islamic model.

Their thoughts on science and technology are centred on the

argument that 'knowledge is divine wisdom' and human beings can not live independently from knowledge of God.[253] According to them, contemporary Western science and technology encompass in their essences atheism, colonialism, and imperialism.[254] From an Islamic point of view, the Muslims should give the greatest effort and priority to make humans more virtuous and enrich their souls. Hence science and technology are meaningful and essential as long as they serve this purpose.[255] The statements and findings of science, which exclude spirituality, are erroneous and deficient.[256]

Moreover they suggest that the non-Western world should not follow this model of science and technology. In relation to this argument, Western technology should be reshaped according to one's own culture before adopting it.

Apart from science and technology, the Muslim intellectuals contend that religion is an all-encompassing phenomenon that determines our actions and every aspect of life. Additionally they point out the current revival of religion concomitant to the crisis of modernity. Accordingly, religion is regaining its importance as a counter-model of modernity. The Muslim intellectuals demonstrate the distinctiveness of Islam and make constant reference to the period of Asr-ı Saadet (Age of Happiness). They strive to bring back this period, which, they are convinced, will solve all the problems and troubles of humanity.

Finally, the contemporary Turkish Muslim intellectuals' beliefs regarding the issue of history have parallels with the medieval as well as Marxist understanding of history. They firmly emphasize the existence of the divine rationale behind the course of history. Moreover according to them, history offers humanity a 'genuine and revolutionary consciousness when it is interpreted with correct methods'.[257] In their views, history should neither be glorified blindly nor convicted or despised obstinately.[258]

This chapter has reviewed the current Muslim intellectuals' thoughts and arguments. In the next chapter, these intellectuals will be compared to some of the leading Muslim intellectuals in the Muslim world and in Turkey since the 1930s and 1950s.

Chapter 4

Comparison of Turkish Muslim Intellectuals across Time and Space

Introduction

This chapter is dedicated to a comparative study of the Turkish Muslim intellectuals' rhetorics, ideas, position, and views *vis-à-vis* some other Muslim intellectuals in the Muslim world and Turkey since the 1930s and 1950s. Since they do not exist independent and isolated from the process of Islamic revival as well as Islamist intellectual developments in the whole Muslim world, I found it necessary to put them in a global and larger context. This will enable us to see their particularities and uniqueness as well as similarities and evaluate them from the perspective of a broader picture. The following questions will be asked. What is different in contemporary Turkish Muslim intellectuals? What are their similarities? Do they have a totally different outlook? What are they? What are they not? In which aspects are they distinctive? Which conditions and circumstances make them different? I contend that this will help us to understand their type, position and particularities more clearly.

The current chapter will consist of two sections. In the first section, a brief historical account of Islamic revival since the nineteenth century in the Arab world will be given in order to have an idea about the resurgence of Islam in other parts of the Muslim world. Then, I will compare the current Turkish Muslim intellectuals firstly with their counterparts in the contemporary Islamic world (Muhammed Arkoun [Algeria], Seyyed Hossein Nasr [Iran], Nasr Hamid Abu Zaid [Egypt]), and Abdolkarim Soroush (Iran) and then with of the three most significant former Muslim thinkers in Turkey: Bediuzzaman Said Nursi, Necip Fazıl Kısakürek, and Sezai Karakoç. I chose specifically these intellectuals because they are the most significant representatives of their genre and at the same time the contemporary Muslim intellectuals in Turkey are mainly influenced and inspired by them.

First section: Historical review of leading Muslim revivalists and their ideology since the nineteenth century in the Arab World

Before embarking upon a comparative analysis of the Islamist intellectuals in the Muslim world, it is imperative to look firstly at the historical evolution of the Islamic resurgence and ideology of various essential Muslim revivalists in the Arab world since the nineteenth century with reference to the historical, social, and political conditions of their age.

The distinguished Islamic scholar Ibrahim Abu Rabi characterized the evolution of the Arab thought, in three phases: 'nahdah (renaissance), thawrah (revolution), and awdah (return to the foundations)'.[1] Accordingly, these three terms refer to the following:

> (1) reviving Muslim thought from within by affirming continuity with the past, and from without by borrowing from western sources; (2) emergence of the nation state in the wake of resisting the political and economic domination of the West, and (3) translating Islam as an ideology of combat which indicates, besides the nonfeasibility of

> nationalism as an alternative to the current state of affairs, a deep confrontation between the status quo upheld by a basically secular and military state and all sorts of Islamist movements carrying the banner of awdah (return) to what they hold to be the true 'religion'.[2]

Let me now elucidate briefly these phases.

The Muslim world's exposure to Western ideas and modernity initiated the need for reforming and modernizing their societies. In other words, in the age of Western hegemony and scientific and technological superiority, the Muslim world began to grasp its powerlessness and ineffectiveness more and more, as a result of which 'a new educated class looking at itself and the world with eyes sharpened by western teachers, and communicating what it saw in new ways' emerged by the end of the nineteenth century.[3] Apart from the urge for modernization and reform against the Western challenge, the inability of the traditional ulema (the doctors of Islamic sciences) to provide effective remedies to the problems of the Islamic societies paved the way to the emergence of new secular intellectuals.[4]

> Not since the high Middle Ages had an educated elite arisen in the Arab world that was distinctly separate from the closed religious stratum of the ulema, who for generations had monopolized learning and intellectual activity. The impact of education and of the new ideas slowly but inexorably broke this monopoly; by the end of the nineteenth century a new intelligentsia had emerged.[5]

These secular intellectuals are similar to as well as influenced and generated by the modern intelligentsia in West Europe and North America.[6]

Apart from the traditional ulema and pro-Western secular intelligentsia in the Muslim world, there was also a third grouping, who were neither satisfied with the classical ulema nor with the newly emerging, pro-Western secular intelligentsia, who were considered as being 'too secular' and 'agents of imperialism' as the nineteenth century was characterized with Western colonialism and domination.[7] These intellectuals, who belonged to this third group, tried to construct a new Muslim attitude, which is both genuinely Islamic and modern.[8] They initiated the nahdah (renaissance) movement, which is:

> a vast political and cultural movement that dominated the period from 1850 to 1914. Originating in Syria and flowering in Egypt, the nahdah sought thorough translation and vulgarization to assimilate the great achievements of modern European civilization while reviving the classical Arab culture that antedates the centuries of decadence and foreign domination.[9]

So, *nahdah* intellectuals 'saw the need for a total revitalization of Islam in the face of an encroaching Western culture' and questioned 'how Muslims can be authentic and modern at the same time.'[10] They can be considered as Islamic modernists. In fact, they aimed to save 'Islamic Reason' from its sluggishness and stagnancy.[11] By employing authentic sources of Islam in their discourses, they tried to ameliorate the conditions of Muslim societies and overcome Western political and intellectual hegemony.[12] Unlike the contemporary Turkish Muslim intellectuals, they argued for the possibility of 'Islamic reasoning' because they thought that rationality is part of the intrinsic nature of Islam.[13]

Rifa'a al-Tahtawi (1801–73), one of the leading Muslim nahdah intellectuals of Egyptian origin, believed in the compatibility of rejuvenation of Islam and adoption of the 'positive features of the West'.[14] Moreover, he believed that 'it was necessary to adapt the Shari'a to new circumstances and that it was legitimate to do so. ... If the "ulama" are to interpret the Shari'a in the light of modern needs, they must understand what the modern world is.'[15]

Another significant and influential modernist Muslim intellectual, Jamal al-Din al-Afghani (1838–97), was an Iranian. His main aim was to struggle against European hegemony and re-establish the glory of Islam. He was not solely a modernist Muslim thinker but a political activist too.[16] Afghani believed in the necessity of interdependence among Muslims to resist the European powers and thus strongly defended the idea of Pan-Islamic union.[17]

Furthermore, he called for the achievement of scientific and technological progress in the Muslim world.[18] According to him, modernization and reform of Islam was necessary because

> religion was the moral basis of technical and scientific achievement and of political solidarity and power. Islam was quintessentially suited to serve as the basis of a modern society. Islam was a religion of reason and the free use of the mind. The Qur'an should be interpreted by reason and was open to reinterpretation by individuals in every era of history. By stressing the rational interpretation of the Qur'an, al-Afghani believed that Islam could be made the basis of a modern scientific society, as it had once been the basis of a medieval society built upon faith.
>
> Islam properly understood, he also argued, was a dynamic faith, for it encouraged an active, responsible approach to worldly affairs. ... As a religion of rationality, science, activism, and patriotism, Islam embodied precisely those virtues that had made the European countries world powers. Al-Afghani saw Islam as a religion that could be a wellspring of a rationally guided, active, responsible life, compatible with modern science, dedicated to the restoration of the autonomy of Muslim nations and to the revival of the political and cultural glory of Muslim peoples.[19]

Aside from Al-Afghani, another important Islamist intellectual is Muhammad Abduh (1849–1905), who was Egyptian and politically less active.[20] That is to say, unlike al-Afghani, he was mainly interested in the religious aspects of the resistance against the European powers, and was also primarily preoccupied with the following question: 'how, when Muslims were adopting Western ways and Western values, could they maintain the vitality of Islam in the modern world?'[21] In his opinion, the reformulation of Islam should be achieved by conserving the principle elements and removing insignificant and incidental factors.[22] More elaborately, although Abduh took the Qur'an and Sunnah as the principal source, he believed in the importance of 'reason and judgement' by explaining the facts that are unrevealed in the Qur'an and Sunnah.[23] He condemned the traditional ulama for being 'dogmatic' and inflexible in matters related to theology and jurisprudence.[24] He contended that 'individual judgement, or ijtihad, was essential to regulate social relations', and 'general principles of Islam had to be reinterpreted in each age, rather than an eternal, detailed blueprint for social and political organization'.[25] So, he defended the rationality of Islam based on Western thought and accepted the adoption of Western ideas with the condition that Islam operates as a restrictive power.[26]

Muhammad Abduh experienced the British occupation of Egypt and realized the threat of augmented secularization and superficiality of the imitated Western culture because he believed that 'there is no profit in that unless they perfect their knowledge of its sources'.[27] He explained his objective as:

> liberating thought form the shackles of imitation (taqlid) and understanding religion as it was understood by the community before dissension appeared; to return, in the acquisition of religious knowledge, to its first sources, and to weigh them in the scale of human reason, which God has created in order to prevent excess or adulteration in religion, so that God's wisdom may be fulfilled and the order of the human world preserved; and to prove that, seen

> in this light, religion must be accounted a friend to science, pushing man to investigate the secrets of existence, summoning him to respect established truths and to depend on them in his moral life and conduct.[28]

Apart from the above mentioned modernist Muslim intellectuals, there emerged a new kind of non-secular, anti-modern Muslim intellectuals during and after the interwar period in the Arab world.[29] Among these intellectuals, Egyptian Hasan al-Banna (1906–49) is very important, as he prepared the ideological ground of a large-scale movement that affected the Islamic world profoundly.[30] Although he has been influenced by Jamal al-Din al-Afghani and Muhammad Abduh to a great extend, his thoughts and attitude were distinctive because he was strictly anti-imperialist, anti-Western, and anti-modern, and rejected secularism.[31] He founded the Muslim Brotherhood movement (Ikhwan al Muslimeen) in Egypt in 1928, which was 'the social movement par excellence in the modern Arab world against the backdrop of both reformism and modernism'.[32] The main objective of the movement was to provide 'Islamic solutions to the problems of education, economic organization, and social justice, advocating an Islamic nation without separation of religion and state. It proposed an Islamic educational system whose goal was to create 'the Muslim individual, the Muslim house, Muslim nation, and the Muslim government' and an economic infrastructure based on Islamic principles to solve social injustice'.[33]

Moreover, the Muslim Brotherhood was considered by Christina Harris as 'militant reactionary reform group' and 'religious revivalist movement' because: 'Their founders believed that "modernism" had already gone too far in Islamic society; they were convinced that the fundamental beliefs and institutions of Islam were thereby threatened. And because they blamed Western politico-economic intrusion in their world for the Westernization of their society, they became xenophobic and anti-Western.'[34]

We also have to pay attention to the political activism of Hasan al-Banna in contrast to the present Muslim intelligentsia in Turkey, which is determined by the distinctive local political and social conditions under which Hasan al-Banna has lived. He explained the fundamental drive behind his actions as follows:

> After the last war [First World War] and during the period I spent in Cairo, there was an increase in spiritual and ideological disintegration in the name of intellectual freedom. There was also a deterioration of behaviour, morals, and deeds in the name of individual freedom. ... I saw that the social life of the beloved Egyptian nation was oscillating between her dear and precious Islamism which she had inherited, defended, lived with, and become accustomed to, ... and this severe Western invasion which is armed and equipped with all the destructive and degenerative influence of money, wealth, prestige, ostentation, material enjoyment, power, and means of propaganda.[35]

In fact, the elimination of British occupation and prevention of the moral corruption of his country were his most important concerns.[36] And to achieve these ideals, he proposed the reintroduction of the Shari'a as the only solution.[37]

Hasan al-Banna was assassinated in 1949 and was followed by Sayyid Qutb (1906–66), who consolidated al-Banna's ideology.[38] He is considered as the most important ideologue of Islamic revival in modern Arab society.[39] That is to say, his thoughts on religion, philosophy, society, and the economy affected current Islamist ideology.[40] Ibrahim Abu Rabi describes the evolution of Qutb and his ideas under the light of the historical conditions in the following manner:

> He joined the Ikhwan movement in 1951, a year before the Egyptian revolution that brought Nasser and his comrades to power broke out. He started his intellectual life in the

1930s as a secular and, somewhat, romantic poet and literary critic. He preached art for art's sake, and supported the modern school of Arabic poetry against the classical school. He was mostly influenced by the secular and liberal orientation of Taha Hussayn, the blind Egyptian man of letters, though he came to reject these influences at a later period of his life, especially after joining the Muslim Brotherhood in 1951.

Qutb's transition to Islamic subjects is expressed clearly in the great theme he adopted as a title of his 1949 book *Social Justice in Islam.* This was followed by another powerful critique of capitalism from an Islamic point of view: *The Battle between Islam and Capitalism.*

In the period between 1947 and 1952, Qutb became totally disillusioned by the social and economic situation in Egypt. He proposed a remedy in his Social Justice in Islam. Second, his work on the battle between Islam and capitalism reflects his mature and realistic social understanding of conditions in Egypt. It is clear that Qutb paid close attention to the expansion of capitalism in his native land.

After 1950, Qutb's main emphasis was to search for an Islamic ideological discourse that would change the social situation. He focused his attention on issues such as Islam vs. Jahiliyah, the modern world, including the Muslim world, is subject to neo-jahiliyah, Islamic doctrine is a priori superior to other doctrines, be they are secular or religious, Islam is the solution to the social and religious malaise in human society, the Islamic doctrine, besides being theoretical, is also social and ideological, and the overall purpose of Islam is to establish the true Islamic society.[41]

So, we should evaluate Qutb's ideology and political actions with reference to the nationalist, socialist, authoritarian, as well as military regime of Nasser; the worsening economic and political conditions in Egypt during the 1950s and 1960s, and the colonial experience.[42] As Yvonne Haddad pointed out, he 'moved from a stance of an observer and interpreter of society, reflecting on its currents of thoughts and goals, to a revolutionary, who chartered the vision of a new order to which he wanted to lead all people. Having been disillusioned by all other solutions, he formulated his own, grounded in the Qur'anic vision yet relevant for the everyday life of Muslims in the Arab world.'[43]

The Muslim Brotherhood was subdued and he was executed by the Nasser government in 1966. But his ideas and thought instigated the future generation of Islamist movements and formations such as Jama'at, al-Takfir wa al-Hijrah (Excommunication and Exile), al-Jihad (Holy War), and Jama'at-i Islamiyah (Islamic Society).[44]

Another important ideologue of the Islamic revival was Abul Ala Mawdudi (1903–79). He founded the Jama'at-i Islami in India in 1941, which aimed to establish an Islamic state as it was in the Golden Age of Islam.[45] This was a Pan-Islamist movement, which repudiated nationalism and called for the unification of all Muslims.[46] He was a strong opponent of Westernization. Abul Ala Mawdudi is described as

> a reformer, fundamentalist, and political organizer, and he called for the formation of a truly Islamic state with Islamic government, banking, and economic institutions and appealed for a return to the Qur'an and Sunna and the use of rational judgement in religious matters so as to apply the principles of Islam in a modern society.[47]

Jama'at-i Islami was outlawed in 1953, but it reacquired its prominence in the late 1970s, when Pakistan became an Islamic state.[48]

The contemporary Muslim intellectuals in Turkey display similarities with these non-secular Muslim revivalists such as Hasan-al Banna, Sayyid Qutb, and Abul Ala Mawdudi in their resistance and repudiation of the West and Western ideas –

capitalism, socialism, liberalism, secularism, and the like, in their longing for the Golden Age of Islam, their quest for authentic Islam, and the belief that Islam is the only solution to the malaise brought by the West. However, unlike the present Islamist intelligentsia in Turkey that I am analysing, the distinctive political, social, and economic conditions of the Arab world turned these non-secular Muslim intellectuals into political activists seeking to realize their objectives. In other words, they did not remain pure intellectual critics. Generally speaking, they were born against European political, cultural, and economic colonialism.[49] In addition, the absence of democracy, the existence of repressive and authoritarian regimes, which are 'tribal' or 'sectarian', and the failure of the existing political, economic, and social systems created an impulse for political action.[50]

However, in the postcolonial period, which began after the Second World War, there have been major global political transformations, as a result of which there emerged a new type of intelligentsia in the Muslim world. These political transformations include the rise of

> the United States as a leading superpower in the wake of the defeat of Nazi Germany in World War Two, the creation of the state of Israel at the heart of the Arab world, shifting alliances in the Middle East after the 1973 war, and the Open Door policy pursued by the Egyptian state in the 1970s and 1980s.[51]

> The double tensions – Muslim stagnation and Western science Western science and Western hegemony – have defined the parameters of the main challenges facing the Arab mind since the nineteenth century. This double bipolarity became more complex in the mid-1950s after the end of official colonialism in most of the Arab states. The new nation states sought to modernize without sacrificing the common interest – be it derived of Muslim or nationalist

> thought – and sought economic and social independence from the West while still relying on it.[52]

So, in the postcolonial era, in which the independent nation states began to rise in the Islamic world, the struggle for the construction of the national and religious identity replaced the fight against colonialism. However, particularly Israel's defeat of Arab forces in 1967 and its capture of 'Golan Heights, Sinai, Gaza, the West Bank, and East Jerusalem, constituted a devastating blow to Arab/Muslim pride, identity, and self esteem'.[53] John Esposito elucidates this historical turning point in the following manner:

> Several conflicts (for example, the 1967 Arab–Israeli war, Chinese–Malay riots in Malaysia in 1969, the Pakistan–Bangladesh civil war of 1971, and the Lebanese civil war of the mid-seventies) illustrate the breadth and diversity of these turning points or catalysts for change. For many in the Arab and broader Muslim world, 1967 proved to be a year of catastrophe as well as a historic turning point.
>
> ... Most important, the loss of Jerusalem, the third holiest city of Islam, assured that Palestine and the liberation of Jerusalem would not be regarded as a regional Arab issue but rather as an Islamic cause throughout the Muslim world.
>
> ... The aftermath of the 1967 war, remembered in Arab literature as the 'disaster', witnessed a sense of disillusionment and soul searching that gripped both Western-oriented secular elites as well as the more Islamically committed, striking at their sense of pride, identity, and history. Where had they gone wrong? Both the secular and the Islamically oriented sectors of society now questioned the effectiveness of nationalist ideologies, Western models of development, and Western allies who had persisted in supporting Israel.

> ... Politically, modern secular nationalism was found wanting. Neither liberal nationalism nor Arab nationalism/socialism had fulfilled its promises. Muslim governments seemed less interested and successful in establishing their political legitimacy and creating an ideology for national unity than in perpetuating autocratic rule. The Muslim world was still dominated by monarchs and military or ex-military rulers, political parties were banned or restricted, and elections were often rigged. Parliamentary systems of government and political parties existed at the sufferance of rulers whose legitimacy, like their security, depended on a loyal military and secret police. Many were propped up by and dependent upon foreign governments and multinational corporations as well.[54]

Consequently, these dramatic events engendered the creation of a new kind of intelligentsia in the Arab world during the 1970s and 1980s, which began to make 'Islamist self-criticism for the first time'.[55]

Iranian Ali Shari'ati (1933–77) was one of the most significant and influential intellectuals of this kind, whose religious critiques shaped the Islamic discourse of the 1970s. He provided the inspiration and laid the intellectual and ideological ground for the Iranian Revolution. He was politically active and opposed to the monarchy and the shah's regime.[56]

He criticized both the secularists 'for their ignorance of metaphysical thought, their uncritical invocation of such foreign-made doctrines as Marxism and liberalism, and their lack of contact with the masses', and the clerics 'for their obscurantism, apolitical views, quietism, and their inattentiveness toward the important contributions and influences of modern sciences and technological breakthroughs'.[57] Most importantly, he indicated the need for a major reconfiguration of Islam on a 'theoretical' as well as 'organizational' basis, just as the Lutheran Reformation had achieved in opposition to the clerical hierarchy and 'Christian orthodoxy'.[58] He believed that 'the Muslim intellectual should begin by embracing an Islamic Protestantism similar to that of Christianity in the Middle Ages, destroying all the degenerating factors which, in the name of Islam, have stymied and stupefied the process of thinking and the fate of the society, and giving birth to new movements.'[59] In order to realize this, he urged the return to the 'Islamic roots', and restore authenticity rather than resorting to foreign Western ideologies.[60]

He created a 'revolutionary' and 'radical' Islamic ideology, which he believed was crucial for the transformation of the status quo.[61] Accordingly, it is the revolutionary understanding of Islam that can only activate people to struggle for social transformation.[62]

Second Section: Analysis of Turkish Muslim intellectuals' similarities, differences and particularities in comparison to other Muslim intellectuals in the Muslim world and Turkey since the 1930s and 1950s

In this section I will explain and analyse the thoughts and ideologies of four leading modernist Muslim intellectuals from the Middle East and three earlier Muslim thinkers/revivalists from Turkey as compared to present-day Turkish Muslim intellectuals. My purpose for comparing them across time and space is to find out their similarities/differences as well as to identify to what extend they are influenced by them. Let me begin with Muhammed Arkoun.

Muhammed Arkoun

Muhammed Arkoun is one of the outstanding Muslim thinkers, critics, and historians. He was born in Algeria in the village of Tourirt-Mimoun in Kabylia region in 1928.[63] After studying at the Faculty of Literature of the University of Algiers, he received his Ph.D. from the University of the Sorbonne in Paris.[64] He is currently Emeritus Professor of Islamic Thought at the

University of the Sorbonne in Paris and Senior Research Fellow and member of the Board of Governors of the Institute of Ismaili Studies.[65]

Before explaining his ideology, let me mention the social and political circumstances that affected and shaped his intellectual mindset as described by him in the following way:

> My full ambition as a Muslim intellectual is not the result of my academic training. Rather it is rooted in my existential experience. I entered a Koranic High School and then university in Algiers. It was colonial times in Algeria, and like all Algerians I was continually shocked by the sharp confrontation between the French culture and language and my own Algerian culture. I speak Berber and Arabic. When I heard lectures on Islam at the University of Algiers I was like others deeply disappointed at the intellectual poverty of the presentations, especially when the burning issues were raised in Algerian society between 1950 and 1954.
>
> The National Movement for Liberation was countering the colonial claim to represent Algerian civilization by emphasizing the Arab–Muslim personality of Algeria. As a result of this brutal confrontation I resolved to understand the Arab Muslim personality claimed by the nationalist movement and to determine the extent to which a modern civilization represented by the colonial powers should be considered a universal civilization.[66]

His exposure to Maghrebian, Arab–Islamic, and European culture through French colonialism enabled him to develop a more pluralist, global, and dynamic worldview, as a result of which he was able to grasp and realize the deficiencies and problems of Islamic tradition as well as modernity.

First of all, Arkoun criticizes the 'apologetic' and 'ideological' use of Islam, which worsened Islamic thought.[67] He is in search of the unorthodox, genuine truth that is 'in a structural situation of tension, of conflict, of mutual exclusion with the official truth'.[68] His aim is affirmed by himself as to 'deconstruct all rationalities, all types and levels of reasoning in the history of thought' and free traditional Islamic discourse

> from all limitations and contradictions by systematically choosing a dynamic vision rather than a static presentation, a bundle of methods taught by the social sciences rather than one method privileged over all others, and a comparative approach rather than the ethnographic view taken by those who tend to enclose and marginalize Islam in 'specificity', particularism, and singularities.[69]

In contrast to the contemporary Turkish Muslim scholars' insistence on the 'transhistorical' nature of Shari'a and Islamic principles, he proposes to examine these principles in conformity with historical realities with the aid of modern methods of historical enquiry.[70] In order to explore the 'objective' essence of the Qur'an, he suggests that:

> we must undo the intolerable amalgamations, the abusive simplifications, the emotional formulations, the arbitrary demands, the neurotic obsessions that feed false consciousness, which is utilized nonetheless to raise the consciousness of the masses for the realization of an historic mission; we must at the same time reinsert in the area thus liberated the positive findings of a critical re-examination of the whole Islamic tradition in the light of the most recent conquests of scientific understanding.[71]

In his opinion, current Islamic thought lacks a solid, consistent, and dependable 'political theology and philosophy'.[72] His struggle is to uncover these 'unthinkable' aspects of Islamic religion, which remained unthought for centuries, through the lenses of history, as well as epistemology, sociology, and anthropology.[73] He emphasizes the importance of historical analysis as follows:

> My starting point is historical. History means opening the full space and giving the floor not only to the big voices which spoke loudly and wrote big books, which we still read today and teach from today. We will also give the voice to those silenced voices. It is extremely important to give the floor to the silenced voices through history. Today, if we want to be a democracy in any society we have to give the floor to those marginalized voices. This is the heart of the issue. You can call it democracy or you can call it religion. It produces the same results. Silencing voices and giving the floor to some voices. What is at stake in doing this? The stake is the pluralism of meaning.[74]

Although he employs the methods of modern science, he does not surrender to modernity. By emphasizing the re-evaluation of the Islamic tradition with the tools of modernity, he also pushes for a criticism of modernity, which, he thinks, will be enriched with the aid of the Islamic pattern.[75]

In contradiction to the current Turkish Islamist intellectuals, who subordinate reason to faith, Arkoun claims that 'reason must intervene independently of revelation, as is established by the existence of aesthetic judgements outside the Islamic framework. Reason is based upon natural, necessary, and therefore universal knowledge.'[76] In his ideology, since the history of Islamic communities and Western people are intertwined, there is no contradiction between Islamic and Western reason.[77] In other words, the two affected each other in the course of history and therefore we have to consider their history as a unified history of the 'peoples of the Book/book', in which there exist distinctiveness within the framework of universalism.[78]

His endorsement of democracy places him into a different group from his Turkish contemporaries. He does not interrogate the compatibility of democracy and Islam. Arkoun approaches the issue again from a comparative historical point of view. Furthermore his approval of democracy is not without criticism of the West:

> I believe in democracy and I am not only criticizing the Islamists side. We lost a lot of time through history. What I am explaining about democracy applies to Europe because in Europe there are voices that are silenced. We know that ... democracy is still an exceptional experience and it is still a project for the future because it still has to be designed not for some people in some societies. You have to remember that in Europe they have been proclaiming human rights since the 18th century. Women didn't participate or benefit from these human rights and they did not vote in France until 1945. That was two centuries after the declaration of human rights. This simple fact shows how democracy is imperfect and imperfectly developed.
>
> All religions and systems of ethics are a matter for scientific research, philosophical debate, and sociological and anthropological reassessment. This cannot be done without the protection of a rule of law and the support of a pluralist civil society in which many traditions of thought, many postures of mind, and many religious experiences can be tackled.[79]

Secularism indicates, in his words, a

> continuous effort by human beings to achieve the greatest adequacy between imagined, represented reality, and objective, positive reality, and in this perspective, the forms, trends, and content of secularism in its European/Western achievements is one possible historical expression of the search for more adequacy pursued in other cultural, historical performances.[80]

Unlike the Muslim intellectuals in present-day Turkey, he claims that secularism exists both in a disguised and apparent manner in the Qur'anic discourse and Islamic experience.[81] According to this argument,

> The Umayyad-Abbasid state is secularist in its sociological and anthropological basis, its military genesis and expansion, its administrative practice, its ideological discourse of legitimacy. The theological and jurisprudential endeavour developed by the ulama contributed to concealing behind a religious vocabulary and sacralizing conceptualization literary devices, the secularist, ideological basis of the so-called 'Islamic' polity, and governance. Only Sufi personalities developed a sense of religious experience of the divine in an autonomous spiritual sphere that was not only independent of the state management of religious affairs but also from the demands of the lay believers.
>
> ... Very early in the history of the state, military power played a pre-eminent role in the caliphate, the imamate, the sultanate, and all later forms of governing institutions in Islamic contexts.[82]

Moreover he opposes the argument that secularism can not exist in Islam due to the non-existence of a class of clergy – a view also shared by the contemporary Muslim intellectuals in Turkey – and states that this belief overlooks historical as well as sociological realities. He argues that 'these are confiscation of spiritual autonomy by the top (the state) and by the bottom (lay believers mobilized by "saints" in brotherhoods) that began in 661 and has lasted until today.'

Likewise on the human rights issue, he criticizes the apologetic tendencies of Muslims, who affirm that those rights already exist in the Qur'an. He affirms that the Muslim intellectuals have to struggle for the liberation and development of the human beings, their thoughts, and their actions instead of reaffirming values that are related to an old culture and deceased procedures of civilization.[83] 'Much remains to be done in all societies,' Arkoun says, 'so that human rights are not mere words designed to assuage the thirst for liberty, justice, dignity, and equality all human beings experience':

> Religions have performed significant educative and therapeutic functions over the centuries, but their effectiveness has always been limited either by misuse at the hands of clerics or by weaknesses inherent in traditional cultural systems.
>
> ... Religion, like language, is a collective force that governs the life of societies. Secular religions have taken over for traditional religions in this regard. It is illusory and dangerous to ask of religions more than they can give. Only human beings, with their creativity and their innovative boldness, can constantly renew and augment opportunities for their own liberation.[84]

So in a nutshell, as a liberal and radical Muslim, he stands with the same distance and reservation towards the dogmatism of Islamists and Eurocenteredness of the Orientalists, who marginalized and categorized Islamic societies and their tradition ethnographically and ideologically rather than anthropologically and scientifically within the context of universal history.[85] In fact, what he tries to do is to challenge the entire inherited systems of thought without distinguishing religious or modern.[86]

Consequently, he strives for the re-examination of Islamic tradition under the light of history, philosophy, epistemology, semiotics, and sociology with an open, pluralist, and free mind and 'reweave it into the broader cloth of the world of which it always been a part'.[87]

Seyyed Hossein Nasr

Seyyed Hossein Nasr is another contemporary distinguished and leading Muslim intellectual and philosopher. He was born in Tehran in 1933 to a highly intellectual and prominent family. This scholarly environment in which he was raised equipped him not only with the knowledge of Persian and Islamic culture and tradition but also with Western philosophy and other religions as well.[88] As a consequence, he developed a universalistic ideology without abandoning his Persian culture.[89]

After finishing high school in the United States, he studied physics and mathematics at the Massachusetts Institute of Technology (MIT). He received his Master's degree in geology and geophysics from Harvard University. The 'intellectual and spiritual crisis' that he was experiencing since his eighteenth year in his search for the Truth led him to study history of science and philosophy at Harvard University, where he received a Ph.D. degree in 1958.[90] He became Professor of philosophy and history of science at the Faculty of Letters at Tehran University. After the Islamic Revolution in Iran in 1979, he moved to the United States, where he taught at various universities until his current position in the Islamic Studies Department at George Washington University.

His attitude towards modernism and the West as a whole is shaped by the conjuncture of historical and political circumstances. The most impressive of these events is his experience of foreign occupation. He describes it in the following way:

> I witnessed the invasion of Persia by the Allied Forces, with all the traumas that followed. Our own family was fairly well protected from the extreme effects of this occupation, including poverty and the outbreak of epidemics, but the sense of humiliation experienced by having to submit to the dictate of foreign powers was deeply felt even by a young boy like myself.[91]

Consequently, this sense of humiliation affected significantly his critical understanding and evaluation of the West and its modernity.

Moreover, his completion of most of his study in the West – in the United States (secondary school, undergraduate and graduate study) – and his intense involvement both in the physical and mathematical sciences and history of science and philosophy provided him with more elaborate, multidimensional, and first-hand knowledge of the West and Western science and philosophy in comparison to the Turkish Muslim intellectuals. In addition, as he explains, his deep knowledge of traditional Islam does not only include theology or philosophy but also cosmology and Sufism.[92] Besides he does not only concentrate on Christianity but also on other religions and beliefs such as Buddhism, Hinduism, and Taoism. Therefore, he has a broader and more global perspective than the Turkism Muslim intellectuals. Moreover although all denounce West and modernity, his criticisms are intensely philosophical and scientific.

He is mainly concerned with the relation between Islam and science as well as issues of 'Islamic cosmology', Sufism, modernism, and the environmental crisis. He considers the re-evaluation of indisputable Islamic doctrines vital within the framework of current Muslim societies.[93] He is neither a conservative[94] nor a liberal. He defines himself not as a 'reformer' but a 'renewer of the Islamic intellectual tradition and a follower of the perennial philosophy within that tradition'.[95] His endeavour is to revitalize and regenerate the traditional life of Islam and its intellectual heritage.[96]

In Nasr's conception tradition is, in his words, 'sacred principles rooted in revelation and their application in the context of a living religious universe'.[97] That is to say, tradition does not mean the continuity of what is modern or non-divine but the survival and diffusion of the 'sacred message', which requires knowing and evaluating West and Western science from the perspective of Islamic ideology and confronting with the challenges of modernity rather than imitating it blindly.[98]

It is imperative here to mention one of his most significant conceptions, that of 'philosophia perennis' or 'traditional school'. This notion implies 'universal knowledge', which is provided and achieved through traditions and 'methods, rites, symbols, images, and other means sanctified by the message from Heaven or the Divine that gives birth to each tradition'.[99] So, like the current Muslim intellectuals in Turkey, Nasr put his emphasis on the divine origin as the 'Ultimate Truth'. According to his notion of philosophia perennis, metaphysics are considered as

> divine science and not purely mental construct which would change with every alteration in the cultural fashions of the day or with new discoveries of a science of the material world. This traditional metaphysics, which in reality should be used in the singular as metaphysics, is a knowledge which sanctifies and illuminates; it is gnosis if this term is shorn of its sectarian connotations going back to early Christian centuries. It is a knowledge which lies at the heart of religion, which illuminates the meaning of religious rites, doctrines and symbols and which also provides the key to the understanding of both the necessity of the plurality of religions and the way to penetrate into other religious universes without either reducing their religious significance or diminishing our own commitment to the religious universe to which we who wish to study other religions belong.[100]

In this approach of philosophia perennis, Seyyed Hossein distinguishes 'reason' (ratio) from 'the Intellect' (intellectus). He defines the Intellect as

> the instrument through which knowledge is obtained, which is at once the source of revelation and exists microcosmically within man. The 'aql is at once both intellectus or nous and ratio or reason. It is both the sun that shines

> within man and the reflection of this sun on the plane of the mind which we call reason.[101]

So, reason cannot attain the knowledge of the essence by itself.[102]

In relation to this, let me elucidate his notion of 'scientia sacra' in order to analyse his thoughts on modern science, which are analogous to those of the contemporary Muslim intellectuals in Turkey. *Scientia sacra* is defined by Nasr as 'sacred knowledge, which lies at the heart of every revelation and is the centre of that circle which encompasses and defines tradition'.[103] In fact, although *scientia sacra* is the Latin version of the term 'sacred science', he makes a distinction between their meanings. Whereas the first reflects his traditional understanding of the ultimate science of the Supreme Being, the latter implies holy science, which is embedded in and emanates from it.[104]

In relation to these explanations, like the Muslim scholars in contemporary Turkey, he asserts that reason is dissociated from its divine source and revelation with the advent of modernity.[105] He condemns Cartesian dualism and positivism too, as a result of which knowledge became 'desacralized'.[106] For this reason, modern science, which is divorced from the Supreme knowledge or 'Ultimate Reality', is identified by Nasr as an 'anomaly'. He explains this degenerative process in the following way:

> What characterizes the whole dialectical thought process in its nineteenth century development, and in contrast to many traditional philosophies of change, is not its concern with becoming or process but the reduction of reality to the temporal process, of being to becoming, of the immutable categories of logic, not to mention metaphysics, to everchanging thought processes. This loss of the sense of permanence in schools of philosophy standing in the mainstream of modern Western thought marks, along with the crass positivism of an Auguste Comte, a more advanced phase of not only desacralization of knowledge

> but also of the loss of the sense of the sacred which characterizes modern, but not necessarily contemporary, man as such.
>
> ... To this mentality the very concept of *scientia sacra* appeared as a contradiction in terms and, in fact, it still appears as either contradictory and meaningless not only to those who either consciously or unconsciously follow the rationalism inherent in Cartesian epistemology but also to those who have rebelled against this rationalism from below with the kinds of irrationalism which characterize so much of modern thought.[107]

As a consequence, he denounces modernism and Western civilization and describes them as a total failure.[108]

His thoughts on modern technology resemble to the rhetorics of Turkish Muslim intellectuals. Similar to them, he emphasizes the destructive and exploitative nature of modern technology, which, according to Nasr, prepares the demise of humanity. To illustrate his views on technology let me quote the following statements of Seyyed Hossein Nasr:

> Modern technology, which is the direct application of modern science, is of quite another order. It has sought until quite recently to manipulate nature with the maximum use of energy and total indifference to the qualitative aspects of nature and what is done consequently to the environment, both human and natural. That is why it has caused the profound crisis which has now brought its own future into serious question. Modern technology has reached such a state in its destruction of the environment that for the first time in human history, man, or more precisely modern man, now threatens the harmony of the whole natural order. There are in fact numerous critics of modern technology in the West who doubt very much that human civilization can survive unless a complete end is put

> to that whole enterprise called the modern world including its science and technology.[109]

By the same token, he equates the crisis of the environment and ecology with the atrophy and contamination of the human spirit through the modernization process, as a result of which human beings dissociated themselves from the Divine Being and began to imitate its role.[110] He also believes strongly that sacred science and traditional culture can replace modern science by enlarging its horizons and offering a new philosophy of life and knowledge.[111] To realize this, he argues that the Muslim intelligentsia has to depend on its own culture.[112] According to Nasr, this is the only way for the salvation and survival of the Islamic societies. 'The survival of oriental cultures', he claims,

> does not depend so much upon their immediate success in the material domain, no matter how important this success may appear at the moment, as upon the degree to which they are able to preserve this vision of Unity binding the various levels of knowledge and of reality, of the spiritual and material into an inseparable whole. This is a vision which is contained in sacred knowledge and which modern man in search of a way to save himself from the devastating effects of his own activity is also seeking, but having lost the direction of the sky he is for the most part searching for the Sun in the bottom of a well. Nothing could be more tragic for the world as a whole than if, at the moment when Western man who had long forgotten this sense of Unity is searching to rediscover it in order to save himself, Oriental cultures should forget and discard this precious vision of Unity and knowledge of the sacred sciences which lie at the heart of their cultures.[113]

So like present-day Turkish Muslims intellectuals, Nasr urges

Muslims not to imitate the West but to learn from their own faults and failures.[114]

Moreover, parallel to the Turkish Muslim intellectuals' contentions on religion, Seyyed Hossein Nasr argues that religion is more than faith. In other words, it has as its prototype the 'Divine Intellect' and comes from 'Divine Origin', which is meta-historical, metaphysical, and not limited by time and space.[115] Moreover, other than metaphysics, which is related to the essence of the Divine Being, religion also correlated to 'cosmological sciences, which see all that exists in the cosmos as manifestations of that Source'.[116]

In addition, he also gives considerable importance to Sufism.[117] He argues that Sufism is the highest point of the esoteric aspect or 'inner dimension' of Islam.[118] The first and the foremost essential principle, Unity, on which Islam is constructed, is very effectively presented by Sufism.[119] In his view, this consolidating power of Sufism enables the total integration of the body and soul, which are separated by modernity.[120] He contends that in this sense Sufism is an efficient cure for the alienated and disintegrated modern man.[121] Finally, similar to the Turkish Muslim intellectuals, he thinks that modernism is already dead.[122]

Let me conclude the analysis of Seyyed Hossein Nasr's ideology with his remarks on his conception of the Islamic renaissance:

> A true Islamic renaissance is not just the birth or rebirth of anything that happens to be fashionable at a particular moment of human history but reapplication of the principles of a truly Islamic nature. The primary condition for a genuine Islamic renaissance becomes clear. This condition in our day resides in independence from the influence of the West and from all that characterizes the modern West. A Muslim far away from the influences of modernism can experience spiritual renewal while remaining oblivious to

what is going on in the modern world. But a Muslim intellectual or religious leader who wishes to renew the intellectual and religious life of the Islamic world, now under such heavy pressure from the West and from modernism in general, cannot hope to bring about an Islamic renaissance on either the intellectual or the social level except through a profound criticism of modernism and of the modern world itself.

The Muslim intelligentsia must face all the challenges with confidence in themselves. They must cease to live in a state of a psychological and cultural sense of inferiority.[123]

Nasr Hamid Abu Zaid

Another important Muslim intellectual in the contemporary Islamic world is Nasr Hamid Abu Zaid. He was born on 10 July 1943, in Quhafa, Egypt. He obtained his Ph.D. in Arabic and Islamic studies in 1981 from Cairo University and became a professor in the same department. He also worked as a visiting professor in the Department of Arabic at Osaka University, Japan during the years 1985–89. He received the Republican Order of Merit from the President of Tunisia in May 1993 for his services to Arab culture.[124] After his expulsion from Cairo University, he and his wife fled to the Netherlands and since 1995 he has been a professor of Arabic and Islamic Studies at Leiden University. He concentrates his research on Qur'anic exegesis and on the critique Islamic discourse.

Nasr Hamid Abu Zaid is one of the most striking Muslim intellectuals, and has been fighting for intellectual freedom and critical thinking. He is accused of being *kafir* (apostate) and he was expelled from the Cairo University, where he was teaching.[125] Moreover, he was forced to divorce his wife, since a Muslim woman can not be married to a heretic. The reason for his expulsion is due to his statement that 'history and culture must be taken into account when interpreting the Qur'an.'[126] In other words, he is in favour of 'a metaphoric interpretation of the

Qur'an rather than an inflexible, literal understanding of that sacred text'.[127]

Nasr Hamid Abu Zaid is a modern Muslim intellectual, who is committed to critical and rational thinking and freedom of thought. He is neither a traditionalist nor a Marxist or an unbeliever/heretic. He criticizes the orthodox, traditional religious discourse. His primary interest is concentrated on the interpretation of the Qur'anic texts by applying the methods of the science of hermeneutics.[128] He defines himself as follows:

> Never do I want to give the impression that I am against Islam. Far from it. Nor do I want to give the impression that I am a new Salman Rushdie. I am not. One of my worst fears is that Westerners will consider me only as a critic of Islam. That is not the whole picture at all. I am a teacher, a scholar, an intellectual, and a researcher. I see my role as a producer of concepts. I treat the Qur'an as a text given by God to the Prophet Muhammad. That text came to us in a human language, Arabic. As a result of my work, I have been critical of Islamic religious discourse. I show how social, political, and economic institutions use religious discourse to get hold of power. Nonetheless, I identify myself as a Muslim. I was born a Muslim, I was raised a Muslim, and I live as a Muslim. God willing, I will die a Muslim.[129]

In comparison to the Muslim intellectuals in present Turkey, the diverse political and socio-economic conditions of the Arab world behind the formation of his critical discourse and his use of modern scientific methods in Islamic studies need to be mentioned. He explains the historical background of the evolution of his thought as follows:

> I became preoccupied with the idea that interpretation of Quranic texts was, within Arab culture, the base upon

> which any idea had to be founded. At that time, during the 1970s, Sadat's regime released Muslim Brothers from prison to offset the left in the universities and outside. The Ikhwan (Brotherhood) began to organize and the Jama'at Islamiyya (Islamic Group) began to be active.
>
> Sadat's speeches were fertile ground for me, because they showed how the matter of interpretation isn't just connected to classical Arab culture. I was raised in the 1960s. The common understanding was about the Islam of social justice, the Islam of the underclass. With the change in the regime's political tendencies, a different kind of Islam came into being. I began to wonder whether or not religious texts were open enough to accept these different types of interpretation. I became influenced by the science of hermeneutics, and the role of the interpreter, the commentator, in reading texts and making them understood.[130]

So, the socio-political and historical conditions in which his ideas developed are different from the conditions of Turkish Muslim intellectuals. Beside colonial experience, the absence of freedom of expression and 'free market of ideas' contributed to the evolution of his critical religious discourse.[131] In other words, the repressive and authoritarian nature of the state, where ideas can not be freely expressed and where the media are kept under strict government control, motivated him to fight for the freedom of expression.

In contrast to the contemporary Turkish Muslim intellectuals, Nasr Hamid Abu Zaid approaches Islam not purely as a faith or religion but also as a subject of scientific investigation. In other words, by employing hermeneutical principles in interpreting the Qur'an, he benefits from the methods of modern science, such as textual, historical analysis, linguistics, and semiotics. That is to say, he applies 'the rules governing the study of a text to the

Qur'an itself'.[132] He says: 'when I study the Qur'an and other religious texts, I attempt to create an objective and scientific framework to analyse and interpret those texts.'[133]

In contrast to the contemporary Turkish Muslim intellectuals, he contends that 'it is not possible to speak about the Qur'an as an absolute that transcends space, time, and place.'[134] He believes that social as well political events manipulate Qur'anic interpretation.[135] According to him, the understanding of the text is contingent on 'individual and cultural experience':[136]

> We must keep in mind that the Qur'an comes to us via a historical and ever-changing human community. Because interpretation of a text often intertwines with the actual text, it's important to understand how the original Muslim community interpreted the Qur'an. However, we ought not to accept their conclusions as final or absolute. Neither should we think of the interpretations that succeeding generations arrived at as being etched in stone. After the text is decoded in the light of history, culture, and language, it must then be recoded into the current cultural and linguistic context. The Qur'an's message has to be continuously discovered and rediscovered.
>
> ... Every text has its context. Social and political forces influenced the chronology of the Qur'an as well as its content. The text, when it was revealed to Muhammed, responded to current problems experienced within the community and answered specific questions regarding those problems.
>
> ... The Qur'an is a mode of communication between God and humanity. When we take the historical aspect of that communication as divine, we lock God's Word in time and space. We limit the meaning of the Qur'an to a specific time in history. [137]

Moreover, as compared to current Islamist intellectuals in

Turkey, he has a flexible approach with regard to Islamic rituals. He states that he 'never considered ritual to be the essential part of Islam. The emphasis was on orthopraxis (proper behaviour), not orthodoxy (proper belief or doctrine).'[138]

In sharp contrast to the present-day Turkish Muslim intellectuals, Nasr Hamid Abu Zaid believes that Shari'a law is not divine:

> Shari'a law is human law. There is nothing divine about it. When we look at certain legal stipulations spoken about in the Qur'an, such as the penalties for fornication, robbery, murder, or causing social disorder, we need to ask certain questions. Are the stipulated penalties initiated by Islam? Can we consider them to be Islamic? Definitely not. The penalties meted out for such offenses were used in pre-Islamic times – some of them come from Roman law and some from Jewish tradition. Others go further back. In modern times – times in which all kinds of human rights legislation is initiated – many people balk at the thought of amputating parts of the human body or taking life of an individual as divinely inspired and, therefore, obligatory as punishment for crime.
>
> Other aspects of Shari'a, such as those dealing with religious minorities, women's rights, and other human rights (such as those of homosexuals) need to be reconsidered as well. The job of the jurists has always been to look for principles of law within Shari'a and then apply those principles in different social contexts. The Qur'an is not a law book. There are legal principles found within the Qur'an. These principles leave a wide space for human interpretation and reinterpretation. To claim that the body of Shari'a literature is binding for all Muslim communities, regardless of time and place, is to ascribe divinity to human thought as it has developed throughout history.[139]

So, he makes a distinction between divine and human aspects of the Qur'an. The divine Word of God transcends the historicity of the Qur'an.[140] He argues that not everything that exists in the Qur'an is initiated by the Qur'an. According to him,

> if anything spoken about in the Qur'an has a precedent in pre-Islamic tradition – whether Jewish, Roman, or anything else, we need to understand that its being mentioned in the Qur'an does not automatically make it Qur'anic and therefore binding on Muslims. When we speak of something Qur'anic, we are talking about that which was initiated by the Qur'an and therefore is binding on Muslims.[141]

With regard to the issue of secularism, Abu Zaid's views also differ from that of the Turkish Muslim intelligentsia. He strongly believes in the effectiveness of the separation of the religion and the state, which will according to him secure religion from being manipulated by politics.[142] In other words, secularism does not give religion an inactive, secondary position but rather secures its integrity.[143] In his words 'a secular state – one that gives no official sanction to any particular religion – gives religion the space it needs to meet the needs of the people. Otherwise, religion easily becomes a weapon in the hands of those in power.'[144]

It should be noted here that both Nasr Hamid Abu Zaid and the contemporary Muslim intellectuals in Turkey are very sensitive to the politicization of Islam. They severely oppose the use of Islam for ideological ends. Furthermore, contrary to the present-day Turkish Muslim intellectuals, he exalts the Western concepts of rational thinking, democracy, and secularism (as already mentioned above) and renounces the idea that Islam and modernity clash. He points out that 'it is not Islam that prevents Muslims from accepting democracy but rather a religious and political dogmatic trend of thought, ever prevalent, which claims that Islam and modernity contradict one another.'[145] He argues that since democracy is based on the rational choice of the people, the absence of rational thought hinders the establishment of democracy in the Islamic world.[146] He believes that the age of ignorance can only be overcome with the establishment of rational thought.[147]

In opposition to the Turkish Muslim intellectuals' call for return to the Golden Age of Islam, Abu Zaid thinks that

> Our current problems stem, so we're told, from our having strayed so far from Islam. The solution? Return to Islam. Within the phrase 'Return to Islam' there is the sense that Islam as practiced by the earliest community enjoyed a purity which subsequent generations lost. As a result of this – dare I call it thinking? – the saying 'Islam is the solution' has taken hold in Muslim society. (Not any different from bumper stickers I've seen in the States that say, 'Jesus is the answer.') Just exactly what is the question? Those who glibly spout such a simplistic formula as a cure-all for our present-day problems offer no plan, nor do they speak about what kind of solution they envision Islam would bring to the social, political, and economic problems that plague us. They fill the gap between the past and the present by simply stating that since Islam solved the problems of the seventh century, it can just as easily solve our problems today.[148]

In a nutshell, he rejects the idea that there exist two kinds of Islam as most of the Muslim revivalists argue: one is 'pure Islam, which existed during the lives of the Prophet and the four guided caliph'; the other is 'contaminated or corrupted Islam, affected by foreign influences'.[149] According to Abu Zaid, these twofold views of Islam derive from the assumption that Islam is 'static'. In contrast, Abu Zaid argues that Islam is a 'historical' and 'dynamic' fact that progresses through time.[150]

His critical and unorthodox approach on Islamic discourse is considered as marginal, radical – if not revolutionary – for the fundamentalists in the Islamic world. Therefore he is considered as heretic in his country. He is still in exile in the Netherlands.

Abdolkarim Soroush

Abdolkarim Soroush is one of the most profound and original critical Islamic thinkers and philosophers in the Muslim World. He is even called as 'the Luther of Islam'.[151] He was born in 1945 in Tehran, Iran. Upon finishing his education in pharmacology at Tehran University, he went to London to study analytical chemistry at London University.[152] Later he decided to study history and philosophy of science at Chelsea College. He noted that his interest in history and philosophy of science was a turning point in his intellectual life.[153] He was introduced to the theories of Karl Popper, Paul Feyerabend, and Imre Lakatos, and began to reconsider and re-evaluate his former knowledge of 'metaphysics and Aristotelian philosophy'.[154] At the same time, he was following the works of Ali Shari'ati, who also contributed to his intellectual development.[155]

Soroush left London for Iran just after the Iranian Revolution 1979. He became the chair of the department of Islamic culture at Tehran's Teacher's College, which was followed by his appointment to the Advisory Council on the Cultural Revolution for reviewing Iran's academic syllabus and reopening the universities, which were closed after the Revolution, to Islamize the curriculum.[156] He began to teach philosophy of science and philosophy of history at Tehran University and still works as a researcher at the Institute for Cultural Research and Studies.[157]

The most important aspect of Soroush's thought is the theory of 'the contraction and expansion of religious knowledge and religious interpretation'.[158] He distinguishes religion from religious knowledge. He describes this distinction as follows:

> Religion is sacred and heavenly, but the understanding of religion is human and earthly. That which remains constant is religion (*din*); that which undergoes change is religious

> knowledge and insight (*ma'refat-e dini*). Religion has not faltered in articulating its objectives and its explanations of good and evil; the defect is in human beings' understanding of religion's intents. Religion is in no need of reconstruction and completion. Religious knowledge and insight that is human and incomplete, however, is in constant need of reconstruction. Religion is free from cultures and unblemished by the artifacts of human minds, but religious knowledge is, without a shadow of a doubt, subject to such influences.[159]

So allegedly, our understanding of religion 'changes, evolves, contracts, expands, waxes, and wanes' over time as the human comprehension and knowledge is enhanced.[160] Therefore, he asserts that 'no religious interpretation is ever final.'[161]

According to Soroush, the execution of human rights is essential for the survival of both the democratic and religious natures of a regime.[162] Furthermore, he states that 'the idea of human rights lies outside religion because it prefigures belief; that is to say, in order to follow a particular religion, the freedom to exercise that option must be open to you. And the only form of government that ensures human rights is democracy.'[163] Moreover, unlike the current Muslim thinkers in Turkey, Soroush states that democracy[164] and Islam are not mutually exclusive things; in other words, they are compatible and 'their association is inevitable. In Muslim society, one without the other is not perfect.'[165] To elaborate, one should be free to choose or quit a faith, and democracy secures this freedom.[166] In addition, Shar'ia has a flexible character, and 'in an Islamic democracy, you can actualize all its potential flexibilities'.[167]

More precisely, his conception of a religious democratic government entails the following principles:

- The combination of religion and democracy is an example of the concordance of religion and reason.

- The combination of religion and democracy is a metareligious artifice that has at least some extrareligious epistemological dimensions. Therefore, the exclusive reliance on the religious laws and myopic focus on intra-religious adjucations (*ijtihad-e fiqhi*) in order to confirm or reject democratic religiosity is ill-considered and unsound.
- It is the religious understanding that will have to adjust itself to democracy, not the other way around; justice, as a value, can not be religious. It is religion that has to be just. Similarly, methods of limiting power are not derived from religion, although religion benefits from them.[168]

In essence, he believes that all these 'extrareligious values (justice, freedom, democracy, human rights, etc.) are authentic and autonomously significant and they even affect the understanding of religion itself.'[169]

On the other hand, Soroush criticizes the people, who reject democracy since it has originated in the West.[170] In his opinion, this false conviction arises from their identification of 'religious democracy with religious jurisprudence.' However according to Soroush, 'religious law (shari'ah) is not synonymous with the entirety of religion; nor is the debate over the democratic religious government a purely jurisprudential argument. Moreover, jurisprudential statements are different from epistemological ones, and no methodic mind should conflate the two realms.'[171]

As against to the beliefs of the Turkish Muslim scholars, in Soroush's view, 'religious ideology should not be used to rule a modern state, for it tends toward totalitarianism and the use of religious ideology in governance blocks the growth of religious knowledge.'[172] He strongly expresses the need for the creation of a democratic regime in Iran.[173]

As regards the issue of modern science, Abdolkarim Soroush's views also differ from those of the contemporary Islamist intellectuals in Turkey. Unlike them, he believes in the compatibility of 'religious' and 'scientific knowledge'.[174] He points out that

It is modern knowledge that has splashed novel colors over the worn-out mat of our existence. The new color will not fade. If there is any controversy here, it is not about science but about discovering the proper relationship between knowledge and justice and forging a desirable connection between them.

Rejection of science betrays new narrow-mindedness reminiscent of the dark ages. This attack on science has become prevalent in our society in various disguises: positivism, humanism, materialism, Occidentalism, existentialism, phenomenology, or hermeneutics. All of these have but one root cause: uncertainty about the veracity of the new science and neglect of the truth. No truth-seeking human being can afford to be oblivious, neutral, and cold toward this steadfast new guest of humanity. Those who spread nonsense about development do so because they have no clear sense of science and cannot separate the realm of epistemology from the other aspects of Western civilization. Thus, they have a contradictory and duplicitous encounter with development. On the one hand, they fail to reconcile themselves with it because of their anti-Western hollow pretensions. On the other hand, they fail to run away from it because of their historicistic view about the historic destiny of the West.

... Science is different from customs, morality, art, and the habits of Westerners and 'infidels'. Customs and mores are noncognitive phenomena (although some argue that they inform epistemology). Science, however, is a cognitive phenomenon. Customs are themselves realities that may become subject to scientific inquiry. Science, on the other hand, is a handiwork of reason and a creature of criticism. It is the mirror of reality and a guide to action. It is exactly this reflective, criticizable, and rational nature of science that sets it apart from other Western phenomena. Yes, science is not utterly impartial, but what could be more

> impartial than science? If a path has to be beaten to take us forward, it has to originate in science.
>
> We should make room for science because the values that encourage science are the same values that encourage development. ... Science, while conjectural, is, in practice, very effective.
>
> ... Human beings can remain spiritual and religious while enjoying the benefits of rational administration of their affairs. Those who consider modern science blasphemous or try to break its majesty with a thousand ifs and buts have no appreciation of the truths that have been uncovered by science. They are naïve.[175]

On the other hand, Soroush does not question the compatibility of secularism with Islam. He defines it as 'scientification and rationalization of social and political thought and deliberation'.[176] In elaboration, with the arrival of modernity, scientific and rational knowledge replaced religion as the source of legitimacy; so secularization represents this process.[177] Moreover, the separation of religion and state does not imply the rejection or opposition to religion.[178] So, in contrast to current Turkish Muslim intellectuals, Soroush does not see secularism contradictory to Islam. He also suggests that Islamic societies should secularize their states, since these have 'non-religious' duties.[179] In effect, 'religious governments', he argues,

> are not answerable to the people. In such a society, the best form of government would be a secular democratic regime. However, it is not valid to argue that nowhere and under no conditions may one perceive the desirability of a religious democracy, even in a religious society. The truth of the matter is that a religious government can be an appropriate reflection of a religious society. Indeed, in such a society any purely secular government would be undemocratic. Whether religious regimes are democratic or undemocratic,

> though, depends on two conditions: (1) the extent to which governments partake of collective wisdom, and (2) the extent to which governments respect human rights. A combination of democracy and religion would entail the convergence of reason ('aql) and revelation (shar').

In contradiction to the current Turkish Muslim intellectuals' deterministic approaches to history, Soroush does not believe in the existence of a 'predetermined plan' in history.[180] He contends that the occurrence of history is not 'artificial' but 'natural:'

> There is an essential difference between our arguments and those of the fatalistic and deterministic school. Our views are in no way based on the assumption that history unfolds according to a predestined plan. History is made out of human choice, which emanates from human nature. Only in this sense is history 'natural': it reveals the nature of humanity. There is no trace of Hegel's 'cunning of reason' in our understanding of history. One hundred per cent of what transpires in history is caused by human volition, not a predetermined plan. The free action of humanity is the very core and domain of history. History is human, humanity is not 'historical' in the Hegelian sense of the term.[18]

He criticizes the Islamist thinkers who put forward the idea of West toxication (Gharbzadegi). This concept is argued by an important Iranian philosopher Jalal Al-e Ahmad, who criticized the West struckness of the Pahlavi regime in Iran during the 1960s. He condemned the monarchy for its excessive imitation of the West. In contrast to Jalal Al-e Ahmad, Soroush warns against the risk of 'Arab toxication'. In essence, what he denounces is the irrational rejection of foreign elements just because they are not created within one's own culture.[182] In response to this thinking, he recommends that:

> The reformers who intend to serve this country must not take as their point of departure the assumption that what has not originated among us is necessarily alien to us. Second, they must not seek to establish the hegemony of one culture at the expense of others. Third, the criterion for belonging to a culture has nothing to do with its native origins. Fourth, each culture contains elements for which it must repent and aspects it should uphold… We must stand in the agora of cultural exchange, fit, able, and willing to assume the task of defending the truth. We must not deem our ethnic and Islamic culture as terminus, but as a point of departure.[183]

One should not derive the conclusion from these facts that Soroush welcomes Western culture and concepts uncritically or in their totality. On the contrary, he suggests taking Western concepts 'selectively' and 'consciously' and warns against blind copying Western culture as a whole.[184] He elucidates his position more clearly as follows: 'We do not mean to neglect the significance of preserving authenticity and rejecting cultural imitation, intimidation, and alienation. We distinguish between servile and dignified varieties of exchange. Our aim is to warn against two pitfalls: blind emulation and blind rejection.'[185]

In a nutshell, in contrast to the Turkish Islamist intelligentsia, Soroush tries to accommodate Islam with the necessities of modern age. His discourse has a critical, modern, and secular tone. However, we should accept that the ideology and thoughts of Soroush developed not in a vacuum but under certain conditions specific to Iran and the Arab world. In other words, his experience of the turmoil of the Islamic Revolution and the authoritarian rule and inflexible, monolithic, and anti-modern attitudes of the clergy in Iran; the prevalent traditional understanding of Islam, the relative absence of freedom of expression and democracy and related factors have been influential in the formation of his ideas and thinking system.

Concluding Remarks (a)

It has been my contention that although both the contemporary Turkish Muslim scholars and non-Turkish Muslim intellectuals in other parts of the Islamic world write and think as Muslim believers from an Islamic perspective and approach the West and modernity critically, there are remarkable ideological, methodological, stylistic, and epistemological differences in general. Unlike the Turkish Muslim intellectuals, their exposure to the authoritarian, despotic, and undemocratic regimes; their experience of foreign invasion and imperialism; the existence of strict political control, and restrictions on ideological, intellectual, and cultural expression, and the conditions of the post-colonial setting have been influential in the formation of their thoughts and agendas. As a consequence, they became actively involved in the politics of their countries. However the Turkish Muslim intelligentsia is concerned predominantly with cultural and social issues instead of political and practical ones. They work in a more open, pluralist, and democratic environment, and they do not have to struggle with superstitious, ignorant fundamentalists or with dogmatic and a narrow-minded, monolithic clergy class. Nor do they have to save the country from foreign occupation or colonial domination.

Whereas they are intensively concerned with philosophical and epistemological issues and debates on the Qur'anic exegesis and Islamic tradition overall, the current Muslim intelligentsia in Turkey are more involved in the reclamation of Islamic values in the social, political, and cultural life and criticism of the West and modernity. Unlike the non-Turkish Muslim intellectuals analysed in this section, the Turkish Muslim intellectuals are unrealistic and utopian. In other words, they are disconnected from the realities of this world.

Moreover, the Turkish Islamists intellectuals are not producers of original ideologies or novel thinkers like Muhammed Arkoun, Seyyed Hossein Nasr, Nasr Hamid Abu Zaid, or Abdolkarim Soroush. They can be considered more as independent public intellectuals, who raise the consciousness, awareness, and knowledge of the masses through their intellectual work than as being deep, original philosophers.

Furthermore, I contend that the Muslim intellectuals in other Islamic countries that are examined in this section are intellectually, scholastically and philosophically more profound and more sophisticated than their Turkish contemporaries. That is to say, their refined and complicated style, their utilization of the intricate techniques of modern social sciences such as hermeneutics, epistemology, linguistics, semiotics, history, philosophy, sociology, anthropology, and the like make them distinctive compared to the Muslim intellectuals of present-day Turkey. Moreover their extensive stay in Western countries for study and work equipped them with deeper, firsthand knowledge and observation of the West, which made them international intellectuals known and influential not only in their countries but also in other parts of the world.

In a nutshell, all of the Muslim intellectuals I analysed in this section are struggling to reconfigure, re-evaluate, reconceptualize, and deconstruct orthodox Islamic thought. They brought a new and fresh understanding to the understanding of Islamic concepts and interpretation of the Qur'an.

Bediuzzaman Said Nursi (1876–1960)

Said Nursi is a profound Muslim thinker and revivalist, whose teachings and ideology are still being followed today. He was born in eastern Turkey. He was trained in a medrese and belongs to the class of ulama (doctors of religion).[186] He has witnessed the overthrow of the Ottoman Empire, which is equated with the defeat of Islam since the Ottomans were the owners of the Caliphate, foreign occupation, the turmoil of long lasting wars, the increase of nationalism, and materialist, rationalist, positivist thought, which contributed to the formation of his thoughts and position as a Muslim revivalist.[187] He tried to rejuvenate Islam and its values in an age of crisis against the rising values of positivism and materialism and secularism. Essentially he fought against materialism and irreligiousness.[188] That is to say, he opposed first the penetration of these values into the Ottoman society and then the secular, anti-clerical attitude of the Kemalist state, which took Western civilization as a model. Parallel to the present-day Turkish Muslim intellectuals' arguments, he considers the return to Islam as the only cure for the social and political problems of his age, which arise mostly from industrialization and materialist philosophy.

His commentaries of the Qur'an are collected in his famous work *Risale-i Nur* (Epistle of Light). In the *Risale-i Nur*, he 'developed the teachings of the Qur'an on the truths of belief that incorporates the traditional Islamic sciences and modern scientific knowledge and that, while instilling those truths, effectively refutes the bases of materialist philosophy'.[189] To elaborate, it was not only religious study that exalts the Islamic faith but also

> a commentary on the status of the Islamic sciences in the twentieth century, and an inquiry into why the modern Muslim world has fallen into a religious abyss, and why the 'other', that is to say, Europe, superseded the Muslim world in matters of science and civilization. It offers a creative, although subtle, method for reconstructing Islamic thought and practice in an era that is no longer dominated by Islamic doctrinal or political teaching. The Risale is an ideological text that wrestles with the most urgent questions facing the modern Muslim mind, especially in Turkish case.[190]

As Şükran Vahide proposes, it brings both 'modern' and 'religious sciences' together and thus 'Qur'anic' and 'modern' simultaneously.[191]

In his early life, he concentrated his efforts on maintaining the unity of the Ottoman Empire and supported the Young Turks in their struggle for reform and the establishment of constitutional government.[192] In fact, he was influenced by the liberal ideas of the nineteenth century, which were introduced by the Young Ottomans.[193] He took also an active role in the Independence War. Later he devoted his efforts intensively to intellectual work and religious meditation. However, after 1950, when the Democratic Party came to power after the long period of One-Party rule by the Republican People's Party (RPP), he supported and gave advice to the Democrats in their pro-Islamic policies.[194]

Nursi utilized scientific data and rational methods to verify and prove the Qur'an's statements on the universe and cosmos.[195] Unlike the current Muslim intellectuals, he asserted that the findings of modern science are not irreconcilable with religion. In contradiction to them, Nursi states that 'he had in part accepted the principles of … European philosophy … [and] … submitted unshakably to some of [its] principles in the form of the physical sciences.'[196] In fact, he tried to prove in his *Risale-i Nur* that all the scientific achievements of Western civilization confirm and support the truths of the Islamic religion. In other words, he benefited from the findings of modern science in verifying the existence and unity of God and challenge materialistic ideology.[197] According to Nursi, 'since the Qur'an was revealed for all men in all ages, these questions … are not defects but evidence for the Qur'an's elevated miraculousness.'[198] Essentially, what he was repudiating is the materialist and profane interpretation of scientific progress.

The following statements of Said Nursi explain the importance he gave to science and technology: 'no doubt, mankind will, in the future, turn to science and technology. It shall take its strength from science. Sovereignty and force will pass into the hands of science.'[199]

In contrast to current Muslim revivalists, he puts great emphasis on 'reason and on the rationality of Islam'.[200] In his words: 'the Qur'an indicates … that Islam is founded on reason, wisdom (*hikmet*), and logic. … The source of Islam is knowledge (*'ilm*), its basis is reason. … The Islamic Shari'a is founded on rational proofs (*burhan*).'[201]

He also encouraged the study of science.[202] In fact, he was convinced that Europe owes its superiority to the advancements in science and technology.[203] Therefore in his project of an Islamic university (*Medresetu'z Zehra*), he aimed to 'completely reconcile European civilization and the truths of Islam', which would combine 'the modern physical sciences' and 'the sciences of religion'.[204]

Moreover his support for secularism put him into a different category from current Muslim intellectuals. He contends that secularism guarantees the right of religious people to practice their faith as it ensures the rights of others, who do not believe.[205] In other words, in his view, the separation of religious things from worldly affairs 'ensures freedom of conscience, and of expression, and other liberties'.[206]

However, his thoughts on Western civilization have the same tone as the new genre of the Muslim intellectuals in his denunciation and criticism of it. In Nursi's view,

> Western civilization as it stands today has contravened the divine fundamental laws, its evils have proved greater than its benefits. The real goals of civilization, which are general well-being and happiness in this world, have been subverted. Instead of economy and abstemiousness (*kanaat*) we have waste and debauchery; instead of work and service, we have laziness and sloth. Thus humanity has simultaneously become very poor and very lazy. The fundamental law of the Qur'an, which originated in the firmament (semavi), is that the happiness in the life of humanity is in economy and in concentration on work and it is around this principle which is already in the Risale-i Nur let me add one or two points.
>
> First, in the state of nomadism, people only needed three of four things. And those who could not obtain these three or four products were two out of ten. The present oppresssive Western civilization, in consequence of its

> consumption and waste and the stimulation of its appetites has brought non-essentials to become essentials and because of mores and habituation, this so called civilized man instead of four has twenty needs. And yet he can only obtain two of these twenty. He still needs eighteen. Therefore, contemporary civilization impoverishes man very much.
>
> Second: As the Risale-i Nur points out, while the radio is a great boon (nimet), which has partly been used for social purposes (and, therefore, should elicit our gratefulness), four fifths of it is being devoted to fancy, to superficial matters.[207]

By the same token, he also believes that Western civilization, which is detached from divinity, has reached deadlock.[208]

Like the current Muslim intellectuals, Nursi approaches philosophy with disdain and suspicion due to its non-divine origin and profanity.[209] In his view, the materialist, positivist, and rationalist philosophy, which 'is based on futility', is a threat to Islam and humanity.[210]

Şerif Mardin points out that 'Said Nursi's contribution was a reaffirmation of the norms set by the Qur'an in such a way as to re-introduce the traditional Muslim idiom of conduct and of personal relations into an emerging society and industry and mass communication.'[211] So, like the Islamist intelligentsia in contemporary Turkey, he benefited from the technological advances of Western civilization. With further proliferation of mass media and improvements in communication technology, his teachings reached and influenced wide masses, especially the young generations, who even today continue to follow his path at an increasing pace.

Nevertheless, his followers split into two different groups after the *coup d'état* of 1980: the group called as Yeni Asya (New Asia), who opposed the New Constitution; and the other group, which approved the New Constitution.

Necip Fazıl Kısakürek (1905–83)

Necip Fazıl Kısakürek is another important conservative Turkish Muslim thinker and famous poet. He has been an inspirational figure for subsequent Muslim revivalists in Turkey. He first attended the Naval School and then is graduated from the department of philosophy at Istanbul University. Afterwards, he was sent by the government to Paris for study, where his negative feelings about Western values and lifestyle began to emerge. He described his feelings about Paris in the following way:

> Paris, which with its civilization symbolized the West, exhibited on its front page designs of miraculous refinement which, however, turned out to be etched on a background of plastic, the latter, in fact attracting to one's eye what it disguised, namely, ruin and darkness; a civilization that was condemned to hit its head against one wall after another and play hide and seek from one crisis to another.[212]

After his return to Turkey he took positions in several banks and worked as a literature professor at Robert College and the Istanbul Academy of Fine Arts.[213] The year 1934 marked the beginning of a new life for Kısakürek. That year he met with a Nakşibendi[214] shaykh, Abd al-Hakim Arvasi, as a result of which his bohemian life style and modernist worldview was transformed into an Islamist stance.[215] 'It is under Arvasi's influence' says Şerif Mardin, 'that Necip Fazıl seems to have opted for an increasingly spiritualist orientation, which with time became that of a true believer.'[216]

Like the contemporary Turkish Muslim intellectuals, Necip Fazıl Kısakürek was in opposition to the Jacobin secularism of the Kemalist state.[217] He had to struggle with the Republican People's Party's (RPP) restrictive and oppressive policies on religion. He was the great enemy of İsmet İnönü, the second president of Turkey, and the one party regime. So he was engaged in a political struggle, unlike the current Muslim intellectuals. His journal

Büyük Doğu (The Great East), initially published in 1943, was suspended several times by the government.[218] Moreover, he was incarcerated many times by the state for violating secularism by spreading his religious views and ideas.[219]

Like the current Islamists scholars, the style of his discourse in his artistic and intellectual work as well as his condemnation of modernity, secularism, and the Kemalist state has a modern and western flavour.[220] That is to say, it is not hard to find French and Western influences in his writings, as a result of where studied for several years.[221]

Moreover, like İsmet Özel and Rasim Özdenören, he benefited from the effect of literature and poetry in his search for the Ultimate Truth. Thereby he contributed to the revival of Islam by combining his intellectual and artistic creativity.

His 'Great East Ideal' aimed to establish an Islamic system, which, he thought, 'is the only formula for the salvation of the Turks and the whole humanity'.[222] In his mission, he gave great importance to the young generation. His effort was to assemble and mobilize them around this great ideal.[223] Like current Islamist intellectuals, he dreamed of the emergence of a new Islamist generation, similar to the Islamic society which existed during the time of Prophet Muhammad and his Companions.[224] He envisaged that Turkey will be the leading nation in the realization of an Islamic life, which will be the model for the entire Muslim community.[225]

However, different from the current Muslim intellectuals in Turkey, he identified himself as nationalist. In fact, he put considerable emphasis on Turkish culture and nation as against Western culture and imperialism.[226] The historical circumstances, his experience of two world wars, and the prevalence of high nationalist spirit that existed in the newly established Republic have affected in his nationalistic and cultural sentiment. In his opinion, Turkish culture consists of three fundamentals: 'Ottoman, western, and eastern'.[227] He alluded that these three essences should be absorbed, internalized, assimilated, and reintegrated.[228] He thought that it is ineffective and chimerical to adopt the material aspects of the West without comprehending its spirit and essence.[229]

His thoughts on secularism are analogous to those of the contemporary Muslim intelligentsia. Secularism, in his mind, is incompatible and unthinkable within Islam.[230] In effect, he finds the notion of secularism 'insincere and unreal'. Consequently, the formation of his quest for the creation of Islamic unity and his dream of the Great East is very much related with the historical transitions and transformations of his age, in which the secularization process and the authoritarian policies of the Kemalist state and its removal of Islam from the public space played a significant role. The earlier years of his life, before he adopted an Islamist worldview, constitute an important example for the first type of Westernized elites of the young Republic, which are the products of its modernization process. That is to say, his unconscious and superficial adoption of the Western life style created a spiritual deprivation and crisis that is filled with Islam, when he met with the Nakşibendi shaykh. In a nutshell, as Mardin puts it, 'Islam was used as a building block in reconstructing his self.'[231]

As a conclusion, he has a great deal of influence on the contemporary Muslim intellectuals in Turkey. However, they have little in common with Necip Fazıl. He was a political activist and radical, and even the militant Islamist groups such as IBDA–C (Great East Raiders Front) and Hizbullah have been influenced to a great extend by his thoughts.

Sezai Karakoç (1933–)

Sezai Karakoç is another distinguished Islamist thinker and poet. He was born in the eastern part of Turkey, in Diyarbakir, Ergani in 1933. He graduated from the Finance Department in the Faculty of Political Science of Ankara University. He held bureaucratic positions in several places in Turkey as a revenue inspector and controller.

More importantly, like Necip Fazıl Kısakürek, he is also one of the most distinguished poets. In addition, he began to publish his intellectual magazine *Diriliş* (Revival) in 1974, which has been quite effective in raising the Islamic consciousness of the public, particularly the young generation. Generally speaking, together with Necip Fazıl's *Büyük Doğu*, Sezai Karakoç and his journal *Diriliş* have been quite influential and inspirational for the contemporary Muslim intellectuals in Turkey.[232]

His doctrine *Diriliş* (Revival) resembles very much the rhetorics of the current Islamist intellectuals. It aims to establish the ideal Islam in contemporary society.[233] In other words, he strives for the regeneration and revitalization of Islamic culture and civilization, which is based on the Qur'anic principles. For him, the current age should be questioned and transformed in conformity with Islam. Thus he calls believers to a jihad in the realms of culture and civilization.[234] In fact, this call is a rebellion against the materialism and profanity of the modern age.[235] In a sense, the resurgence of Islam will be at the same time the rejuvenation of his spirit.[236]

In his view, unconditional Western democracy is manipulative and inefficient.[237] Like the current Islamists scholars, he contends that it is irrational and meaningless to compare and assess Islam with the values of Western civilization.[238] So they are incompatible. According to him, the ideal democracy is an Islamic one, which is based first and foremost on morality and virtue.[239] In such an idealized state, the corrupted system and values of the West such as capitalism, communism, materialism, will be excluded.[240]

This project reminds us Ali Bulaç's Islamic state model, which is based on the Medina Contract. Karakoç is aware of the utopian nature of his idealistic plan. In actuality, what he is suggesting is to realize this plan as much as possible, if not completely. So he attempted to create an Islamic revival around his Diriliş ideology.

It is noteworthy that Sezai Karakoç formulated his ideology during the Cold War period, when the world was divided into the democratic/capitalist and the communist blocs. In this context, like other Muslim revivalists in the Islamic world (Seyyed Qutb, Mawdudi, Necip Fazıl Kısakürek) Karakoç visualizes an Islamic system as a third bloc in opposition to the other two blocs.[241] Thus he urges all Islamic countries to unite around this ideal in the same league.[242] Thereby he repeatedly emphasizes that the Turkish people belong to the Middle East.

Consequently, his discourse is ideological and political, unlike that of the present-day Muslim intellectuals in Turkey. He also engaged in politics and founded the Diriliş Party in 1990 in order to 'spread his opinions to the public more effectively and to mobilize the intellectuals around his ideology', which he led until 1997, when it was closed by the Supreme Court.[243]

It is essential to state that he was influenced and inspired by the Islamic resurgence movements, which gained momentum after the bankruptcy of nationalist, socialist, and secularist policies in Middle Eastern countries. He puts emphasis on the sociological and historical aspects of the spiritual revival of the Muslim people, who had been liberated from the oppression and subjugation of their Western colonizers.[244] In his view, this spiritual awakening will make the realization of an ideal Islamic society possible.[245]

Let me conclude with his statements on the Islamic revival:

> Religion has not changed and will not be changed. But human beings have changed and fallen into the abyss of their vanity. They should be get out of this abyss and search for the secret of change. This secret, is reserved in religion, in the Holy Qur'an, and in the acts and life of the Prophet Mohammad. Human beings, who damaged nature, should return to its authentic heritage. This ageless heritage is not the heritage of death, but the inheritance of revival… The asset of the future and of the coming ages is Islam. As humans orient themselves towards this asset, they will find themselves before a great salvation.[246]

Concluding Remarks (b)

Firstly, we have to conclude that the contemporary Muslim intellectuals in Turkey are freer than former Muslim conservatives to express their religious opinions. In other words, although Jacobin secularism is still on the scene in Turkey, religion is no longer a private issue as it was half century ago. Rather, it was carried from the private sphere to the public space with all its expression by the Muslim revivalists. In other words, they are not confronted with the authoritarian policies of the One Party regime, with which Bediuzzaman Said Nursi, Necip Fazıl Kısakürek, and Sezai Karakoç had to struggle once. Moreover, their political activism beside their intellectualism put them in a different category than the contemporary Muslim intelligentsia.

In addition, the Muslim intellectuals of the 1930s and 1950s witnessed the bipolarity of the Cold War period, in which global politics was determined by the rivalry of two opposing camps; namely the Western capitalist and democratic bloc versus the communist bloc. Consequently they regarded Islam as a distinctive third bloc. However, after the collapse of communist regimes worldwide during the late 1980s, the Cold War period ended, and communism ceased to be a threat for Western democracies. Hence, the contemporary Muslim intelligentsia sees Islam as the only alternative and challenge of Western capitalism. In other words, they evaluate the rise of Islam in the context of Samuel Huntington's famous 'clash of civilization' theory, in which international politics will be shaped by the rivalry between the Islam(ic civilization) and the Western civilization (Christianity).[247]

Conclusion

In Turkish intellectual life, a distinctive, unique kind of formation has been taking place since the 1980s, in which a new religious class of intelligentsia with an Islamist worldview began to dominate both the intellectual and public discourse. I contend that their ascendance constitutes a challenge to the Kemalist and secularist intellectual discourse. Their importance and effect is increasing considerably. This study aims to analyse and elucidate this phenomenon with reference to the disestablishment of the legacy of the Kemalist ideology and its modernization process.

It has been my contention that Turkish modernity, which is a typical paradigm of non-Western modernization, has been a blind imitation of the West, which disregarded the indigenous characteristics of Turkish society. That is to say, the Kemalist project of Westernization, which is also considered as modernization, was an unconscious adoption of Western concepts and principles at the expense of local culture and values. The Kemalist elite disestablished the Islamic inheritance, abolished religion from public life, and overlooked the cultural diversity of Turkish society. As a result, there existed both distance and resentment between the secular, urban elite and the provincial population.

Consequently, I am arguing that the alienation of the neglected rural people, their exclusion from the benefits of rapid capitalistic development, and the inability of the secular westernization project to accommodate local religious and cultural structures with the values of the West engendered and facilitated the emergence of Muslim intellectuals and the revival of Islamic discourse. That is to say, these Muslim thinkers, who share the same sentiments and thoughts, become the ideologues and representatives of these disappointed, resented, and unsatisfied people, and Islam served as 'the uniting bond, the common social-moral context, and the common language.'[1]

Moreover, the political vacuum created by the demise of the national developmentalism paradigm, the bankruptcy of socialism and ideologies of the 1960s, and the advance of globalization, are filled by the recently emerged Islamic intellectual discourse.[2] Additionally, relatively tolerant attitudes of the state towards religious activities since the 1950s with demise of the One-Party era; improvements in educational facilities; unbalanced and unequal economic growth and rapid industrialization together with fast urbanization due to increasing social mobility during the 1960s and 1970s; the crisis of the state led, planned import substituting industrialization model; the state's changing laissez faire attitude towards Islam after 1980s through the adoption of a Turkish–Islamic synthesis and consequent 'islamization of secularism'; together with economic and political liberalization under the regime of Turgut Özal; subsequent gradual development towards liberal democracy and a multicultural open democratic society; privatization of education and mass media; improvements in communication technology prepared and facilitated the ground for the appearance of a group of people who were in search of a self-definition for their Islamic identity as opposed to that imposed by the state.

Hence, the critical analysis of the official Kemalist ideology and its reforms helped me to understand the rise of the Islamist intellectuals and their attacks on Kemalism and its plan for modernity. Their criticisms concentrated on its authoritarianism, the enforcement of modernization, and restrictive and oppressive policies on religion.What is striking is their perceptions of Kemalism as an unchanging, static phenomenon independent from recent discussions and developments on the subject matter.

During my analysis of the current Muslim intellectuals in Turkey, I noticed that they generally come from provincial regions of Turkey and that they are increasing their domination in the intellectual life of Turkey with their critical religious discourse against modernity and Westernization thorough their writings, publications, public debates, and other means of expressions. They are widely read, and their thoughts and ideas have a significant impact dominantly on conservative provincial as well as recently migrated middle and lower urban population and especially 'upwardly mobile' high school and university students. It should also be said that their readers and audiences are not limited to religious or Islamist people. On the contrary, their followers are also composed of people who are not actively religious.

The Muslim intellectuals in contemporary Turkey are preoccupied with Islamic models, to solve the problems of political corruption, economic inequality, and social and moral decadence. According to them, Islam is the single remedy for every illness and plague, which is caused by modernity. Therefore, they often refer to the Qur'an and Sunnah as the only authentic sources of knowledge. In relation to this, I have also observed that present-day Muslim intellectuals in Turkey come across as apologists due to their defense and exaltation of Islam and Islamic principles.

In effect, they consider Islam not only as a religion but as a philosophy and life style. That is why they strive for the establishment of an Islamic society. In their mind, the ideal Islamic society existed only in the time of Prophet Mohammad through the first four Caliphs. Therefore, they strive for the creation of this ideal society, in which all the accumulations and traces of non-Islamic elements of traditions will be purged. In this sense, they can be identified as puritans. Moreover, unlike former conservative Muslim thinkers, they do not identify themselves as traditionalist or nationalist. In fact Islamic sources and principles constitute the single reference point for them.

The common argument I have observed in their writings and conversations is their contention that nationalism is the major source of conflict and means of oppression. Thus it is very dangerous. Additionally, in their view, nationalism, like other Enlightenment values, is a part of Western culture.

In essence, not only nationalism but also capitalism, democracy, secularism, modernism, liberalism, socialism, modern science and technology are identified with Western civilization by Muslim intellectuals. Since these concepts did not originate from divine sources – the Qur'an and Sunnah (the acts and deeds of the Prophet Mohammad) – they can not be accepted. According to the Muslim intellectuals, the above mentioned concepts are irreconcilable with Islam because they are the products of a profane culture, which subjugated faith to reason and desacralized knowledge and society.

In the course of my study, I noticed that secularism is one of the most rejected concepts within the Islamist discourse of current Muslim revivalists. They argue that the separation of religion and state is not reasonable since in Islamic religion state and religion are united. To put it another way, they claim that the division between church and state did not exist in Islam because, in contrast to Christianity, Islam appeared in the form of a state from the beginning.[3] In addition, they oppose the elimination of religion from social and individual life.[4] This fact lies at the heart of their criticisms of the Kemalist ideology.

What is equally important is their belief in the revival of Islam since the beginning of twentieth century after a long stagnation period.[5] They claim that the glorious days of Islam are forthcoming, in which Islam and Muslims will again be powerful.

Furthermore, it should be demonstrated that they act as public intellectuals, who aim to reform and enlighten society by educating it and raising its awareness of Islamic values. In fact, they are aware of their position as public intellectuals. So, it can be concluded that Muslim intellectuals empathize with the large sections of the public, who have similar backgrounds and who are negatively influenced by the modernization project. They share their feelings, problems, and desires.

In addition to their intellectual mission, some of them are prominent poets and littérateurs. It would not be wrong to claim that they combine artistic creativity and mental skills in their effort to disseminate their ideas and reform society in compliance with Islamic principles. Moreover, they try to reach their goal through intellectual effort by educating the public both mentally and spiritually. According to them, real reform will be in the mind and soul of the people, so they are not revolutionary or radical.

Generally speaking, their writing style is charming, eloquent, ironic and, didactic. The language they use is plain, modern-day Turkish, unlike that of the former Islamist intellectuals.[6] İsmet Özel and Abdurrahman Dilipak, are distinguished by their aggressive, derisive, and witty writing style.

Equally importantly, they write not only about religious or metaphysical issues but also about almost every aspect of life, from local and global politics and economics to history and culture. Interestingly, they are preoccupied with the same problems as the secular intellectuals. They differ from them in their Islamist approach and the solutions they provide to the problems of Turkey and the world.

As I researched their professional backgrounds, I observed that they have their own columns in major newspapers and journals and that all of them are authors of numerous books; or they have posts in government; some of them are university professors, and most of them are involved in many of these professions simultaneously. They are educated in the social sciences. Most of them are bilingual and have international experience.

Paradoxically, they benefit from the advantages of modernity, which they repudiate.[7] They are educated in modern, secular universities. As a result, this education has equipped them with critical and rational thinking as secular intellectuals, although they reject rational reasoning. Furthermore, they use the facilities of modernity. Thanks to developments in technology, information, and communications systems, they are able to reach and influence more people than before. As Şerif Mardin pointed out, the enlargement and proliferation of mass media contributed to the strengthening of Islamic discourse rather than weakening it.[8] Consequently 'the inability to think the culture through – a result of Jacobin strictures – was reshaped by the translation of religiosity onto a new ideological level where media images took the place of the soul.'[9]

In my study, I attempted to provide comparative, global, and broader insight into the evaluation and understanding of Muslim intellectuals' attitude, nature and distinctiveness in present-day Turkey rather than limiting myself to the analysis of their writings and speeches. Therefore, I compared them with the contemporary, unorthodox, critical Muslim intellectuals of the Arab world: Muhammed Arkoun, Seyyed Hossein Nasr, Nasr Hamid Abu Zaid, and Abdolkarim Soroush, as well as former three leading conservative and Islamist intellectuals – Bediuzzaman Said Nursi, Necip Fazıl Kısakürek, and Sezai Karakoç – who affected and inspired the contemporary Turkish Muslim intellectuals mostly. What I observed – with the exception of Seyyed Hossein Nasr – was the latters' approval of independent reasoning, rationality, democracy, and secularism, unlike the position of current Turkish Muslim intellectuals, who attempt to reconceptualize, reassess, and deconstruct orthodox Islamic discourse. Generally speaking, the Arab intellectuals in question are trying to accommodate the realities and necessities of the contemporary world with Islam in contrast to the Turkish Muslim intellectuals in question.

In effect, social, political, and historical dynamics play a significant role in the differences between Turkish and other Muslim intellectuals. That is to say, the prevalence of undemocratic and autocratic regimes, the colonial heritage and foreign occupation, traces of imperialism, the existence of superstitious fundamentalists, and a monolithic, orthodox clergy as well as control and restrictions on freedom determined the differences in the ideology and agenda between these Muslim thinkers and intellectuals in other Islamic countries.

Moreover, I also realized that Turkish Muslim intellectuals are preoccupied with problems of social, political, and cultural life, unlike their counterparts in the Arab world, who deal with more sophisticated philosophical, epistemological, and hermeneutic issues. In contrast, Turkish Islamists intellectuals are not original ideologues or deep philosophers. Instead, they are contributing the rejuvenation of Islamic awareness within the society, and they have been very effective in this.

In a nutshell, contemporary Muslim intellectuals not only transformed intellectual life in Turkey, but also the nature of Islamist discourse. It has been my contention that their prominence and attractiveness will increase and that they will be followed by more people as the role of religion increases more and more. In fact, their attraction comes neither from their originality or strength as philosophers and ideologues nor from their programme. Rather, they fulfill a need, which the Western lifestyle creates a demand for. Furthermore, their utopianism is very important and influential attracting people, who have little to hope for in their daily lives. This is understandable if we consider the electoral process in Turkey, which shows examples of totally unrealistic promises. That is to say, significant portion of the voters believe in miraculous economic and political commitments and show a tendency to vote for unattainable promises.

Moreover, their stress on religion and morality has a positive effect on the marginalized and dispossessed poor classes, who feel themselves rejected or outsiders. So they also fulfill a psychological need. In addition, they are highly educated and can argue in a modern way by using the tools of modern social science. Finally, contemporary Muslim intellectuals in Turkey share a similar background with university students, who empathize with them.

All in all, these Muslim thinkers constitute one of the dominant intellectual oppositional forces, whose rhetorics will continue to shape the discourse of Turkish intellectual life as long as the conditions for the revival of Islam persist within the domain of Turkish political, cultural and social life.

Notes

Introduction

1. Ali Bulaç, *Nuh'un Gemisine Binmek* (*Embarking on Noah's Ark*) İz Yayıncılık, 1995, p. 86.
2. The following articles on Islamist intellectuals are worth mentioning: Michael Meeker, 'Muslim Intellectuals', in Richard Tapper (ed.) *Islam in Modern Turkey'*; Ahmet Çiğdem, 'Batılılaşma, Modernite ve Modernizasyon', in *Modern Türkiye'de Siyasi Düşünce*, (*Political Thought in Modern Turkey*) Vol. 3; Nilüfer Göle, 'Secularism and Islamism in Turkey: The Making of Elites and Counter-Elites', *Middle East Journal,* Vol. 1, Winter 1997; Binnaz Toprak, 'Islamist Intellectuals of the 1980s in Turkey', *Current Turkish Thought*, No. 62, Spring 1987, Binnaz Toprak, İki Müslüman Aydın: Ali Bulaç ve İsmet Özel (Two Muslim Intellectuals: Ali Bulaç and İsmet Özel), *Toplum ve Bilim*, Vol. 29/30, 1985.
3. Ali Bulaç, *Nuh'un Gemisine Binmek*, p. 43.
4. John L. Esposito and John O. Voll, *Makers of Contemporary Islam*, Oxford University Press, 2001, p. 4.

Chapter 1

1. Haldun Gülalp, 'Political Islam in Turkey: The Rise and Fall of the Refah Party', *Muslim World*, Vol. 89, 1999, p. 23.
2. The literal meaning of the "*The Golden Age*" is the 'Age of Happiness', (Asr-ı Saadet), which began with the emergence of Islam with the Prophet Muhammed and lasted during the rule of the first four Caliphs.
3. Levent Köker, 'Kemalizm/Atatürkçülük: Modernleşme, Devlet ve Demokrasi' in Uygur Kocabaşoğlu (ed.) *Modern Türkiye' de Siyasi Düşünce,* Vol.3, İletişim Yayıncılık, 2002, p. 98.
4. Nadia Urbinati, 'From the Periphery of Modernity: Antonio Gramsci's Theory of Subordination and Hegemony', *Political Theory*, Vol. 26, June 1998, p. 370.

5. Seçil Deren, 'Kültürel Batılılaşma', in Uygur Kocabaşoğlu (ed.) *Modern Türkiye' de Siyasi Düşünce,*Vol.3, İletişim Yayıncılık, 2002, p. 382.
6. Hakan Yavuz, 'Turkey's Fault Lines and the Crisis of Kemalism', *Current History*, January 2000, p. 34.
7. Paul Dumont, 'The Origins of Kemalist Ideology', in Jacob Landau (ed.) *Atatürk and the Modernization of Turkey,* Westview Press, 1984, p. 41.
8. Ibid.
9. Murat Belge, 'Mustafa Kemal ve Kemalizm', in Ahmet İnsel (ed.) *Modern Türkiye'de Siyasi Düşünce*, Vol. 2, İletişim Yayıncılık, 2002, p. 33.
10. Ibid.
11. Şerif Mardin, *Jön Türklerin Siyasi Fikirleri 1895-1908, (The Political Thoughts of the Young Turks)*, İletişim Yayıncılık, 1983, p. 228.
12. Paul Dumont, 'The Origins of Kemalist Ideology', in Jacob Landau (ed.) *Atatürk and the Modernization of Turkey,* Westview Press, 1984, p. 37.
13. Şerif Mardin, 'Religion and Secularism in Turkey', in Ali Kazancigil & Ergun Özbudun (eds) *Atatürk: The Founder of a Modern State*, London, C. Hurst, 1981, p. 205.
14. Ibid.
15. Binnaz Toprak, *Islam and Political Development in Turkey*, Leiden, The Netherlands, E. J. Brill, 1981, p. 35.
16. Nuray Mert, 'Cumhuriyet Türkiye'sinde Laiklik ve Karşı Laikliğin Düşünsel Boyutu' in Ahmet İnsel (ed.) *Modern Türkiye'de Siyasi Düşünce*, Vol. 2, İletişim Yayıncılık, 2002, p. 198.
17. Ibid.
18. Peter Gay, 'The Enlightenment', in Jose Sanchez (ed.) *Anticlericalism: A Brief History*, University of Notre Dame Press, 1972, p. 60.
19. Ibid.
20. Paul Dumont, 'The Origins of Kemalist Ideology', in Jacob Landau (ed.) *Atatürk and the Modernization of Turkey*, Westview Press, 1984, p. 41.
21. Alper Kaliber, 'Türk Modernleşmesini Sorunsallaştıran Üç Ana Paradigma Üzerine', in Uygur Kocabaşoğlu (ed.) *Modern Türkiye' de Siyasi Düşünce,*Vol.3, İletişim Yayıncılık, 2002, p. 110.
22. Quoted by Kemal H. Karpat from 'Nutuk (Speeches of Atatürk)' Ankara, 1935, in his book *Turkey's Politics, The Transition to A Multi-Party System*, Princeton University Press, 1959.
23. Nilüfer Göle, 'Batı Dışı Modernlik: Kavram Üzerine' in Uygur Kocabaşoğlu (ed.) *Modern Türkiye' de Siyasi Düşünce,* Vol. 3, İletişim Yayıncılık, 2002, p. 65.
24. Ibid.
25. Feroz Ahmad, 'Politics and Islam in Modern Turkey', *Middle Eastern Studies*, Vol. 27, January 1991.

26. Paul Dumont, 'The Origins of Kemalist Ideology', in Jacob Landau (ed.) *Atatürk and the Modernization of Turkey*, Westview Press, 1984, p. 30.
27. Ibid. p. 29.
28. Ahmet İnsel, 'Introduction' in Ahmet İnsel (ed.) *Modern Türkiye'de Siyasi Düşünce*, Vol. 2, İletişim Yayıncılık, 2002, p.19.
29. Reşat Kasaba & Sibel Bozdoğan, *Rethinking Modernity and National Identity in Turkey*, University of Washington Press, 1997.
30. Haldun Gülalp, 'Political Islam in Turkey: The Rise and Fall of the Refah Party', *Muslim World*, Vol. 89, 1999.
31. Erik J. Zürcher, 'The Core Terminology of Kemalism: Mefkure, Millî, Muasir, Medenî', in François Georgeon (ed.) *Les mots de politique de l'Empire Ottoman a la Turquie kemaliste*, Paris, EHESS/ESA, CNRS, 2000, pp. 55–64.
32. Erik J. Zürcher, *From Empire to Republic-Problems of Transition, Continuity and Change*, http://www.let.leidenuniv.nl/tcimo/tulp/Research/Fromtorep.htm.
33. Binnaz Toprak, *Islam and Political Development in Turkey*, p. 20.
34. Ibid. p. 24.
35. Ibid. pp. 25, 31, 32.
36. Hakan Yavuz, *Turkey's Fault Lines and the Crisis of Kemalism*, p. 33.
37. Ibid.
38. Feroz Ahmad, *Politics and Islam in Modern Turkey*, p. 8.
39. Erik J. Zürcher, *Turkey: A Modern History*, London, I.B. Tauris, 1993, p. 201.
40. Binnaz Toprak, *Islam and Political Development in Turkey*, p. 47.
41. Özay Mehmet, 'Turkey in Crisis: Some Contradictions in the Kemalist Development Strategy', *International Journal of Middle East Studies*, Vol. 15, February 1983, p. 51.
42. Paul Dumont, 'The Origins of Kemalist Ideology', p. 36.
43. Şerif Mardin, 'Religion and Secularism in Turkey', p. 191.
44. Nuray Mert, 'Cumhuriyet Türkiye'sinde Laiklik ve Karşı Laikliğin Düşünsel Boyutu', p. 206.
45. Ibid.
46. Source: Binnaz Toprak 'The Religious Right' in Ertuğrul Ahmet Tonak & Irvin C. Schick (eds) *Turkey in Transition: New Perspectives*, Oxford University Press, 1987, p. 223.
47. Binnaz Toprak, *Islam and Political Development* in Turkey, p. 125.
48. Levent Köker, 'Kemalizm/Ataürkçülük: Modernleşme, Devlet ve Demokrasi', in Ahmet İnsel (ed.) *Modern Türkiye'de Siyasi Düşünce*, Vol. 2, İletişim Yayıncılık, 2002, p. 106.
49. Ibid.

50. Nimet Arsan, *Atatürk'ün Söylev ve Demeçleri* 1918-1937, *(The Speech and Statements of Atatürk)* Vol. 3, Ankara, Türk Tarih Kurumu Basımevi, 1961, p. 68.
51. Joseph R. Gusfield, 'Tradition and Modernity: Misplaced Polarities in the Study of Social Change', *American Journal of Sociology*, Vol. 72, 1967, p. 361.
52. Dean C. Tipps, 'Modernization Theory and the Comparative Study of Societies: A Critical Perspective' *Comparative Studies in Society and History*, Vol. 15, No. 2, March, 1973.
53. Ibid, p. 202.
54. Samuel P. Huntington, 'The Change to Change: Modernization, Development, and Politics', *Comparative Politics,* Vol. 3, No. 3, April 1971, pp. 288–90.
55. Şerif Mardin, *Makaleler 4 Türk Modernleşmesi*, İletişim Yayınları, 1995, p. 248.
56. Quoted by Bernard Lewis from '*Nutuk*', (Speeches of Atatürk) Ankara, 1950–52, in his book *The Emergence of Modern Turkey,* Oxford University Press, 1961, p. 263.
57. Ibid.
58. Nilüfer Göle, 'Batı Dışı Modernlik: Kavram Üzerine', p. 63.
59. Ibid.
60. Ibid.
61. Ibid.
62. Ibid.
63. Levent Köker, 'Kemalizm/Atatürkçülük: Modernleşme, Devlet ve Demokrasi', p. 109.
64. Taha Parla, 'Kemalizm, Türk Aydınlanması mı?' in Ahmet İnsel (ed.) *Modern Türkiye'de Siyasi Düşünce*, Vol. 2, İletişim Yayıncılık, 2002, p. 314.
65. Quoted in Kemal Karpat, *Turkey's Politics, The Transition to A Multi-Party System,* Princeton University Press, 1959, p. 61.
66. Şerif Mardin, 'Projects as Methodology Some Thoughts on Modern', in Reşat Kasaba & Sibel Bozdoğan (eds) *Rethinking Modernity and National Identity in Turkey*, University of Washington Press, 1997, p. 65.
67. Ibid., p. 214.
68. Ibid., p. 215.
69. Çağlar Keyder, 'Whither the Project of Modernity? Turkey in the 1990s', in Sibel Bozdoğan & Reşat Kasaba (eds) *Rethinking Modernity and National Identity in Turkey,* University of Washington Press, 1997, p. 39
70. Heinz Kramer, *A Changing Turkey: The Challenge to Europe and the United States,* Brookings Institution Press, 2000, p. 90.

71. Kemal Karpat, *Turkey's Politics, The Transition to A Multi-Party System*, p. 271.
72. Ibid.
73. Şerif Mardin, 'Religion and Politics in Modern Turkey' in James Piscatori (ed.) *Islam in the Political Process*, Cambridge University Press, 1983, p. 155.
74. Kemal Karpat, Turkey's *Politics The Transition to A Multi-Party System*, p. 60.
75. İlter Turan, 'Continuity and Change in Turkish Bureaucracy', in Jacob Landau (ed.) *Atatürk and the Modernization of Turkey*, Westview Press, 1984, p.108.
76. Ibid.
77. Mehmet Altan, 'Batılılaşmanın Sosyo-Politik Temelleri, Düşünsel ve Toplumsal Yapısı', in Uygur Kocabaşoğlu (ed.) *Modern Türkiye' de Siyasi Düşünce*,Vol. 3, İletişim Yayıncılık, 2002, p. 142.
78. Çağlar Keyder, 'The Political Economy of Turkish Democracy', in *Turkey in Transition: New Perspectives*, Irvin C. Schick & Ertuğrul A. Tonak (eds) Oxford University Press, 1987, p. 42.
79. Ömer Turan, 'Son Dönemde Kemalizme Demokratik Meşruiyet Arayışları' in Ahmet İnsel (ed.) *Modern Türkiye'de Siyasi Düşünce*, Vol. 2, İletişim Yayıncılık, 2002, p. 593.
80. Çağlar Keyder, 'The Political Economy of Turkish Democracy', in Ertuğrul A.Tonak & Irvin C. Schick (eds) *Turkey in Transition: New Perspectives*, Oxford University Press, 1987, p. 59.
81. Binnaz Toprak, *Islam and Political Development in Turkey*, p. 19.
82. Samuel P. Huntington, 'The Change to Change: Modernization, Development, and Politics', p. 295.
83. Hakan Yavuz, 'Political Islam and Welfare Party in Turkey', *Comparative Politics*, Vol.30, No.1, Oct., 1997, p. 67.
84. Kramer, Heinz, *A Changing Turkey: The Challenge to Europe and the United States*, p. 65.
85. Ümit Cizre Sakallıoğlu, 'Parameters and Strategies of Islam-State Interaction in Republican Turkey', *International Journal of Middle East Studies*, Vol. 28, 1996, p. 242.
86. Ibid., p. 244.
87. Schools designed for the training of preacher and prayer leaders.
88. Sami Zubaida, 'Turkish Islam and National Identity: Insolvent Ideologies, Fractured State', *Middle East Report*, No. 199, April–June, 1996, p. 13.
89. Ziya Öniş, 'The Political Economy of Islamic Resurgence in Turkey: The Rise of the Welfare Party in Perspective', *Third World Quarterly*, Vol. 18, No. 4, 1997, p. 750.

90. Hakan Yavuz, 'Turkish-Israeli Relations Through the Lens of the Turkish Identity Debate', *Journal of Palestine Studies*, Vol. 27, No. 1, Autumn 1997, p. 25.
91. Nilüfer Göle, 'Secularism & Islamism in Turkey: The Making of Elites and Counter-Elites', *Middle East Journal*, Vol.51, Winter 1997, p. 47.
92. Ümit Cizre Sakallıoğlu, 'Parameters and Strategies of Islam-State Interaction in Republican Turkey', p. 244.
93. Ziya Öniş, 'The Political Economy of Islamic Resurgence in Turkey: The Rise of the Welfare Party in Perspective', p. 761.
94. Hakan Yavuz, 'Political Islam and Welfare Party in Turkey', p. 69.
95. Kramer, Heinz, *A Changing Turkey: The Challenge to Europe and the United States*, p. 2.
96. Binnaz Toprak, 'Religion and State in Turkey', she delivered her lecture at a Dayan Center conference on *Contemporary Turkey: Challenges of Change*, on 20 June 1999.
97. Kramer, Heinz, *A Changing Turkey*, p. 16.
98. Ümit Cizre Sakallıoğlu, 'Parameters and Strategies of Islam-State Interaction in Republican Turkey', p. 245.
99. Samuel P. Huntington, 'Political Development and Political Decay', *World Politics*, Vol. 17, No. 3, April 1965, pp. 406–8.
100. Nilüfer Göle, 'Batı Dışı Modernlik: Kavram Üzerine', p. 66.
101. Emile Sahliyeh, *Religious Resurgence and Politics in the Contemporary World*, State University of New York Press, 1990, p. 9.
102. Binnaz Toprak, *Religion and State in Turkey*, 1999, p. 5.
103. Heinz Kramer, *A Changing Turkey: The Challenge to Europe and the United States*, p. 82.
104. Samuel P. Huntington, 'Political Development and Political Decay', p. 406.
105. Ezel Kural Shaw and Stanford J. Shaw, *History of the Ottoman Empire and Modern Turkey*, Volume II: Reform, Revolution and Republic: The Rise of Modern Turkey, 1808–1975, Cambridge University Press, 1977, p. 387.
106. Taha Parla, 'Kemalizm, Türk Aydınlanması mı?'

Chapter 2

1. Sayyid Qutb, 'Dirasat Islamiyyah' (Islamic Studies), in Lamia Rustum Shehadeh (ed.) *The Idea of Women Under Fundamentalist Islam*, University Press of Florida, 2003.
2. Alvin W. Gouldner, *The Future of Intellectuals and the Rise of the New Class*, The Seabury Press, 1979, p. 57.
3. Cemil Meriç, in Murat Belge (ed.) *Cumhuriyet Dönemi Türkiye Ansiklopedisi*, Iletişim Yayınları, Vol. 1, 1983, p. 131.

4. Tibor Huszar, 'Changes in the concept of intellectuals', in Alexander Gella (ed.) *The Intelligentsia and the Intellectuals: Theory, Method and Case Study*, London, Sage, 1976, pp. 79.
5. Paul Johnson, *Intellectuals*, Harper & Row Publishers, 1988, p. 1.
6. Ibid., pp. 1–2.
7. Random House Webster's College Dictionary; Random House, Inc. 2001.
8. *The Oxford Dictionary and Thesaurus*, American Edition, Oxford University Press Inc. 1996.
9. *Oxford English Dictionary*, 5th Edition (Vol. 1) Oxford University Press, 2002.
10. Edward Shills, 'Intellectuals', in David L.Sills (ed.) *International Encyclopedia of the Social Sciences*, Vol. 7, New York, Macmillan, 1991, p. 399.
11. Joseph Schumpeter, *Capitalism, Socialism, and Democracy,* New York, Harper & Row, 1950, p. 147.
12. Ibid., p. 146.
13. Anthony Kemp-Welch, Jeremy Jennings, *Intellectuals in Politics from the Dreyfus Affair to Salman Rushdie,* Routledge, 1997, p. 1.
14. Ibid.
15. Ibid., p. 12.
16. Abdolkarim Soroush, *The Powerless Wielders of Power*, in *Conversation with Abdolkarim Soroush*, 29 March 2002, http://www.seraj.org/conversation2.htm.
17. Lennert G. Svensson, Roy Eyerman and Thomas Soderqvist, *Intellectuals, Universities and the State in Western Modern Societies,* University of California Press, 1987, p. 6.
18. Pierre Bourdieu, 'Towards a Theory of Practice', in Roy Eyerman, Lennert G. Svensson and Thomas Soderqvist (eds) *Intellectuals, Universities and the State in Western Modern Societies*, University of California Press, 1987, p. 22.
19. Nilüfer Göle, *Secularism and Islamism in Turkey*, pp. 46–7.
20. Roy Eyerman, Lennert G. Svensson and Thomas Soderqvist, *Intellectuals, Universities and the State in Western Modern Societies*, p. 28.
21. George Konrad and Ivan Szelenyi, *The Intellectuals on the Road to Class Power*, New York, Harcourt Brace Jovanovich, 1979, p. 6.
22. Renate Holub, *Antonio Gramsci: Beyond Marxism and Postmodernism,* Routledge, 1992, p. 153.
23. Ibid., p. 156.
24. Ibid., p. 165.
25. Ibid., p. 165.
26. Carl Boggs, *Intellectuals and the Crisis of Modernity,* Albany, State University of New York Press, 1993, p. 146.

27. Alvin W. Gouldner, *The Future of Intellectuals and the Rise of the New Class*, p. 5. Eyerman, Svensson and Soderqvist explained the language behaviour as 'a key element in the culture acquired through higher education and which refers to a critical – reflective attitudes as well as to the technical languages and pragmatic orientations of science and scientists'.
28. Ibid., pp. 20–1.
29. Murat Belge, *Cumhuriyet Dönemi Türkiye Ansiklopedisi*, p. 123.
30. Ibid., p. 123.
31. As Şerif Mardin explains in his book *The Genesis of Young Ottoman Thought* (p. 3), Tanzimat 'refers to period of Turkish history (1839–78) during which a considerable number of Western-inspired political and social reforms were carried out in the Ottoman Empire'.
32. Michael Meeker, 'The New Muslim Intellectuals in the Republic of Turkey', in Richard Tapper (ed.) *Islam in Modern Turkey: Religion, Politics and Literature in a Secular State*, St. Martin's Press, 1991, p. 218.
33. Namık Kemal, Mustafa Fazıl Paşa, Ali Suavi, Ziya Paşa are the leading Young Ottomans.
34. Şerif Mardin, *The Genesis of Young Ottoman Thought, A Study in the Modernization of Turkish Political Ideas,* Syracuse University Press, 2000, p. 3.
35. Ibid. p. 4.
36. Ibid., p. 397,404.
37. Ibid., p. 9.
38. Ibid., p. 4.
39. Ibid., p. 316.
40. Ibid., p. 283.
41. Ibid., p. 295.
42. Ahmet Rıza Bey, Abdullah Cevdet, Murat Bey, Ziya Gökalp are the most important figures of this generation.
43. Erik J. Zurcher, *The Young Turks: Children of the Borderlands?* Turkology Update Leiden Project Working Papers Archive, October 2002, http://www.let.leidenuniv.nl/tcimo/tulp/Research/ejz16.htm, p. 2.
44. Şükrü Hanioğlu, *The Young Turks in Opposition*, Oxford University Press, 1995, p. 23.
45. Ibid., p. 32.
46. Şerif Mardin, 'Religion and Secularism in Turkey', p.207.
47. Şükrü Hanioğlu, *The Young Turks in Opposition*, p. 211.
48. Ibid., p. 216.
49. Paul Dumont, 'The Origins of Kemalist Ideology', p. 41.
50. Ibid., p. 41.

51. Erik-Jan Zürcher, *Ottoman Sources of Kemalist Thought*, Turkology Update Leiden Project Working Papers Archive Department of Turkish Studies, Universiteit Leiden, March 2002, http://www.let.leidenuniv.nl/tcimo/tulp/Research/MUNCHEN2.htm, p.16.
52. Murat Belge, *Cumhuriyet Dönemi Türkiye Ansiklopedisi*, p.126.
53. Ibid. p. 126.
54. Ibid., p. 124.
55. Ibid., p. 126.
56. Yalçın Küçük, *Cumhuriyet Dönemi Türkiye Ansiklopedisi*, İletişim Yayınları, İstanbul, 1983, p. 139.
57. Politician, founder and member of the Turkish Socialist and Farmers Party.
58. Marxist theoretician, writer, member of the Turkish Communist Party and founder of Vatan (Patrie) Party.
59. Yalçın Küçük, *Cumhuriyet Dönemi Türkiye Ansiklopedisi*, p. 140.
60. Ibid., p. 140.
61. Şerif Mardin, *Cultural Transitions in the Middle East*, Leiden, The Netherlands, E.J. Brill, 1994, p. 199.
62. Ibid., p. 192.
63. Yalçın Küçük, *Cumhuriyet Dönemi Türkiye Ansiklopedisi*, p. 140.
64. Ibid., p. 141.
65. Ibid., p. 143.
66. Ibid., p. 143.
67. Murat Belge, *Cumhuriyet Dönemi Türkiye Ansiklopedisi*, p. 126.
68. Ibid., p. 128.
69. Ibid., p. 128.
70. Nilüfer Göle defines them as 'engineers and technicians, which through secular and modern education, have acquired a 'cultural capital' namely, a universal scientific language and professional skills'. Nilüfer Göle, 'Secularism and Islamism in Turkey: The Making of Elites and Counter-Elites', p. 55.
71. Nilüfer Göle, 'Secularism and Islamism in Turkey: The Making of Elites and Counter-Elites', p. 55.
72. Murat Belge, *Cumhuriyet Dönemi Türkiye Ansiklopedisi*, p. 128.
73. The term *Islamist* designates Muslim people who are striving to implement Islamic values in all spheres of life.
74. Interview with İsmet Özel, July 2003, Istanbul.
75. Michael Meeker, 'The New Muslim Intellectuals in the Republic of Turkey', p. 211.
76. Ibid.
77. Ibid., 201.

78. Ibid., p. 189.
79. Nilüfer Göle, 'Secularism and Islamism in Turkey: The Making of Elites and Counter-Elites', p. 47.
80. Practices and doings of the Prophet Muhammed are defined as Sunnah, whereas his words and deeds handed down by His companions are called as Hadith.
81. Binnaz Toprak, 'Islamist Intellectuals of the 1980s in Turkey', *Current Turkish Thought*, No. 62, Spring 1987, p. 15.
82. Interview with Ali Bulaç, June 2003, Istanbul.
83. İsmet Özel, Milli Gazete, 25 August 2003.
84. Rasim Özdenören, *Müslümanca Yaşamak* (Living like Muslim) p. 115.
85. Interview with Ersin Gürdoğan, June 2003, Istanbul.
86. Sufism is explained in the *Historical Dictionary of Islam* as follows: 'a mystical path (*tariqa*) or discipline that consists of graded esoteric teachings leading through a series of initiations to the status of an adept. The objective of the path is to achieve direct experiential knowledge (*ma'rifah*), which through illumination (*kashf*), leads to communion with God (*fana'fillah*); it is achieved through personal devotion and a mastery of the techniques taught by the shaykh.'
87. Rasim Özdenören, *Kafa Karıştıran Kelimeler* (Confusing Words) İz Yayıncılık, 1997.
88. Ali Bulaç, Zaman, 12 April 2002.
89. Ali Bulaç, *Nuh'un Gemisine Binmek*, p. 220.
90. Ibid., p. 160.
91. Interview with Ersin Gürdoğan, June 2003, Istanbul.
92. Michael Meeker, 'The Muslim Intellectual and His Audience: A New Configuration of Writer and Reader Among Believers in the Republic of Turkey', in Dale F. Eickelman (ed.) *Knowledge and Power in Morocco*, Princeton University Press, 1985, p. 154.
93. Ibid., pp. 153–4.
94. Ali Bulaç writes: 'We benefit from the Western sources. We should refer to them. In this sense to limit ourselves to the 'local' is only an illusion.'
95. Interview with İlhan Kutluer, July 2003, Istanbul.
96. Michael Meeker, 'The Muslim Intellectual and His Audience: A New Configuration of Writer and Reader Among Believers in the Republic of Turkey', in Dale F. Eickelman (ed.) *Knowledge and Power in Morocco*, Princeton University Press, 1985, p. 189–2.
97. Interview with Ersin Gürdoğan, July 2003, Istanbul.
98. İsmet Özel, who spent almost ten years of his youth as a socialist during the 1960s until early 1970s, constitutes an exception here. He later adopted an Islamic way of life.

99. There are certain typologies to define traditional as against modern societies. According to Friedrich Tonnies, gemeinschaft represents traditional society, which 'is the lasting and genuine form of living together. In contrast to Gemeinschaft, Gesellschaft is transitory and superficial. Accordingly, Gemeinschaft should be understood as a living organism, and Gesellschaft as a mechanical aggregate and artifact.' Similarly, Emile Durkheim examined pre-historic and pre-agricultural societies in terms of 'mechanical solidarity' and modern and industrial society in terms of organic solidarity. As modernity and industrialization advance, division of labor and differentiation occurs within traditional society. Durkheim argues that 'there is, then, a social structure of determined nature to which mechanical solidarity corresponds. What characterizes it is a system of segments, homogeneous and similar to each other. Quite different is the structure of societies where organic solidarity is preponderant. They are constituted, not by a repetition of similar, homogeneous segments, but by a system of different organs each of which has a special role, and which are themselves formed of differentiated parts.'(Durkheim, *The Division of Labor in Society*, p. 192) (1933, p. 181).
100. Michael Meeker, 'The Muslim Intellectual and His Audience: A New Configuration of Writer and Reader Among Believers in the Republic of Turkey', in Dale F. Eickelman (ed.) *Knowledge and Power in Morocco*, Princeton University Press, 1985, p. 195.
101. Ibid., pp. 195–6.
102. George Konrad and Ivan Szelenyi, *The Intellectuals on the Road to Class Power*, p. 5.
103. Jeremy Jennings and Anthony Kemp-Welch, *Intellectuals in Politics from the Dreyfus Affair to Salman Rushdie*, p. 2.
104. Michael Meeker, 'The Muslim Intellectual and His Audience: A New Configuration of Writer and Reader Among Believers in the Republic of Turkey', in Dale F. Eickelman (ed.) *Knowledge and Power in Morocco*, Princeton University Press, 1985, pp. 161–2.
105. Carl Boggs, *Intellectuals and the Crisis of Modernity*, p. 8.
106. Ibid., p. 9.
107. Ali Bulaç, *İslam ve Fundamentalizm* (Islam and Fundamentalism) İz Yayıncılık, 1997, p. 51.
108. Ersin Gürdoğan, *Kültür ve Sanayileşme* (Culture and Industrialization) İz Yayıncılık, 1997, p. 119.
109. Ali Bulaç, *Din ve Modernizm*, (Religion and Modernism) p. 78.
110. Ibid., p. 78.
111. İsmet Özel, *Üç Mesele* (Three Problems) *Teknik-Medeniyet-Yabancılaşma*, Şule Yayınları, 1998, p. 149.

112. Interview with Rasim Özdenören, June 2003, Ankara.
113. Interview with İsmet Özel, July 2003, Istanbul.
114. Ersin Gürdoğan, *Kültür ve Sanayilesme*, p. 120–2.
115. Ali Bulaç, *Din ve Modernizm*, p. 78.
116. Ibid., pp. 115, 298.
117. Ali Bulaç, *Çağdaş Kavramlar ve Düzenler* (Modern Concepts and Orders) İz Yayıncılık, 1997, p. 57.
118. Ali Bulaç, *Yağma Özgürlüktür* (Pillage is Freedom) Zaman, 21 April 2003.
119. Abdurrahman Dilipak, *Coğrafi Keşiflerin İçyüzü* (The Reality of Geographical Explorations) Inkılab Yayınları, 1984, p. 223.
120. Ibid., p. 156.
121. Ibid.
122. Ibid.
123. Ali Bulaç, *İnsanın Özgürlük Arayışı* (Man's Search for Freedom) İz Yayıncılık, 1995, p. 28.
124. Ibid., p. 28.
125. Ali, Bulaç, *İslam Dünyasında Düşünce Sorunları* (Problems of Thought in the Islamic World) İz Yayıncılık, 1995, p. 179.
126. Rasim Özdenören, *Yumurtayı Hangi Ucundan Kırmalı?* (On Which Side Should One Break the Egg?) İz Yayıncılık, 1999, p. 49.
127. Ibid., p. 50.
128. Ibid., p. 52.
129. Ali Bulaç, *İnsanın Özgürlük Arayışı*.
130. İsmet Özel, *Üç Mesele*, p. 168.
131. İsmet Özel, *Bakanlar ve Görenler* (Those who Look and those who See) Şule Yayınları, 1996, p. 47.
132. Ali Bulaç, *Çağdaş Kavramlar ve Düzenler*, p. 43.
133. Ibid.
134. Ali Bulaç, *Nuh'un Gemisine Binmek*, p. 96. It is important to note here that the concept of West not only include Europe but also the United States.
135. Ibid.
136. Rasim Özdenören, *Çapraz İlişkiler*, p. 8.
137. İlhan Kutluer, *Modern Bilimin Arka Planı* (The Unseen Agenda of Modern Science) İnsan Yayınları, 1985, p. 95.
138. Rasim Özdenören *Yeni Dünya Düzeninin Sefaleti* (The Misery of the New World Order) İz Yayıncılık, 1998, p. 174.
139. Ali Bulaç, *İslam ve Fanatizm* (Islam and Fanaticism) İz Yayıncılık, 1995, pp. 146–7.
140. Ibid.

141. Ersin Gürdoğan, *Kültür ve Sanayileşme*, p. 117
142. Ibid.
143. Ibid., p. 118.
144. Ibid., p. 123.
145. Ibid.
146. Rasim Özdenören, *Müslümanca Yaşamak*, p. 34.
147. Ali Bulaç, *Bir Aydın Sapması* (A Deviation of an Intellectual) İz Yayıncılık, 1995, p. 38.
148. Rasim Özdenören, *Yeni Dünya Düzeninin Sefaleti*, p. 28.
149. Ibid.
150. Ibid., p. 55.
151. Interview Rasim Özdenören, June 2003, Ankara.
152. Ibid.
153. Ibid.
154. Ali Bulaç, *Din, Devlet ve Demokrasi* (Religion, State and Democracy) Zaman Kitap, 2001, p. 30.
155. Ibid.
156. Ibid., p. 34.
157. Rasim Özdenören, *Yeni Dünya Düzeninin Sefaleti*, p. 40.
158. Ali Bulaç, *İslam ve Demokrasi* (Islam and Democracy) İz Yayıncılık, 1995, p. 19.
159. Ibid.
160. Ali Bulac, *Din ve Modernizm*, p. 204.
161. Ali Bulaç, *Din, Devlet ve Demokrasi*, p. 37.
162. Ibid., p. 47.
163. Ali Bulaç, *İslam ve Demokrasi*, p. 70.
164. Ibid.
165. Ibid., p. 17.
166. The time of pre-Islamic paganism.
167. İlhan Kutluer, *Erdemli Toplum ve Düşmanları* (The Virtuous Society and its Enemies) İz Yayıncılık, 1995, p. 16.
168. Ibid.
169. Ali Bulac, *İslam ve Demokrasi*, p. 31.
170. Ibid.
171. Ibid.
172. Ibid., p. 56–7.
173. Ibid.
174. Ibid.
175. Ibid., p. 148.
176. Ibid., p. 177.
177. Ibid., 185,186.

178. Ibid., p. 147.
179. Ibid.
180. Ali Bulaç, *Bir Aydın Sapması*, p. 35. Bulaç explains the protection of generation as the assurance of its continuity and provision of a decent, virtuous life.
181. Ibid., p. 36.
182. Ibid.
183. İsmet Özel, *İrtica Elden Gidiyor*, Şule Yayınları, 1998, p. 70.
184. Interview with İsmet Özel, July 2003, Istanbul.
185. Ali Bulaç, *Nuh'un Gemisine Binmek*, p. 37.
186. Ibid.
187. Rasim Özdenören, *Yeni Dünya Düzeninin Sefaleti*, p. 173.
188. Ibid., p. 201.
189. Ibid., p. 201.
190. Ibid., p. 203.
191. Ibid., p. 203.
192. Ibid., p. 212.
193. Abdurrahman Dilipak, *Laisizm* (Laicism) Beyan Yayınları, 1991, p. 17.
194. Ibid., p. 17.
195. Ali Bulaç, *Çağdaş Kavramlar ve Düzenler*, p. 178.
196. Infidelity, unbelief.
197. Ali Bulaç, *İslam ve Fundamentalizm*, p. 206.
198. Interview Ali Bulaç, June 2003, Istanbul.
199. Interview Ali Bulaç, June 2003, Istanbul.
200. Interview Ali Bulaç, June 2003, Istanbul.
201. Abdurrahman Dilipak, *Laisizm*, p. 103.
202. Ibid., p. 17.
203. Ibid., p. 9.
204. Ibid., p. 127.
205. Ibid., 28.
206. A going back; political reaction
207. Abdurrahman Dilipak, *Laisizm*, p. 114.
208. Dilipak draws attention to Coskun Üçok's argument that laicism is dictated by the West and enforced by the state elite, so is a top down process.
209. Ali Bulaç, *İslam ve Fanatizm*, p. 51.
210. Abdurrahman Dilipak, *Laisizm*, p. 43.
211. Ibid., 43.
212. Ibid., 44.
213. Ibid., 52.
214. Ibid., p. 101.
215. Ibid., p. 157.

216. Ibid., p. 157.
217. Ibid., p. 158.
218. Ibid., p. 98.
219. Ibid., p. 159.
220. İsmet Özel, *Cuma Mektupları* (Friday Letters) Şule Yayınları, 1998, p. 35.
221. Ibid., p. 86.
222. Ibid., p. 86.
223. Ersin Gürdoğan, *Kirlenmenin Boyutları* (The Dimensions of Corruption) İnsan Yayınları, 1989, p. 92.
224. Interview with Ali Bulaç, June 2003, Istanbul.
225. Interview with Ali Bulaç, June 2003, Istanbul.
226. Ali Bulaç, *Din ve Modernizm* (Religion and Modernism) p. 115.
227. Ibid., p. 273.
228. İlhan Kutluer, *Erdemli Toplum ve Düşmanları*, p. 53.
229. Ibid., p. 53.
230. Ibid., p. 53.
231. Ibid., p. 54.
232. Ibid., p. 54.
233. Ibid., p. 54.
234. Ali Bulaç, *Din ve Modernizm*, p. 49.
235. Ibid., p. 49.
236. Daniel Lerner, *Passing of Traditional Society*, Free Press, 1958, p. 45.
237. Interview with Ali Bulaç, June 2003, Istanbul.
238. Ali Bulaç, *Nuh'un Gemisine Binmek*, p. 189.
239. İsmet Özel, *Üç Mesele*, p. 39.
240. Ali Bulaç, *Din ve Modernizm*, p. 67.
241. Ibid., p. 68.
242. Ibid., p .68.
243. Ali Bulaç, *İnsanın Özgürlük Arayışı*, p. 54.
244. Ali Bulaç, *Din ve Modernizm*, p. 71.
245. Ibid., p. 71.
246. Ibid., p. 45.
247. Ibid., p. 222.
248. Ibid., p. 303.
249. Ibid., p. 299.
250. Ibid., p. 188.
251. Ibid., p. 188.
252. Ibid., p. 217.
253. Ibid., p. 193.
254. Ibid., p. 199.
255. Ibid., p. 141.

256. Ibid., p. 219.
257. İsmet Özel, *Üç Mesele*, p. 44 .
258. Ali Bulaç, *Din ve Modernizm*, p. 141.
259. Ibid., p. 223 .According to Islamic mysticism God is unique (Vahdet) and the manifestations that express His diverse features are numerous. (Kesret) All these manifestations take the human being to the unity of God.
260. Ibid., p. 325.
261. Ali Bulaç, *Çağdaş Kavramlar ve Düzenler*, p. 30.
262. Ibid., p. 29.
263. Ali Bulaç, *Kutsala, Tarihe ve Hayata Dönüş*, (Return to the Sacred, History and Life) İz Yayıncılık, 1995, p. 20.
264. Ali Bulaç, *Çağdaş Kavramlar ve Düzenler*, p. 38.
265. Ibid., p. 75.
266. Ibid., p. 75.
267. Rasim Özdenören, *Yeniden İnanmak* (Believing Again) İz Yayıncılık, 1999, p. 17.
268. Ali Bulaç, *Çağdaş Kavramlar ve Düzenler*, p.74
269. Ibid., p. 74.
270. Ibid., p. 76.
271. Rasim Özdenören, *Yeniden İnanmak*, p. 16.
272. Ibid., p. 17.
273. İsmet Özel, *Ve'l Asr*, Şule Yayınları, 2003, p. 54.
274. Ibid., p. 54.
275. Ali Bulaç, *Bir Aydın Sapması*, p. 105.
276. Ibid., p. 105.
277. İsmet Özel, *Cuma Mektupları 8*, Şule Yayınları, 2002, p. 131.
278. Ali Bulaç, *Bir Aydın Sapması*, p. 105.
279. Rasim Özdenören, *Yeni Dünya Düzeninin Sefaleti*, p. 113.
280. Ibid., p. 127.
281. Ibid., p. 132.
282. Ali Bulaç, *İslam ve Fanatizm*, p. 138–9.
283. Ali Bulaç, *Nuh'un Gemisine Binmek*, p. 107.
284. Ibid., p. 112.
285. Ibid., p. 112.
286. Ersin Gürdoğan, *Zamanı Aşan Şehirler* (Cities That Transcend Time) İz Yayıncılık, 1997, p. 42.
287. Ersin Gürdoğan, *Günler Akarken* (As the Days Past By) İz Yayıncılık, 1996, p. 96.
288. Ibid., p. 96.
289. Ali Bulaç, *Nuh'un Gemisine Binmek*, p. 110.
290. Ali Bulaç, *Çağdaş Kavramlar ve Düzenler*, p. 127.

291. Ibid., p. 127.
292. Ibid., pp. 86, 129.

Chapter 3

1. See Chapter 1.
2. Rasim Özdenören, *Yumurtayı Hangi Ucundan Kırmalı*, p. 127.
3. Ibid., p. 127.
4. Ibid., p. 135.
5. Ibid., p. 140.
6. Ali Bulaç, *İslam ve Demokrasi*, p. 149. Here, 'Athan: means call to prayer.
7. Ersin Gürdoğan, *Günler Akarken*, p. 117.
8. Abdurrahman Dilipak, *Laisizm*, p. 55.
9. Ibid., p. 57.
10. Ersin Gürdoğan, *Kirlenmenin Boyutları*, p. 117.
11. İsmet Özel, *Cuma Mektupları I*, p. 30.
12. Ibid., p. 24.
13. Ali Bulaç, *Kutsala, Tarihe ve Hayata Dönüş*, p. 226.
14. Ibid., p. 226.
15. İsmet Özel, Cuma *Mektupları 1*, Şule Yayınları, 1998, p. 155.
16. Ali Bulaç, *Modern Ulus Devlet* (Modern Nation State) İz Yayıncılık, 1998, p. 270.
17. Ersin Gürdoğan, *Günler Akarken*, p. 94.
18. Ali Bulaç, *Modern Ulus Devlet*, pp. 50–3.
19. Rasim Özdenören, *Yeni Dünya Düzeninin Sefaleti*, p. 110.
20. Ibid., p. 111.
21. Ibid., p. 111.
22. Interview with Ali Bulaç, June, 2003, Istanbul.
23. Ali Bulaç, *Din ve Modernizm*, p. 271.
24. Pronouncing the oneness and uniqueness of God.
25. Ali Bulaç, *Din ve Modernizm*, p. 271.
26. Ibid., p. 271.
27. Interview with Ali Bulaç, June, 2003, Istanbul.
28. İsmet Özel, *Milli Gazete*, 9 May 2002.
29. Ibid
30. Ibid.
31. Interview with İsmet Özel, July 2003, Istanbul.
32. Interview with İsmet Özel, July 2003, Istanbul.
33. Gale Stokes, 'How is Nationalism Related to Capitalism? A Review Article', *Comparative Studies in Society and History*, Cambridge University Press 1986, p. 593.

34. Ernest Gellner, 'Nations and Nationalism', in Gale Stokes (ed.) 'How is Nationalism Related to Capitalism? *A Review* Article', *Comparative Studies in Society and History*, Cambridge University Press, 1986, p. 594.
35. Charles Tilly, Book Review, 'Nations and Nationalism', *The Journal of Modern History*, 1985, p. 528.
36. Interview with İsmet Özel, July 2003, Istanbul.
37. Interview with İsmet Özel, July 2003, Istanbul.
38. Interview with Rasim Özdenören, July 2003, Istanbul.
39. Ali Bulaç, *Din ve Modernizm*, p. 271.
40. İsmet Özel, *Cuma Mektupları 1*, p. 152.
41. Ibid., p. 153.
42. 'Ummah' means the community of Muslims.
43. İsmet Özel, *Neyi Kaybettiğini Hatırla* (Remember What You Forget) Şule Yayınları, Nisan 2000, p. 88.
44. Ibid., p. 89.
45. Ibid., p. 89.
46. Abdurrahman Dilipak, *Vakit*, 25 February 2004.
47. Ali Bulaç, *İslam ve Fanatizm*, p. 98.
48. İsmet Özel, *Cuma Mektupları 1*, p. 154.
49. Ali Bulaç, *Din ve Modernizm*, p. 120.
50. Ibid., p. 120.
51. Ibid., p. 120.
52. Ali Bulaç, *Bir Aydın Sapması*, p. 15.
53. Ersin Gürdoğan, *Günler Akarken*, p. 94.
54. Ali Bulaç, *Din ve Modernizm*, p. 91
55. Abdurrahman Dilipak, *Vakit*, 23 February 2004.
56. Ali Bulaç, *Din ve Modernizm*,. p. 95.
57. Ersin Gürdoğan, *Günler Akarken*, p. 95.
58. Ali Bulaç, *İslam ve Demokrasi*, pp. 136–7.
59. Ibid., p. 137.
60. Ibid., p.138.
61. Ibid., p. 143.
62. Ibid., p. 25.
63. Ali Bulaç, *Din, Devlet ve Demokrasi*, p. 35.
64. Ali Bulaç, *Modern Ulus Devlet*, p. 25.
65. Ali Bulaç, *Din, Devlet ve Demokrasi*, p. 133.
66. Ibid., p. 154.
67. Ali Bulaç, *Din, Devlet ve Demokrasi*, p. 133.
68. Ibid., p.133.
69. Ibid., p. 151.
70. Ibid., p. 138.

71. The Medina Charter is explained in the Oxford Encyclopedia of Islam as 'a contract between Muhammad, the prophet and statesman, and his Muslim/Jewish community (ummah), 'peoples of the book,' (ahl-al kitab, monotheists with a revealed scripture), who enjoyed freedom of worship in return for loyalty and a payment of a poll-tax (jizyah).'
72. Ali Bulaç, *Din, Devlet ve Demokrasi*, p. 225.
73. Adamec, Ludwig, *Historical Dictionary of Islam*, Rowman & Littlefield Publishers, Inc, March 2001, p. 181.
74. Ali Bulaç, *Sözleşme Temelinde Toplumsal Proje* (Social Project on the Basis of Contract) *Birikim*, Vols 38–9, June–July 1992, p. 62.
75. Ali Bulaç, *İslam ve Demokrasi*, p. 162.
76. Ibid., p. 163.
77. Ali Bulaç, 'Sözleşme Temelinde Toplumsal Proje', p. 62.
78. Ali Bulaç, *İslam ve Demokrasi*, pp. 174–5.
79. Ali Bulaç, *İslam Düşüncesinde Din–Felsefe/Vahiy–Akıl İlişkisi* (The Relation of Religion–Philosophy/Revelation–Reason in the Islamic Thought) İz Yayıncılık, 1995, p. 113.
80. Ersin Gürdoğan, *Kültür ve Sanayileşme*, p. 28.
81. Ibid., p. 29.
82. Ibid., p. 29.
83. Ibid. p. 29.
84. Ersin Gürdoğan, *Teknolojinin Ötesi* (Beyond Technology) İz Yayıncılık, 2003, p. 68.
85. Ali Bulaç, *İslam Dünyasında Düşünce Sorunları*, p. 39.
86. Ibid., p. 37.
87. Ali Bulaç, *Nuh'un Gemisine Binmek*, p. 193.
88. Ibid., p. 213.
89. İlhan Kutluer, *Modern Bilimin Arka Planı*, p. 31.
90. Ali Bulaç, *İslam ve Fundamentalizm*, p. 141.
91. Ali Bulaç, *Çağdaş Kavramlar ve Düzenler*, p. 180.
92. Ersin Gürdoğan, *Teknolojinin Ötesi*, p. 68.
93. Ali Bulaç, *İslam ve Fundamentalizm*, p. 27.
94. Ibid., p. 179.
95. İlhan Kutluer, *Modern Bilimin Arka Planı*, p. 29.
96. Ersin Gürdoğan, *Kültür ve Sanayileşme*, p. 28.
97. Ibid., p. 29.
98. Ibid., p. 29.
99. Ali Bulaç, *Kutsala, Tarihe ve Hayata Donüş*, p. 262.
100. İlhan Kutluer, *Modern Bilimin Arka Planı*, pp. 185–6.
101. Ibid., p. 179.
102. Ibid., p. 180.

103. Rasim Özdenören, *Müslümanca Düşünme Üzerine Denemeler* (Essays on Thinking as a Muslim) İz Yayıncılık, 2002, p. 16.
104. Abdurrahman Dilipak, *Vakit*, 13 February 2004.
105. İlhan Kutluer, *Modern Bilimin Arka Planı*, p. 45.
106. Ibid., p. 46.
107. Ali Bulaç, *İnsanın Özgürlük Arayışı*, p. 52.
108. Ibid., p. 18.
109. Ali Bulaç, *Nuh'un Gemisine Binmek*, p. 137.
110. Ibid., pp. 137–8.
111. Ali Bulaç, *Çağdaş Kavramlar ve Düzenler*, p. 179.
112. Ibid., p. 181.
113. İsmet, Özel, *Vel'l Asr*, p. 63.
114. Ibid., p. 64.
115. Ali Bulaç, *Kutsala, Tarihe ve Hayata Donüş*, p. 96.
116. Ali Bulaç, *İslam ve Fundamentalizm*, p. 97.
117. Ibid., p. 97.
118. Ibid., p. 101.
119. Ali Bulaç, *İnsanın Özgürlük Arayışı*, p. 51.
120. Ersin Gürdoğan, *Kültür ve Sanayileşme*, p. 49.
121. Interview with Ali Bulaç, June 2003, Istanbul.
122. Ersin Gürdoğan, *Kültür ve Sanayileşme*, p. 41.
123. Ali Bulaç, *Nuh'un Gemisine Binmek*, p. 175.
124. Ali Bulaç, *Din ve Modernizm*, p. 22.
125. Interview with Ersin Gürdoğan, June 2003, Istanbul.
126. Ersin Gürdoğan, *Kültür ve Sanayileşme*, p. 40.
127. Interview with Ali Bulaç, June 2003, Istanbul.
128. Ersin Gürdoğan, *Kültür ve Sanayileşme*, p. 40.
129. Ibid., p.41.
130. Interview with Ersin Gürdoğan, June 2003, Istanbul.
131. Ersin Gürdoğan, *Kültür ve Sanayileşme*, p. 45.
132. Rasim Özdenören, *Müslümanca Düşünme Üzerine Denemeler*, p. 15.
133. İsmet Özel, *Üç Mesele*, pp. 151, 187.
134. Rasim Özdenören, *Yaşadığımız Günler* (Days We Live In) İz Yayıncılık, 1999, p. 142.
135. Ibid., p. 143.
136. Ersin Gürdoğan, *Kültür ve Sanayileşme*, p. 47.
137. Ersin Gürdoğan, *Kirlenmenin Boyutları*, p. 141.
138. Ali Bulaç, *Din ve Modernizm*, pp. 53, 61.
139. İsmet Özel, *Üç Mesele*, p. 187.
140. Ersin Gürdoğan, *Yeni Roma* (New Rome) İz Yayıncılık, 2003, p. 13.
141. Rasim Özdenören, *Müslümanca Düşünme Üzerine Denemeler*, p. 15.

142. Ali Bulaç, *Nuh'un Gemisine Binmek*, p. 30.
143. İlhan Kutluer, *Modern Bilimin Arka Planı*, pp. 186–7.
144. Abdurrahman Dilipak, *Laisizm*, p. 97.
145. Ibid., p. 94.
146. Ibid. p. 97.
147. İsmet Ozel, *Cuma Mektupları 1*, pp. 121–2.
148. Ibid., p. 122.
149. Ali Bulaç, *Çağdaş Kavramlar ve Düzenler*, p. 137.
150. Ali Bulaç, *İslam ve Fanatizm*, p. 74.
151. Ali Bulaç, *İslam ve Fundamentalizm*, p. 210.
152. Ibid., p. 16.
153. Ibid., p. 236.
154. Ibid., p. 236.
155. Abdurrahman Dilipak, *Laisizm*, p. 94.
156. Ali Bulaç, *Tarih, Toplum ve Gelenek* (History, Society and Tradition) İz Yayıncılık, 1997, p. 189.
157. Rasim Özdenören, *Müslümanca Yaşamak*, p. 118.
158. Rasim Özdenören, *Müslümanca Düşünme Üzerine Denemeler*, p. 33.
159. Ali Bulaç, *İnsanın Özgürlük Arayışı*, p. 136.
160. Ibid., p. 136.
161. Abdurrahman Dilipak, *Laisizm*, p. 95.
162. Ibid., p. 95.
163. Ali Bulaç, *İnsanın Özgürlük Arayışı*, p. 134.
164. İsmet Özel, *Cuma Mektupları 1*, pp. 119–21.
165. *Ali Bulaç, Din ve Modernizm*, p. 311.
166. Ibid., p. 311.
167. Ibid., p. 311.
168. Ibid., p. 72.
169. Ibid., p. 311.
170. Ibid., p. 311.
171. Ibid., p. 311.
172. Rasim Özdenören, *Yeniden İnanmak*, p. 82.
173. Ibid., p. 82.
174. Ibid., p. 82.
175. Ibid., p. 82.
176. Ibid., p. 82.
177. Ibid., p. 82.
178. Ibid., p. 82.
179. Ali Bulaç, *Din, Devlet ve Demokrasi*, p. 92.
180. Ibid., p. 92.
181. Rasim Özdenören, *Yumurtayı Hangi Ucundan Kırmalı?* p. 114.

182. Ibid., p. 114.
183. Ibid., p. 114.
184. Ibid., p.115.
185. Ali Bulaç, *Din ve Modernizm*, p. 264.
186. Ibid., p. 304.
187. Ibid., p. 275.
188. Ibid., p. 267.
189. Ibid., p. 304.
190. Ernest Gellner, *Postmodernism, Reason and Religion*, London, Routledge, 1992, p. 5.
191. Ibid., pp. 6–9.
192. Ali Bulaç, *Kutsala, Tarihe ve Hayata Dönüş*, p. 16.
193. Ibid., p. 15.
194. Ibid., p. 15.
195. Rasim Özdenören, *Müslümanca Yaşamak*, p. 74.
196. Ersin Gürdoğan, *Erdemli Tolum ve Düşmanları*, p. 55.
197. Ali Bulaç, *İslam ve Fundamentalizm*, p. 147.
198. Ibid., p. 147.
199. Interview with Ersin Gürdoğan, June 2003, Istanbul.
200. Ali Bulaç, *İslam ve Fundamentalizm*, p. 93.
201. İlhan Kutluer, *Sarp Yokuşu Tırmanmak* (The Steep Ascend) İz Yayıncılık, 1998, p. 143.
202. Ali Bulaç, *Nuh'un Gemisine Binmek*, p. 163.
203. Ibid., p. 163.
204. Ibid., p. 253.
205. Rasim Özdenören, *Müslümanca Yaşamak*, p. 18.
206. Ibid., p. 18.
207. Ali Bulaç, *İslam ve Fundamentalizm*, p. 229.
208. Interview with Ali Bulaç, June 2003, Istanbul.
209. Ali Bulaç, *Nuh'un Gemisine Binmek*, p. 82.
210. Ibid., p. 83.
211. Ali Bulaç, *İslam ve Fundamentalizm*, p. 115.
212. Ali Bulaç, *Modernizm, İrtica ve Sivilleşme* (Modernism, Fundamentalism and Civil Society) İz Yayıncılık, 1995, p. 53.
213. Ali Bulaç, *İslam ve Fundamentalizm*, p. 114.
214. Ibid., p. 82.
215. Ibid., p. 82.
216. Ibid., p. 83.
217. Ibid., p. 93.
218. Ibid., p. 93.
219. Ibid., p. 93.

220. Ali Bulaç, *Ÿslam ve Fanatizm*, p. 46.
221. Ibid., p. 46.
222. Ali Bulaç, *Çağdaş Kavramlar ve Düzenler*, p. 164.
223. Ali Bulaç, *İslam ve Demokrasi*, p. 164.
224. Rasim Özdenören, *Müslümanca Yaşamak*, p. 19.
225. Ibid., p. 19.
226. İsmet Özel, *Üç Mesele*, p. 79.
227. Ali Bulaç, *Çağdaş Kavramlar ve Düzenler*, p. 161.
228. Ali Bulaç, *İslam ve Fundamentalizm*, p. 153.
229. Ali Bulaç, *İslam Dünyasında Toplumsal Değişme* (The Social Change in the Islamic World) İz Yayıncılık, 1995, p. 234.
230. Rasim Özdenören, *Müslümanca Yaşamak*, p. 55.
231. Ali Bulaç, *Din ve Modernizm*, p. 264.
232. Ali Bulaç, *İslam ve Fundamentalizm*, p. 232.
233. Ali Bulaç, *İslam Dünyasında Toplumsal Değişme*, p. 236.
234. Rasim Özdenören, *Yaşadığımız Günler*, p. 13.
235. Ibid., p. 13.
236. Terence Ball, 'History: Critique and Irony, The Cambridge Companion to Marx', in Terrell Carver (ed.) Cambridge University Press, 1991, p.127.
237. Erik Olin Wright, Review Article, 'Is Marxism Really Functionalist, Class Reductionist, and Teleological?' *The American Journal of Sociology*, Vol. 89, 1983.
238. Rasim Özdenören, *Yaşadığımız Günler*, p. 13.
239. Ibid., p. 13.
240. Ali Bulaç, *Tarih, Toplum ve Gelenek*, p. 239.
241. Ibid., p. 77.
242. Ali Bulaç, *İnsanın Özgürlük Arayışı*, p. 50.
243. Rasim Özdenören, *Yaşadığımız Günler*, p. 13.
244. Ali Bulaç, *İnsanın Özgürlük Arayışı*, p. 50.
245. Ibid. p. 50.
246. Ibid., p. 51.
247. Ali Bulaç, *Tarih, Toplum ve Gelenek*, p. 270.
248. Ibid., p. 271.
249. Ibid., p. 82.
250. Ibid., p. 78.
251. Ibid., p. 266.
252. Ibid., p. 266.
253. Ali Bulaç, *Kutsala, Tarihe ve Hayata Dönüş*, p. 262.
254. Ali Bulaç, *İslam Dünyasında Düşünce Sorunları*, p. 186.
255. Ersin Gürdoğan, *Kültür ve Sanayileşme*, p. 49.

256. Ali Bulaç, *Din ve Modernizm*, p. 310.
257. Ali Bulaç, *İslam Dünyasında Düşünce Sorunları*, p. 103.
258. Ibid., p. 103.

Chapter 4

1. Ibrahim M. Abu Rabi, *Intellectual Origins of Islamic Resurgence in the Modern Arab World*, State University of New York Press, 1996, p. 9.
2 Ibid., p. 9.
3. John L. Esposito and John O. Voll, *Makers of Contemporary Islam*, Oxford University Press, 2001, p. 12.
4. Ibid., p. 16.
5. Hisham Sharabi, *Arab Intellectuals and the West: The Formative Years, 1875–1914*, Baltimore, John Hopkins Press, 1970, p. 3.
6. John L. Esposito and John O. Voll, *Makers of Contemporary Islam*, p. 12.
7. Ibid., p. 17.
8. Ibid., p. 17.
9. Abdallah Laroui, 'The Crisis of Arab Intelligentsia: Traditionalism or Historicism?' in Ibrahim Abu Rabi (ed.) *Intellectual Origins of Islamic Resurgence in the Modern Arab World*, State University of New York Press, 1996, p. 6.
10. Ibrahim M. Abu Rabi, *Intellectual Origins of Islamic Resurgence in the Modern Arab World*, p. 9.
11. Ibid., p. 9.
12. Ibid., p. 9.
13. Ibid., p. 9.
14. Ibid., p. 6.
15. John L.Esposito and John O. Voll, *Makers of Contemporary Islam*, p. 15.
16. Ira M. Lapidus, *A History of Islamic Societies*, Cambridge University Press, 2002, p. 517.
17. Ibid., p. 517.
18. Ibid. p. 517.
19. Ibid., p. 517.
20. Derek Hopwood, 'The Culture of Modernity in Islam and the Middle East', in John Cooper, Mohamed Mahmoud and Ronald Nettler (eds) *Islam and Modernity, Muslim Intellectuals Respond*, I.B.Tauris & Co Ltd, 2000, p. 5.
21. Ira M. Lapidus, *A History of Islamic Societies*, p. 517.
22. Ibid. p. 517.
23. Ibid. p. 517.
24. Ludwig W. Adamec, *Historical Dictionary of Islam*, p. 24.

25. Ibid., p. 518.
26. Derek Hopwood, 'The Culture of Modernity in Islam and the Middle East', in John Cooper, Mohamed Mahmoud and Ronald Nettler (eds) *Islam and Modernity, Muslim Intellectuals Respond*, I.B.Tauris & Co Ltd, 2000, p. 6.
27. Ibid., p. 6.
28. Albert Hourani, *A History of the Arab Peoples*, The Belknap Press of Harvard University Press, 1991, p. 308.
29. John L. Esposito and John O. Voll, *Makers of Contemporary Islam*, p. 19.
30. Ibrahim M. Abu Rabi, *Intellectual Origins of Islamic Resurgence in the Modern Arab World*, p. 64.
31. John L. Esposito and John O. Voll, *Makers of Contemporary Islam*, p. 19.
32. Ibrahim M. Abu Rabi, *Intellectual Origins of Islamic Resurgence in the Modern Arab World*, p. 38.
33. Ibid., p. 13.
34. Ibid., p. 70.
35. Hasan al-Banna, 'Mudhakarat' translated by Harris, 'Nationalism and Revolution', in Ibrahim Abu Rabi (ed.) *Intellectual Origins of Islamic Resurgence in the Modern Arab World*, State University of New York Press, p. 65.
36. Derek Hopwood, 'The Culture of Modernity in Islam and the Middle East', pp. 6–7.
37. Ibid., p. 7.
38. Ibid., p. 7.
39. Ibrahim M. Abu Rabi, *Intellectual Origins of Islamic Resurgence in the Modern Arab World*, p. 93.
40. Ibid., p. 94.
41. Ibrahim M. Abu Rabi, *Intellectual Roots of Islamic Revivalism in the Modern Arab World*, The Message International, February 1992, p. 13.
42. Ira M. Lapidus, *A History of Islamic Societies*, p. 523.
43. Yvonne Y. Haddad, 'Sayyid Qutb', in Ibrahim Abu Rabi (ed.) *Intellectual Origins of Islamic Resurgence in the Modern Arab World*, State University of New York Press, 1996, p. 165.
45. Ibid., p. 148.
46. Ibid., p. 148.
47. Ira M. Lapidus, *A History of Islamic Societies*, p. 645.
48. Ludwig W. Adamec, *Historical Dictionary of Islam*, p. 148.
49. Ibrahim M. Abu Rabi, *Contemporary Arab Thought Studies in Post 1967 Arab Intellectual History*, Pluto Press, 2004, p. 17.
50. Ibid., p. 16.
51. Ibid., p. 13.
52. Ibrahim M. Abu Rabi, Review Article, 'Issues in Contemporary Arab

Thought: Cultural Decolonization and the Challenges of the 21st Century', *Intellectual Discourse*, Vol. 5, No. 2, 1997, pp. 169–78.

53. John L. Esposito, *The Islamic Threat Myth or Reality*, Oxford University Press, 1992, p. 12.
54. Ibid., pp. 12, 14–15.
55. Ibrahim M. Abu Rabi, *Contemporary Arab Thought Studies in Post 1967 Arab Intellectual History*, p. 10.
56. Mehrzad Boroujerdi, *Iranian Intellectuals and the West The Tormented Triumph of Nativism*, Syracuse University Press, 1996, p. 113.
57. Ibid., p. 110.
58. Ibid., p. 111.
59. Ali Shari'ati, 'What Is to Be Done: The Enlightened Thinkers and an Islamic Renaissance', in Mehrzad Boroujerdi (ed.) *Iranian Intellectuals and the West The Tormented Triumph of Nativism*, Syracuse University Press, 1996, p. 115.
60. Ali Mirsepassi, *Intellectual Discourse and the Politics of Modernization Negotiating Modernity in Iran*, Cambridge University Press, 2000, p. 116.
61. Ali Rahnema, *An Islamic Utopian A Political Biography of Ali Shari'ati*, I.B.Tauris & Co Ltd, 2000, p. 287.
62. Ali Mirsepassi, *Intellectual Discourse and the Politics of Modernization Negotiating Modernity in Iran*, p. 122.
63. http://www.cis-ca.org/voices/a/arkoun-mn.htm
64. http://www.iis.ac.uk/research/academic_publications/arkoun.htm
65. Ibid.
66. http://www.islam21.net/pages/confrences/june99–1.htm
67. Muhammed Arkoun, *The Unthought in Contemporary Islamic Thought*, Saqi Books, 2002, p. 30.
68. Robert D. Lee, *Overcoming Tradition and Modernity The Search for Islamic Authenticity*, Westview Press, 1997, p. 152.
69. Muhammed Arkoun, *Rethinking Islam Common Questions, Uncommon Answers*, Westview Press, 1994, p. 1.
70. Robert D. Lee, *Overcoming Tradition and Modernity: The Search for Islamic Authenticity*, p. 152. Arkoun states his desire as: 'My ambition was to emancipate Islamic thought from the historiographical, theological framework developed and propogated during the Classical Islamic period, and was, from the thirteenth century onwards, fragmented and impoverished by Muslim scholasticism, then reactivated later in a linear, narrative, descriptive transcription by classical Orientalist erudition'.
71. Muhammed Arkoun, 'Critique', in Robert D. Lee (ed.) *Overcoming Tradition and Modernity The Search for Islamic Authenticity*, Westview Press, 1994, p. 152.

72. Muhammed Arkoun, *The Unthought in Contemporary Islamic Thought*, p. 248.
73. Ibid., p. 249.
74. http://www.islam21.net/pages/confrences/june99–1.htm
75. Muhammed Arkoun, *Rethinking Islam Common Questions, Uncommon Answers*, p.13. He enunciates his position towards modernity in the following way: 'I am careful about modernity. Many people think I am supporting modernity and secularism as an alternative to get rid of religious traditions. This is absolutely wrong. This is not my position. And many from the left side who are supporting modernity say just the opposite. Arkoun is just a reformist like all Muslims. He is going back to very ancient texts and trying to teach us something which is over and is an obstacle to modernity and secularism.'
76. Muhammed Arkoun, 'Morale et Politique', in Robert D. Lee (ed.) *Overcoming Tradition and Modernity The Search for Islamic Authenticity*, p. 155.
77. Muhammed Arkoun, *Rethinking Islam Common Questions, Uncommon Answers*, p. x.
78. Ibid., p. x.
79. http://www.islam21.net/pages/conferences/june99–1.htm; Muhammed Arkoun, *The Unthought in Contemporary Islamic Thought*, p. 323.
80. Muhammed Arkoun, *The Unthought in Contemporary Islamic Thought*, p. 249.
81. Ibid., p. 248.
82. Ibid., pp. 248, 249.
83. Muhammed Arkoun, *The State, the Individual, and Human Rights: A Contemporary View of Muslim in a Global Context*, The Institute of Ismaili Studies, p. 1.
84. Muhammed Arkoun, *Rethinking Islam Common Questions, Uncommon Answers*, p. 113.
85. Muhammed Arkoun, *The Unthought in Contemporary Islamic Thought*, p. x.
86. http://www.islam21.net/pages/confrences/june99–1.htm
87. Muhammed Arkoun, *The Unthought in Contemporary Islamic Thought*, p. xi.
88. Lewis E. Hahn and Randall E. Auxier and Lucian W. Stone, *The Philosophy of Seyyed Hossein Nasr*, The Library of Living Philosophers Vol. 28, Southern Illinois University at Carbondale, 2001, p. 5.
89. Ibid., p. 5.
90. Ibid., p. 16.
91. Ibid., pp. 7-8.
92. Ibid., p. 793.
93. Ibid., p. 800.

94. He describes his position in the following way: 'I consider myself completely orthodox on all levels ranging from the outward aspects of religion to theology, philosophy, and Sufism and do not consider orthodoxy as understood in its universal sense to be any way opposed to intellectual creativity or universality. On the contrary I believe that only in orthodoxy can the full possibilities of the intellect be actualized.'
95. Lewis E. Hahn and Randall E. Auxier and Lucian W. Stone, *The Philosophy of Seyyed Hossein Nasr*, p. 809.
96. Ibid., p. 810.
97. Ibid., p. 810.
98. Ibid., pp. 270,810.
99. Seyyed Hossein Nasr, *The Need for a Sacred Science*, Albany, State University of New York Press, 1993, p. 54.
100. Ibid., p. 54.
101. Seyyed Hossein Nasr , 'Sufi Essays', in Lewis E. Hahn, Lucian W. Stone and Randall E. Auxier (eds) The Philosophy of Seyyed Hossein Nasr, *The Library of Living Philosophers*, Vol. 28, Southern Illinois University at Carbondale, 2001, p. 803.
102. Seyyed Hossein Nasr, *Islam and the Plight of Modern Man*, London, Longman Group Ltd., 1975, p. 10.
103. Seyyed Hossein Nasr, *Knowledge and the Sacred*, State University of New York Press, 1989, p. 130.
104. Lewis E. Hahn, Randall E. Auxier and Lucian W. Stone, *The Philosophy of Seyyed Hossein Nasr*, p. 464.
105. Seyyed Hossein Nasr, *Knowledge and the Sacred*, p. 46.
106. Ibid., p. 46.
107. Ibid., pp. 42–3.
108. Seyyed Hossein Nasr, *Islam and the Plight of Modern Man*, p. 12.
109. Seyyed Hossein Nasr, *The Need for a Sacred Science*, p. 77.
110. Seyyed Hossein Nasr, *Islam and the Plight of Modern Man*, p. 12.
111. Seyyed Hossein Nasr, *The Need for a Sacred Science*, p. 88.
112. Ibid., p. 90.
113. Ibid., p. 92.
114. Seyyed Hossein Nasr, *Islam and the Plight of Modern Man*, p. 13.
115. Seyyed Hossein Nasr, *The Need for a Sacred Science*, p. 56.
116. Lewis E. Hahn, Randall E. Auxier and Lucian W. Stone, *The Philosophy of Seyyed Hossein Nasr*, p. 463.
117. In the Historical Dictionary of Islam, Sufism is described as 'a mythical path (tariqa) or discipline that consists of graded esoteric teachings leading through a series if initiations to the status of an adept.'
118. Seyyed Hossein Nasr, *Islam and the Plight of Modern Man*, p. 58

119. Ibid., p. 58.
120. Ibid., p. 59.
121. Ibid., p. 59.
122. Interview with Seyyed Hossein Nasr, November, 2003.
123. Seyyed Hossein Nasr, *Islam and the Plight of Modern Man*, pp. 126–7, 148.
124. John Cooper, Ronald Nettler and Mohamed Mahmoud, *Islam and Modernity, Muslim Intellectuals Respond*, I.B.Tauris & Co Ltd, 2000, p. vii.
125. Nasr Abu Zaid, *Voice of an Exile Reflections on Islam/Nasr Abu Zaid with Esther R. Nelson*, Praeger Publishers, 2004, p. ix.
126. Ibid., p. ix.
127. Ibid., p. ix.
128. 'Methodological principles of textual interpretation'.
129. Nasr Abu Zaid, *Voice of an Exile Reflections on Islam/Nasr Abu Zaid with Esther R. Nelson*, p. 11.
130. Ayman Bakr, Elliot Colla and Nasr Hamid Abu Zaid, 'Silencing is at the Heart of My Case', *Middle East Report*, November–December 1993, p. 28.
131. Nasr Abu Zaid, *Voice of an Exile Reflections on Islam/Nasr Abu Zaid with Esther R. Nelson*, p. 179.
132. Ibid., p. 60.
133. Ibid., p. 100.
134. Ibid., p. 60.
135. Ibid., p. 60.
136. Ibid., p. 60
137. Ibid., pp. 100, 109, 175.
138. Ibid., p. 64.
139. Ibid., pp. 89–90.
140. Ibid., p. 167.
141. Ibid., p. 167, 174.
142. Ibid., p. 183.
143. Ibid., p. 183.
144. Ibid., p. 183.
145. Ibid., p. 207.
146. Ibid., p. 207.
147. Ibid., p. 203.
148. Ibid., p. 113.
149. Ibid., p. 113.
150. Ibid., p. 114.
151. Abdolkarim Soroush, *Reason Freedom and Democracy in Islam*, Oxford University Press, 2000, p. 20.
152. Mehrzad Boroujerdi, *Iranian Intellectuals and the West the Tormented Triumph of Nativism*, p. 158.

153. Abdolkarim Soroush, *Reason Freedom and Democracy in Islam*, p. 8.
154. Ibid., p. 10.
155. Ibid., p. 11.
156. Ibid., p. 12.
157. Mehrzad Boroujerdi, *Iranian Intellectuals and the West: The Tormented Triumph of Nativism*, p. 158.
158. Abdolkarim Soroush, *Reason Freedom and Democracy in Islam*, p. 30.
159. Ibid., p. 31.
160. Ibid., p. 34.
161. John L.Esposito and John O. Voll, *Makers of Contemporary Islam*, p. 174.
162. Abdolkarim Soroush, *Reason Freedom and Democracy in Islam*, p. 129.
163. Robin Wright, 'Iran's Greatest Political Challenge Abdolkarim Soroush', *World Policy Journal*, Summer 1997, p. 68.
164. He defines democracy as 'a method of harnessing the power of rulers, rationalizing their policies, protecting the rights of the subjects, and attaining the public good.'
165. Robin Wright, *Iran's Greatest Political Challenge Abdolkarim Soroush*, World Policy Journal, Summer 1997, p. 70. Soroush states: 'We no longer merely claim that a genuinely religious government can be democratic but that it can not be otherwise.'
166. Ibid., p. 70.
167. Ibid., p. 70.
168. Abdolkarim Soroush, *Reason Freedom and Democracy in Islam*, pp. 131–2.
169. Ibid., p. 22.
170. Ibid., p. 134.
171. Ibid., p. 134.
172. Robin Wright, 'Iran's Greatest Political Challenge Abdolkarim Soroush', p. 69.
173. John L.Esposito and John O. Voll, *Makers of Contemporary Islam*, p. 151.
174. Ibid., p. 154.
175. Abdolkarim Soroush, *Reason Freedom and Democracy in Islam*, pp. 51–2, 61.
176. Ibid., p. 57.
177. Ibid., p. 57.
178. Ibid., p. 56.
179. Michael Jansen, 'Struggle to Rescue Islam From Zealots', *Irish Times*, 22 November 1997.
180. Abdolkarim Soroush, *Reason Freedom and Democracy in Islam*, p. 195.
181. Ibid., p. 195.
182. Ibid., p. 169.

183. Ibid., p. 170.
184. John L. Esposito and John O. Voll, *Makers of Contemporary Islam*, p. 172.
185. Abdolkarim Soroush, *Reason Freedom and Democracy in Islam*, p. 169.
186. Ibrahim Abu Rabi, *Islam at the Crossroads*, State University of New York Press, 2003, p. 25.
187. Ibid., p. 10.
188. Şerif Mardin, *Religion and Social Change in Modern Turkey The Case of Bediuzzaman Said Nursi*, Albany, State University of New York Press, 1989, p. 9.
189. Ibrahim Abu Rabi, *Islam at the Crossroads*, p. 1.
190. Ibid., p. x.
191. Ibid., p. 21.
192. Ibid., p. 5.
193. Ibid., p. 6.
194. Ibid., p. 23.
195. Ibid., p. 15.
196. Said Nursi, 'Letter', in Ibrahim Abu Rabi (ed.) *Islam at the Crossroads*, State University of New York Press, 2003, p. 26.
197. Ibid., p. 16.
198. Said Nursi, 'Isaratu'l–Icaz', in Ibrahim Abu Rabi (ed.) *Islam at the Crossroads*, State University of New York Press, 2003, p. 10.
199. Bediuzzaman Said Nursi, 'Sözler', in Şerif Mardin (ed.) *Religion and Social Change in Modern Turkey The Case of Bediuzzaman Said Nursi*, Albany, State University of New York Press, 1989, p. 203.
200. Ibrahim Abu Rabi, *Islam at the Crossroads*, p. 10.
201. Said Nursi, 'Isaratu'l–Icaz', in Ibrahim Abu Rabi (ed.) *Islam at the Crossroads*, State University of New York Press, 2003, p. 10.
202. Şerif Mardin, *Religion and Social Change in Modern Turkey The Case of Bediuzzaman Said Nursi,* Albany, State University of New York Press, 1989, p. 203.
203. Ibid., p. 203.
204. Ibrahim Abu Rabi, *Islam at the Crossroads*, p. 25.
205. Ibid., p. 23.
206. Ibid., p. 22.
207. Bediuzzaman Said Nursi, in *Religion and Social Change in Modern Turkey: The Case of Bediuzzaman Said Nursi*, p. 99.
208. Ibid., p. 203.
209. Ibrahim Abu Rabi, *Islam at the Crossroads*, p. 17.
210. Ibid., p. 17.
211. Şerif Mardin, *Religion and Social Change in Modern Turkey: The Case of Bediuzzaman Said Nursi*, p. 13.

212. Necip Fazıl Kısakürek, 'O ve Ben' (He and Me), in Şerif Mardin (ed.) *Cultural Transitions in the Middle East*, p. 197.
213. Şerif Mardin, *Cultural Transitions in the Middle East*, Leiden, The Netherlands, E. J. Brill, 1994, p. 197.
214. Şerif Mardin explains that the 'Nakşibendi revival had begun in India as early as the seventeenth century but had acquired greater expansion and momentum as a reaction against Western colonialism and imperialism; and especially beginning with the nineteenth century and the travails of a Nakşibendi shaykh by the name of Mawlana Khalid (d. 1827), it affected, directly and indirectly, a number of movements of Islamic revitalization.'
215. Şerif Mardin, *Cultural Transitions in the Middle East*, p. 199.
216. Ibid., p. 199.
217. Ibid., p. 192.
218. Ibid., p. 199.
219. Ibid., p. 199.
220. Ibid., p. 200.
221. Ibid., p. 200.
222. Necip Fazıl Kısakürek, *Konuşmalar* (Conversations) Büyük Doğu Yayınları, 1999, pp. 82–128.
223. Ibid., p. 95.
224. Ibid., p. 194.
225. Necip Fazıl Kısakürek, *Dünya Bir Inkilap Bekliyor* (The World is Waiting for a Revolution) Büyük Doğu Yayınları, 2004, p. 53.
226. Necip Fazıl Kısakürek, *Çerçeve* (Framework) Büyük Doğu Yayınları, 1997, p. 104.
227. Ibid., p. 113.
228. Ibid., p. 114.
229. Ibid., p. 113.
230. Necip Fazıl Kısakürek, *Dünya Bir Inkilap Bekliyor*, p. 28.
231. Şerif Mardin, *Cultural Transitions in the Middle East*, p. 212.
232. Interview with İlhan Kutluer, June 2003, Istanbul.
233. Sezai Karakoç, *Diriliş Neslinin Amentüsü* (The Fundamentals of the Revivalist Generation) Diriliş Yayınları, 2001, p. 27.
234. Ibid., p. 29.
235. Ibid., p. 37.
236. Ibid., p. 37.
237. Ibid., p. 45.
238. Sezai Karakoç, *Günlük Yazılar 1 Farklar* (Daily Writings 1 Differences) Diriliş Yayınları, 1997, p. 58.

239. Sezai Karakoç, *Diriliş Neslinin Amentüsü* (The Fundamentals of the Revivalist Generation) Diriliş Yayınları, 1997, p. 46.
240. Ibid., p. 47.
241. Sezai Karakoç, *İslamın Dirilişi* (The Resurgence of Islam) Diriliş Yayınları, 1999, p. 32.
242. Sezai Karakoç, *Günlük Yazılar 1 Farklar*, p. 53.
243. Sezai Karakoç, *Çıkış Yolu 1 Ülkemizin Geleceği* (The Future of Our Country) Diriliş Yayınları, 2002, p. 11.
244. Sezai Karakoç, *İslamın Dirilişi*, p. 33.
245. Ibid., p. 35.
246. Sezai Karakoç, *Çağ ve İlham* (The Age and Inspiration) Diriliş Yayınları, 1999, p. 75.
247. Ali Bulaç, Zaman, 6 December 2004.

Conclusion

1. Binnaz Toprak, *Religion and State in Turkey*, p. 5.
2. Ziya Öniş, *The Political Economy of Islamic Resurgence in Turkey: The Rise of the Welfare Party in Perspective.*
3. Ali Bulaç, *Nuh'un Gemisine Binmek*, p. 37.
4. Ibid., p. 43.
5. Ali Bulaç, *İslam Dünyasında Toplumsal Değişme*, p. 236.
6. Michael Meeker, 'The Muslim Intellectual and His Audience: A New Configuration of Writer and Reader Among Believers in the Republic of Turkey', in Dale F. Eickelman (ed.) *Knowledge and Power in Morocco*, Princeton University Press, 1985, p. 154.
7. Nilüfer Göle, 'Secularism and Islamism in Turkey: The Making of Elites and Counter-Elites', p. 54.
8. Şerif Mardin, *Cultural Transitions in the Middle East*, E. J. Brill, 1994, p. 212.
9. Ibid., p. 212.

Bibliography

Abu Rabi, M. Ibrahim. *Intellectual Roots of Islamic Revivalism in the Modern Arab World*, The Message International, February 1992

— *Intellectual Origins of Islamic Resurgence in the Modern Arab World*, State University of New York Press, 1996

— *Issues in Contemporary Arab Thought: Cultural Decolonization and the Challenges of the 21st Century, Intellectual Discourse*, Vol. 5, No. 2, 1997

— *Islam at the Crossroads*, State University of New York Press, 2003

— *Contemporary Arab Thought Studies in Post 1967 Arab Intellectual History*, Pluto Press, 2004

Abu Zaid, Nasr Hamid. *Voice of an Exile Reflections on Islam/Nasr Abu Zaid with Esther R. Nelson*, Praeger Publishers, 2004

Abu Zaid, Nasr Hamid, Ayman Bakr and Elliot Colla. *Silencing is at the Heart of My Case*, Middle East Report, November–December 1993

Adamec, W. Ludwig. *Historical Dictionary of Islam Historical Dictionaries of Religions, Philosophies, and Movements*, No. 37, The Scarecrow Press, Inc., 2001

Ahmad, Feroz. 'Politics and Islam in Modern Turkey', *Middle Eastern Studies*, vol. 27, no. 6, January 1991

Altan, Mehmet. 'Batılılaşmanın Sosyo-Politik Temelleri, Düşünsel ve Toplumsal Yapısı', in Uygur Kocabaşoğlu (ed.) *Modern Türkiye' de Siyasi Düşünce*, Vol. 3, İletişim Yayıncılık, 2002

Arkoun, Muhammed. *Rethinking Islam Common Questions, Uncommon Answers*, Westview Press, 1994

— 'Critique', in Robert D. Lee (ed.) *Overcoming Tradition and Modernity The Search for Islamic Authenticity*, Westview Press, 1994

— *The State, the Individual, and Human Rights: A Contemporary View of Muslims in a Global Context*, The Institute of Ismaili Studies, 2000

— *The Unthought in Contemporary Islamic Thought*, Saqi Books, 2002

Arsan, Nimet. *Atatürk'ün Söylev ve Demeçleri 1918–1937* (The Speech and Statements of Atatürk) Vol. 3, Ankara, Türk Tarih Kurumu Basımevi, 1961

Auxier, E. Randall, E. Lewis Hahn and W. Lucian Stone. *The Philosophy of Seyyed Hussein Nasr,* The Library of Living Philosophers, Vol. 28, Southern Illinois University at Carbondale, 2001

Ball, Terence. 'History: Critique and Irony', in Terrell Carver (ed.) *The Cambridge Companion to Marx*, Cambridge University Press, 1991

Banna, al-Hasan. 'Mudhakarat', translated by Harris, 'Nationalism and Revolution', in Ibrahim Abu Rabi (ed.) *Intellectual Origins of Islamic Resurgence in the Modern Arab World,* State University of New York Press, 1996

Belge, Murat. 'Mustafa Kemal ve Kemalizm', in Ahmet İnsel (ed.) *Modern Türkiye'de Siyasi Düşünce*, Vol. 2, İletişim Yayıncılık, 2002

Boggs, Carl. *Intellectuals and the Crisis of Modernity,* State University of New York Press, Albany, 1993

Boroujerdi, Mehrzad. *Iranian Intellectuals and the West: The Tormented Triumph of Nativism*, Syracuse University Press, 1996

Bourdieu, Pierre. 'Towards a Theory of Practice', in Roy Eyerman, Lennert G. Svensson and Thomas Soderqvist (eds) *Intellectuals, Universities and the State in Western Modern Societies*, University of California Press, 1987

Bozdoğan, Sibel and Reşat Kasaba. *Rethinking Modernity and National Identity in Turkey,* University of Washington Press, 1997

Bulaç, Ali. 'Sözleşme Temelinde Toplumsal Proje' (Social Project on the Basis of Contract), *Birikim*, Vols 38–9, June–July 1992

— *Bir Aydın Sapması Sağ ve Sol Akımlar*, İz Yayıncılık, 1995

— *Din ve Modernizm Bütün Eserleri 4*, İz Yayıncılık, 1995

— *İnsanın Özgürlük Arayışı*, İz Yayıncılık, 1995

— *İslam ve Demokrasi Bütün Eserleri 7: Teokrasi ve Totaliterizm*, İz Yayıncılık, 1995

— *İslam Dünyasında Düşünce Sorunları*, İz Yayıncılık, 1995

— *İslam ve Fanatizm Bütün Eserleri 10*, İz Yayıncılık, 1995

— *İslam Dünyasında Toplumsal Değişme*, İz Yayıncılık, 1995

— *İslam Düşüncesinde Din-Felsefe/Vahiy-Akıl İlişkisi*, İz Yayıncılık, 1995

— *Kutsala, Tarihe ve Hayata Dönüş Bütün Eserleri 3*, İz Yayıncılık, 1995

— *Modernizm, İrtica ve Sivilleşme Bütün Eserleri 6*, İz Yayıncılık, 1995

— *Nuh'un Gemisine Binmek*, İz Yayıncılık, 1995

— *Çağdaş Kavramlar ve Düzenler Bütün Eserleri 2*, İz Yayıncılık, 1997

— *İslam ve Fundamentalizm Bütün Eserleri 16*, İz Yayıncılık, 1997

— *Tarih, Toplum ve Gelenek*, İz Yayıncılık, 1997

— *Modern Ulus Devlet Bütün Eserleri 1*, İz Yayıncılık, 1998

— *Din, Devlet ve Demokrasi*, Zaman Kitap, 2001
Carver, Terrell. *The Cambridge Companion to Marx*, Cambridge University Press, 1991
Cooper, John, Mohamed Mahmoud and Ronald Nettler. *Islam and Modernity: Muslim Intellectuals Respond*, I.B.Tauris & Co Ltd, 2000
Deren, Seçil. 'Kültürel Batılılaşma', in Uygur Kocabaşoğlu (ed.) *Modern Türkiye' de Siyasi Düşünce*, Vol. 3, İletişim Yayıncılık, 2002
Dilipak, Abdurrahman. *Coğrafi Keşiflerin İçyüzü* (The Reality of Geographical Explorations), Inkılab Yayınları, 1984.
— *Laisizm*, Beyan Yayinlari, 1991
Dumont, Paul. 'The Origins of Kemalist Ideology', in Jacob Landau (ed.) *Atatürk and the Modernization of Turkey*, Westview Press, 1984
Eickelman, F. Dale. *Knowledge and Power in Morocco*, Princeton University Press, 1985
Esposito, L. John. *The Islamic Threat Myth or Reality*, Oxford University Press, 1992
Esposito, L. John and O. John Voll. *Makers of Contemporary Islam*, Oxford University Press, 2001
Eyerman, Roy, Thomas Soderqvist and G. Lennert Svensson. *Intellectuals, Universities and the State in Western Modern Societies*, University of California Press, 1987
Gay, Peter. 'The Enlightenment', in José Sanchez (ed.) *Anticlericalism: A Brief History*, University of Notre Dame Press, 1972
Gellner, Ernest, *Nations and Nationalism*, Ithaca, NY, Cornell University Press, 1983
— *Postmodernism, Reason and Religion*, Routledge, 1992
Gouldner, Alvin. *The Future of Intellectuals and the Rise of the New Class*, The Seabury Press, 1979
Göle, Nilüfer. 'Secularism and Islamism in Turkey: The Making of Elites and Counter-Elites', *Middle East Journal*, Vol. 51, Winter 1997
— 'Batı Dışı Modernlik: Kavram Üzerine', in Uygur Kocabaşoğlu (ed.) *Modern Türkiye' de Siyasi Düşünce*, Vol. 3, İletişim Yayıncılık, 2002
Gülalp, Haldun. 'Political Islam in Turkey: The Rise and Fall of the Refah Party', *Muslim World*, vol. 89, 1999
Gürdoğan, Ersin. *Kirlenmenin Boyutları*, İnsan Yayınları, 1989
— *Kültür ve Sanayileşme*, İz Yayıncılık,1991
— *Günler Akarken*, İz Yayıncılık, 1996
— *Zamanı Aşan Şehirler*, İz Yayıncılık,1997
— *Teknolojinin Ötesi*, İz Yayıncılık, 2003
— *Yeni Roma*, İz Yayıncılık, 2003

Haddad, Yvonne. 'Sayyid Qutb', in Ibrahim Abu Rabi (ed.) *Intellectual Origins of Islamic Resurgence in the Modern Arab World*, State University of New York Press, 1996

Hanioğlu, Şükrü *The Young Turks in Opposition*, Oxford University Press, 1995

Holub, Renate. *Antonio Gramsci: Beyond Marxism and Postmodernism*, Routledge, 1992

Hopwood, Derek. 'The Culture of Modernity in Islam and the Middle East', in John Cooper, Mohamed Mahmoud and Ronald Nettler (eds) *Islam and Modernity, Muslim Intellectuals Respond*, I.B.Tauris & Co Ltd, 2000

Hourani, Albert. *A History of the Arab Peoples*, The Belknap Press of Harvard University Press, 1991

Huntington, Samuel P. 'Political Development and Political Decay', *World Politics*, Vol. 17, No. 3, April 1965

— 'The Change to Change: Modernization, Development, and Politics', *Comparative Politics*, Vol. 3, No. 3, April 1971

Huszar, Tibor. 'Changes in the concept of intellectuals', in Alexander Gella (ed.) *The Intelligentsia and the Intellectuals: Theory, Method and Case Study*, London, Sage, 1976

İnsel, Ahmet. 'Introduction', in Ahmet İnsel (ed.) *Modern Türkiye'de Siyasi Düşünce*, Vol. 2, İletişim Yayıncılık, 2002

Jansen, Michael. 'Struggle to Rescue Islam from Zealots', *Irish Times*, 22 November 1997

Jennings, Jeremy and Anthony Kemp-Welch. *Intellectuals in Politics: From the Dreyfus Affair to Salman Rushdie*, Routledge, 1997

Johnson, Paul. *Intellectuals*, Harper & Row, 1988

Kaliber, Alper. 'Türk Modernleşmesini Sorunsallaştıran Üç Ana Paradigma Üzerine', in Uygur Kocabaşoğlu (ed.) *Modern Türkiye' de Siyasi Düşünce*, Vol. 3, İletişim Yayıncılık, 2002

Karakoç, Sezai. *Günlük Yazılar 1 Farklar*, Diriliş Yayınları, 1997

— *İslamın Dirilişi*, Diriliş Yayınları, 1999

— *Çağ ve İlham*, Diriliş Yayınları, 1999

— *Diriliş Neslinin Amentüsü*, Diriliş Yayınları, 2001

— *Çıkış Yolu 1 Ülkemizin Geleceği*, Diriliş Yayınları, 2002

Karpat, H. Kemal. *Turkey's Politics: The Transition to a Multi-Party System*, Princeton University Press, 1959

Keyder, Çağlar. 'The Political Economy of Turkish Democracy', in Ertuğrul A. Tonak and Irvin C. Schick (eds) *Turkey in Transition: New Perspectives*, Oxford University Press, 1987

— 'Whither the Project of Modernity? Turkey in the 1990s', in Reşat Kasaba and Sibel Bozdoğan (eds) *Rethinking Modernity and National Identity in Turkey*, University of Washington Press, 1997
Kısakürek, Necip Fazıl. *Çerçeve*, Büyük Doğu Yayınları, 1997
— *Konuşmalar*, Büyük Doğu Yayınları, 1999
— *Dünya Bir İnkılap Bekliyor*, Büyük Doğu Yayınları, 2003
— *O ve Ben*, Büyük Doğu Yayınları, 2004
Konrad, George and Ivan Szelenyi. *The Intellectuals on the Road to Class Power*, New York, Harcourt Brace Jovanovich, 1979
Kramer, Heinz. *A Changing Turkey*, Brookings Institution Press, 2000
Kutluer, İlhan. *Modern Bilimin Arka Planı,* İnsan Yayinlari, 1985
— *Erdemli Toplum ve Düşmanları*, İz Yayıncılık, 1996
— *Sarp Yokuşu Tırmanmak*, İz Yayıncılık, 1998
Küçük, Yalçın. *Cumhuriyet Dönemi Türkiye Ansiklopedisi*, İstanbul, İletişim Yayınları, 1983
Landau, M. Jacob. *Atatürk and the Modernization of Turkey*, Westview Press, 1984
Lapidus, M. Ira. *A History of Islamic Societies*, Cambridge University Press, 2002
Laroui, Abdallah. 'The Crisis of Arab Intelligentsia: Traditionalism or Historicism?' in Ibrahim Abu Rabi (ed.) *Intellectual Origins of Islamic Resurgence in the Modern Arab World*, State University of New York Press, 1996
Lee, D. Robert. *Overcoming Tradition and Modernity: The Search for Islamic Authenticity*, Westview Press, 1997
Lerner, Daniel. *Passing of Traditional Society: Modernizing the Middle East*, Free Press, 1958
Lewis, Bernard. *The Emergence of Modern Turkey*, Oxford University Press, 1961
Mardin, Şerif. 'Religion and Secularism in Turkey', in Ali Kazancigil and Ergun Özbudun, *Atatürk: The Founder of a Modern State*, London, C. Hurst, 1981
— *Jön Türklerin Siyasi Fikirleri 1895–1908*, İletişim Yayıncılık, 1983
— 'Religion and Politics in Modern Turkey' in James Piscatori (ed.) *Islam in the Political Process*, Cambridge University Press, 1983
— *Religion and Social Change in Modern Turkey: The Case of Bediuzzaman Said Nursi*, Albany, State University of New York Press, 1989
— *Cultural Transitions in the Middle East*, Leiden, E. J. Brill, 1994
— 'Projects as Methodology Some Thoughts on Modern', in Reşat Kasaba and Sibel Bozdoğan (eds) *Rethinking Modernity and National Identity in Turkey*, University of Washington Press, 1997

— *The Genesis of Young Ottoman Thought: A Study in the Modernization of Turkish Political Ideas,* Syracuse University Press, 2000

Meeker, Michael. 'The Muslim Intellectual and his Audience: A New Configuration of Writer and Reader Among Believers in the Republic of Turkey', in Dale F. Eickelman (ed.) *Knowledge and Power in Morocco*, Princeton University Press, 1985

— 'The New Muslim Intellectuals in the Republic of Turkey', in Richard Tapper (ed.) *Islam in Modern Turkey: Religion, Politics and Literature in a Secular State*, St Martin's Press, 1991

Meriç, Cemil, in Murat Belge (ed.) *Cumhuriyet Dönemi Türkiye Ansiklopedisi*, İletişim Yayınları, Vol. 1, 1983.

Mert, Nuray. 'Cumhuriyet Türkiye'sinde Laiklik ve Karşı Laikliğin Düşünsel Boyutu', in Ahmet İnsel (ed.) *Modern Türkiye'de Siyasi Düşünce*, Vol. 2, İletişim Yayıncılık, 2002

Mirsepassi, Ali. *Intellectual Discourse and the Politics of Modernization Negotiating Modernity in Iran*, Cambridge University Press, 2000

Nasr, Seyyed Hossein. *Islam and the Plight of Modern Man*, Longman Group Ltd, London, 1975

— *Knowledge and The Sacred*, State University of New York Press, 1989

— *The Need for a Sacred Science*, State University of New York Press, 1993

— Nasr, Seyyed Hossein. 'Sufi Essays', in Lewis E. Hahn, Lucian W. Stone and Randall E. Auxier (eds) *The Philosophy of Seyyed Hossein Nasr*, The Library of Living Philosophers, Vol. 28, Southern Illinois University at Carbondale, 2001

Nursi, Bediuzzaman Said. 'Sözler', in Şerif Mardin (ed.) *Religion and Social Change in Modern Turkey The Case of Bediuzzaman Said Nursi*, Albany, State University of New York Press, 1989

— 'Letter', in Ibrahim Abu Rabi (ed.) *Islam at the Crossroads*, State University of New York Press, 2003

— 'Isaratu'l–Icaz', in Ibrahim Abu Rabi (ed.) *Islam at the Crossroads*, State University of New York Press, 2003

Öniş, Ziya. 'The Political Economy of Islamic Resurgence in Turkey: The Rise of the Welfare Party in Perspective', *Third World Quarterly*, Vol. 18 no. 4, 1997

Özay, Mehmet. 'Turkey in Crisis: Some Contradictions in the Kemalist Development Strategy', *International Journal of Middle East Studies*, Vol. 15, No. 1, February 1983

Özbudun, Ergun and Ali Kazancigil. *Atatürk: The Founder of A Modern State*, London, C. Hurst, 1981

Özdenören, Rasim. *Çapraz İlişkiler Bütün Eserleri – 19*, İz Yayıncılık, 1997

— *Kafa Karıştıran Kelimeler Bütün Eserleri* 2, İz Yayıncılık, 1997

— *Müslümanca Yaşamak Bütün Eserleri 3*, İz Yayıncılık, 1998
— *Yeni Dünya Düzenin Sefaleti Bütün Eserleri 11*, İz Yayıncılık, 1998
— *Yaşadığımız Günler, Bütün Eserleri 4*, İz Yayıncılık, 1999
— *Yeniden İnanmak, Bütün Eserleri 14*, İz Yayıncılık, 1999
— *Yumurtayı Hangi Ucundan Kırmalı, Bütün Eserleri 5*, İz Yayıncılık, 1999
— *Müslümanca Düşünme Üzerine Denemeler*, İz Yayıncılık, 2002
Özel, İsmet. *Bakanlar ve Görenler Bütün Eserleri 5*, Şule Yayınları; 1996
— *Cuma Mektupları 1*, Şule Yayınları, 1998
— *İrtica Elden Gidiyor Bütün Eserleri 7*, Şule Yayınları; 1998
— *Üç Mesele Bütün Eserleri 1 Teknik-Medeniyet-Yabancılaşma*, Şule Yayınları, 1998
— *Neyi Kaybettiğini Hatırla*, Şule Yayınları, Nisan 2000
— *Cuma Mektupları 8*, Şule Yayınları, 2002
— *Cuma Mektupları 9*, Şule Yayınları, 2003
— *Vel'l Asr*, Şule Yayınları, 2003
Parla, Taha. 'Kemalizm, Türk Aydınlanması mı?', in Ahmet İnsel (ed.) *Modern Türkiye'de Siyasi Düşünce*, Vol. 2, İletişim Yayıncılık, 2002
Qutb, Sayyid, 'Dirasat Islamiyyah' (Islamic Studies), in Lamia Rustum Shehadeh (ed.) *The Idea of Women Under Fundamentalist Islam*, University Press of Florida, 2003
Rahnema, Ali. *An Islamic Utopian: A Political Biography of Ali Shari'ati*, I.B.Tauris, 2000
Sahliyeh, Emile. *Religious Resurgence and Politics in the Contemporary World*, State University of New York Press, 1990
Sakallioğlu, U. Cizre. 'Parameters and Strategies of Islam-State Interaction in Republican Turkey', *International Journal of Middle East Studies*, Vol. 28, 1996
Schick, C. Irvin and A. Ertuğrul Tonak. *Turkey in Transition: New Perspectives*, Oxford University Press, 1987
Schumpeter, Joseph. *Capitalism, Socialism, and Democracy*, New York, Harper & Row, 1950
Sharabi, Hisham. *Arab Intellectuals and the West: The Formative Years, 1875–1914*, Baltimore: John Hopkins Press, 1970
Shari'ati, Ali. 'What Is to Be Done: The Enlightened Thinkers and an Islamic Renaissance', in Mehrzad Boroujerdi (ed.) *Iranian Intellectuals and the West: The Tormented Triumph of Nativism*, Syracuse University Press, 1996
Shaw, Ezel Kural and J. Stanford Shaw. *History of the Ottoman Empire and Modern Turkey*, Volume II, *Reform, Revolution and Republic: The Rise of Modern Turkey, 1808–1975*, Cambridge University Press, 1977

Shehadeh, R. Lamia. *The Idea of Women in Fundamentalist Islam*, University Press of Florida, 2003

Shills, Edward. 'Intellectuals', in David L. Sills (ed.) *International Encyclopedia of the Social Sciences*, Vol. 7, New York, Macmillan, 1991

Soroush, Abdolkarim. *Reason Freedom and Democracy in Islam,* Oxford University Press, 2000

Soroush, Abdolkarim. *Intellectuals: The Powerless Wielders of Power,* in Conversation with Abdolkarim Soroush, 29 March 2002 http://www.seraj.org/ conversation2.htm

Stokes, Gale, 'How is Nationalism Related to Capitalism? A Review Article', *Comparative Studies in Society and History*, Cambridge University Press, 1986

Tapper, Richard. *Islam in Modern Turkey: Religion, Politics and Literature in a Secular State*, St Martin's Press, 1991

Tilly, Charles. Book Review, 'Nations and Nationalism', *The Journal of Modern History*, 1985

Tipps, C. Dean. 'Modernization Theory and the Comparative Study of Societies: A Critical Perspective', *Comparative Studies in Society and History*, Vol. 15, No. 2, March 1973

Toprak, Binnaz. *Islam and Political Development in Turkey,* Leiden, E. J. Brill, 1981

— 'The Religious Right', in Ertuğrul Ahmet Tonak and Irvin C. Schick (eds) *Turkey in Transition: New Perspectives*, Oxford University Press, 1987

— 'Islamist Intellectuals of the 1980s in Turkey', *Current Turkish Thought*, No. 62, Spring 1987

— *Religion and State in Turkey*, Lecture given at a Dayan Center conference on 'Contemporary Turkey: Challenges of Change', on 20 June 1999

Turan, İlter. 'Continuity and Change in Turkish Bureaucracy', in Jacob Landau (ed.) *Atatürk and the Modernization of Turkey*, Westview Press, 1984

Turan, Ömer. 'Son Dönemde Kemalizme Demokratik Meşruiyet Arayışları' in Ahmet İnsel (ed.) *Modern Türkiye'de Siyasi Düşünce*, Vol. 2, İletişim Yayıncılık, 2002

Urbinati, Nadia. 'From the Periphery of Modernity: Antonio Gramsci's Theory of Subordination and Hegemony', *Political Theory*, Vol. 26, June 1998, p. 370

Wright, Erik Olin. Review Article: 'Is Marxism Really Functionalist, Class Reductionist, and Teleological?' *The American Journal of Sociology*, Vol. 89, 1983

Wright, Robin. 'Iran's Greatest Political Challenge Abdolkarim Soroush', *World Policy Journal*, Summer 1997

Yavuz, Hakan. 'Turkish–Israeli Relations through the Lens of the Turkish Identity Debate', *Journal of Palestine Studies*, Vol. 27, No. 1, Autumn 1997

— 'Political Islam and the Welfare Party in Turkey', *Comparative Politics*, vol. 30, No. 1, 1997

— 'Turkey's Fault Lines and the Crisis of Kemalism', *Current History*, January 2000

Zubaida, Sami. 'Turkish Islam and National Identity: Insolvent Ideologies, Fractured State', *Middle East Report*, No. 199, April–June 1996

Zürcher, J. Erik. *Turkey: A Modern History*, London: I.B.Tauris, 1993

— *From Empire to Republic: Problems of Transition, continuity and Change*, http://www.let.leidenuniv.nl/tcimo/tulp/Research/Fromtorep.htm

— 'The Core Terminology of Kemalism: Mefkure, Millî, Muasir, Medenî', in François Georgeon (ed.) *Les mots de politique de l'Empire Ottoman a la Turquie kemaliste*, Paris, EHESS/ESA, CNRS, 2000

— *Ottoman Sources of Kemalist Thought*, Turkology Update Leiden Project Working Papers Archive Department of Turkish Studies, Universiteit Leiden, March 2002, http://www.let.leidenuniv.nl/tcimo/tulp/Research/MUNCHEN2.htm

— *The Young Turks-Children of the Borderlands?* Turkology Update Leiden Project Working Paper Archive, October 2002, http://www.let.leidenuniv.nl/tcimo/ tulp/Research/ejz16.htm

Journals and newspapers:

Akit
Birikim
Bogaziçi Journal, Review of Social, Economic and Administrative Studies
Bizim Aile
Comparative Politics
Comparative Studies in Society and History
Contention
Economy and Society
Current History
Girişim
Government and Opposition
Gösteri
International Affairs
International Journal of Middle East Studies

International Journal of the Sociology of Science
Middle East Journal
Middle East International
Middle East Report
Middle East Review of International Affairs
Middle Eastern Studies
Milli Gazete
Muslim World Report
New Perspective on Turkey
Praxis International
Telos
The Muslim World
The Message International
Türkiye Günlüğü
Vakit
Yeni Gündem
Yeni Şafak
Yeni Asya
Toplum ve Bilim
Türkiye Günlüğü
Zaman

Index